SCALE
ENCLOSE | BUILD

SCALE

ENCLOSE | BUILD

WALLS, FACADE, ROOF

EDITORS
ALEXANDER REICHEL
KERSTIN SCHULTZ

AUTHORS
EVA MARIA HERRMANN
MARTIN KRAMMER
JÖRG STURM
SUSANNE WARTZECK

Birkhäuser
Basel

FOREWORD

Architecture conveys its message via the facade, the building envelope. Houses, urban spaces and landscapes are initially perceived in terms of their overall outward appearance, and only after that in their details. The facade determines the appearance of the building, and hence the street space and even the landscape where the building is located.

The fifth volume of the *SCALE* series deals with the facades of buildings, which provide their envelope and depend for their appearance on the construction details. The title *Enclose | Build* conveys the ambivalence of the subject: the poetry and volatility on the one hand, and the practical necessities of the production process on the other. This volume, together with the volume *Support | Materialise*, describes all of the building components required for construction and puts them into context, from the design drawing through to technical implementation. It thus makes clear how different design processes influence the idea of construction. Owing to the technical developments of recent decades, facade concepts are increasingly being created almost free of technical restrictions. Furthermore, facades are no longer limited to the vertical plane, but rather envelope the entire building. In consequence, the last chapter but one of this volume deals with the classic structure and principles of roofing, including constructional details.

As the public face of a building, its envelope conveys its immediate expression; it bears witness to the historic era of the building and the architect's approach. Some 150 years ago, Gottfried Semper, a proponent of historicism, postulated that buildings should be cloaked by a facade. He understood buildings to be a fixed volume which should be 'clothed', similar to a man with textile garments. Just about fifty years later, the Deutsche Werkbund and the proponents of the International Style that had evolved from the Bauhaus movement turned their back on this attitude; instead they demanded honesty and the proper application of work and materials, with dramatic consequences for the facade. From today's point of view, the emancipation of architectural form, together with its counter-movement, Post-Modernism, provided the basis of today's diversity of building envelopes. These combine aesthetics, technology and functionality. They can independently enclose space, determine the character of a space, or even create it. Advances in building technology with respect to building physics, energy efficiency and sustainability raise new issues and provide new solutions for the design of facades.

Within this dialogue, we consider it important to discuss the elements that make up envelopes in an authentic and technically correct manner – not just as abstract images, but also in a way that assists the implementation of the respective idea in detail. The diversity of design options is reflected in the diversity of contemporary construction methods. The main part of this volume therefore describes different suspended facade systems and their effects, and presents their principles and characteristics. Following an introductory chapter, we deal with the various envelopes under the categories of self-supporting or non-supporting facade, examining their development and discussing their symbolic, aesthetic and technical possibilities. For the self-supporting envelopes in particular, there are overlaps between the construction methods illustrated in the *Support | Materialise* volume and the discussion of the principle differences in the construction of a building with non-self-supporting envelopes (curtain wall facades).

What comes first – the structural system, or the appearance and effect of a building? This ambivalence permeates the entire design process; it has to be faced by all those involved and can only be resolved via an integrative approach to design. Both this and the aforementioned *SCALE* volume demonstrate that design, material and structure not only depend on each other, but benefit from this interaction: they need this combination to create the desired architectural effect. This also depends on the quality of implementation at the different scales – from the outline design stage through to construction detailing. This volume therefore covers the different stages and includes detailed drawings to illustrate the relationship between design principles and construction details.

Enclose | Build completes the core of the current *SCALE* construction series. It would not have been possible without the prolonged and committed involvement of all its authors and contributors, to whom we express our heartfelt gratitude. We would also like to cordially thank the architects and photographers who have provided us with their projects and photographs. Above all, we would like to thank the volume editor, Eva Maria Herrmann, who has pulled the threads together, and Andrea Wiegelmann, who conceived the series and has continuously supported it. We thank Birkhäuser Verlag for its helpful cooperation over a long period of time. We have enjoyed working on these essential architectural issues and their ramifications. We hope you will be inspired by an enthralling read.

Darmstadt/Kassel, 31 March 2015
Alexander Reichel, Kerstin Schultz

ENCLOSE | BUILD
FUNDAMENTALS

INTRODUCTION

Mankind has been building shelters since time immemorial in order to gain protection from the weather, wild animals and enemies. The envelope of these shelters forms the boundary between the outer environment (specific local and climate conditions) and the sheltered interior, which – with as consistent a room temperature and climate as possible – can be used in all of the necessary ways. As demands for people's general well-being have increased, the requirements have become more complex but the essential, protective function of the building envelope has remained the same. Conversely, the building envelope also has an outward role to play. It enables communication and creates relationships with outdoor space. The term 'building envelope' normally refers to the facade, but that is too simplistic. In this book we shall look at the different building elements such as plinth, wall and roof in combination. These can envelope a building like a skin, and are responsible for dealing with all impacts resulting from the environment. Over the course of centuries, many variants have been developed in response to diverse requirements.

A decisive influence on the design of the building envelope has always been exerted by the location, its climatic and cultural conditions, and the locally available material. Historically, the availability of materials at a location played a decisive role – one that is now regaining importance due to today's ecological criteria.

Buildings have an effect upon each other depending on how close together they are, forming rural and urban patterns of settlement. It follows that the location of a building is paramount in importance and has a fundamental influence on the shape and design of the envelope. While nomads developed element-based envelopes in the form of tent-like constructions for flexible, temporary use, settled populations developed solid forms of enclosure which were place-specific and designed for durability. Likewise, the location of a building involves both cultural and historic influences. For example, depending on the cultural context and the era, the connection or separation of public and private space can become visible and thereby reflect the social structures of the society. To this day the envelope of a building is an expression of the social status and position of its users. In the case of public buildings with a representational function, the facade will always reveal the attitude to society of those who built it; it has always been used to express wealth, influence and power. The function of a building has a significant effect on the construction and design of the facade. The close interplay between facade, internal arrangement and construction determines its composition, transparency and openings.

While up into the twentieth century the building envelope was normally not just a space enclosure but also part of the loadbearing structure, the dematerialisation of the once structural wall to create the suspended facade, which can fulfil structural and symbolic functions, has opened up a range of aesthetic and functional options. Whereas solid structural envelopes impose limits on the design of openings (facade with windows), the continuous development of new building materials is enabling a separation of the envelope from the loadbearing structure, providing greater flexibility and freedom in the facade design. The loadbearing elements of a building can either be concealed by the envelope, be visible in interaction

1 Tent structure in Arabia
In the arid zones of Persia and Arabia where timber is scarce, tent poles were covered with high-strength fabrics in order to create large, well ventilated envelopes that provided protection from the sun. The height of these structures was determined by the length of poles available, the size and strength of the cloth and the process of putting up the structure, which remained unstable until it was tied down.

2 Borie in the south of France
The corbelled vaulting consists of small, unworked flat stones and has been used in rural areas up to modern times. These stone houses have a pointed roof and are built without cement and mortar. The building technique, with its small components, is typical of a manual process.

with the envelope, or become the main design theme. The enclosing envelope is directly related to the type of use, the loadbearing structure and the building services installations. Constant feedback relating to function, construction and expression is necessary to produce a well-integrated overall design.

A building envelope is not just about the building surface. It fulfils a multitude of functions. The quality of an envelope can only be assessed in the overall context of functional, structural, stylistic, ecological and sociological criteria. Depending on the concept, it will have not only a protective function but also those of structural support, climate control, lighting and communication with the surroundings.

The expression and form of a facade result from the multiple requirements the building envelope has to fulfil. For example, the design of a facade may be determined by use, function, or construction respectively; alternatively, a facade may have a purely sculptural and expressive intent. It may represent the function of a building in a symbolic or iconic way to the outside, or fulfil a specific purpose as a landmark (e.g. a lighthouse). The interplay of these factors determines the appearance and overall impression of the building. One contemporary development is to see the envelope as an active system within a sustainable energy concept. Depending on the approach and possibilities, this may take a variety of forms, ranging from simple folding shutters in front of windows for shade, to glass facades with controlled ventilation openings, daylight control systems or integrated photovoltaic panels for the generation of energy.

Increasingly the ecological assessment of a facade not only focuses on the energy demand or energy gain during its service life, but is extended to include the eco-balance over the complete life cycles of its constituent parts – from the production of the raw material to the disposal of the envelope. This highlights the connection between economic efficiency and ecology. The overall assessment of the life cycle can reveal important information about the cost efficiency of a facade during its service life, apart from the cost of construction. This includes the expenses of cleaning, maintenance, renovation and renewing materials.

It follows that building envelopes should be considered not in isolation, but as complex elements that are integrated into the design process. This increases the demands on the design team and the design and implementation processes.

This book complements the Scale volume Support | Materialise in addressing the subjects of enclosure and building with a focus on the fundamental systems and principles of the loadbearing structure and the facade – from the foundations to the roof. It aims to illustrate the breadth of options in designing envelopes, as well as their limitations, and to develop an understanding of their technical implementation.

This publication is intended to encourage solution-oriented thinking, involving constant reference to context, typology and construction, rather than strict obedience to a given design principle.

3 The Curtain Wall House, Tokyo, 1997, Shigeru Ban
The Curtain Wall House is symbolic of the emancipation of the envelope from the loadbearing structure. Weather protection is afforded by a textile curtain which, when open, eliminates the boundary between the interior and the exterior. The private space becomes public, and the public space becomes part of the private sphere.

4 The Opera House, Oslo, 2008, Snøhetta
The plinth, walls and roof of the building merge seamlessly to create a walk-on roof landscape. The additional public urban space thus created adds to the amenity value.

CULTURAL CONTEXT - HISTORY

Original architectural space fulfils the simplest functional requirements – those associated with providing protection – with the use of locally available materials. Gottfried Semper, writing in the middle of the nineteenth century, developed a theory of the facade which he derived from the lightweight but effective construction of nomadic tents – which are still in use today with their system of a separate loadbearing structure and a protective envelope, even in extreme climatic conditions. As in the world of fashion the garment envelopes the space of human existence. Rather than the functional technology of construction, Semper emphasised the symbolic and cultural criteria for the suitability of the architecture. While early buildings were designed along purely functional lines in response to a given situation, over the course of history the concept of buildings as accommodation evolved from one of being purely protective into the discipline of architectural design. The collapsible, enveloping structures of migrating peoples were replaced by buildings designed for permanence. Just as in clothing there are many variations of colour, weaving patterns and textures, so too the positioning of openings, the arrangement of structural elements – such as arches and columns – of friezes, paintings and sculptural, figurative elements developed as independent forms of expression.

The term 'facade' derives from the Latin 'facies' (face), which was used in antiquity to describe the publicly visible side of a building - especially of prestigious buildings (sacral as well as secular). A structure built by the hand of Man symbolises the interaction between the individual, the outside space and society. This encompasses the climate and topographic contexts on one hand, the reflection of societal forms, political intent, religious provenance and ethnic grouping on the other, and even the availability of local resources. A building serves as a store of information, and is at the same time a witness of different epochs.

Since time immemorial, people have availed themselves of the power of expression inherent in built forms. The pyramids are the mighty enclosure of a pharaoh who thus manifested his power and his connection with the heavens to his contemporaries and for posterity. While the early democratic structures of the Greeks and Romans resulted in residential buildings having private, introverted inner courtyards, public temples were designed to be all the more ostentatious.
From the Middle Ages onwards, as a society of citizens and tradesmen developed, the facades of secular buildings were also increasingly decorated for representational purposes. Openings acquired special importance. They served as a filter between the exterior and the interior that could be opened to a greater or lesser degree.

Even though the size of windows in residential buildings was limited for a long time, the openings themselves were often elaborately designed. Coloured or moulded surrounds emphasised their importance in the facade.
In Gothic architecture, parts of the external wall were relieved of their structural functions for the first time, by elements such as columns, flying buttresses, ribs or piers. In place of the masonry came large windows intersected by tracery. While in the Gothic period the envelope consisted chiefly of the supporting structure, in the Renaissance the facade became separated from the building and was understood as a separate design element.
In the time of industrialisation, from the middle of the nineteenth century, new materials and construction methods (such as the skeleton construction method) and new building types (such as industrial buildings and warehouses) brought about a fundamental change. Large glazed facade openings become possible and heralded the transition to the first all-glass facades. With the onset of the Modern age, the influence of the building structure on the enclosing envelope was reduced and the envelope became an independent component of the design.

The separation of the loadbearing structure from the envelope can go as far as completely dissolving their original connection. In Post-Modernism, an architectural style from the 1960s to 1980s, facades were placed as backdrops or stage sets for the space in front of a building and in this way re-applied the principles of the Renaissance. In later developments, some facades became fully independent of the building and developed into standalone, sculptural forms with their own – sometimes iconographic – meaning. The discrepancy between preservation and creative development is considerable. Freezing a supposedly ideal state of affairs can lead to 'pattern book' architecture and regression, just as disregard for the cultural context gives birth to 'foreign bodies' that strain to create an effect at all costs rather than integrating into an urban context.

Today too, the interface between interior and exterior reflects the cultural context in a reference to the social structures of the society and the place where they have developed, and in the sense - propagated by Modernism - that openness, transparency and design are to be understood as expressions of democratic society.
In the future, the functionality of facades will be extended even further. Technical progress has made it possible for facades and roofs to absorb and process energy, to dispose of dirt, to provide acoustic insulation and to transmit information. At a highly technical level, the envelope performs tasks which are also expressed in its appearance – be it imperceptibly or conspicuously.

1 Traditional housing in Cameroon, consisting of pressed, sun-dried clay in the form of a conical shell.

2 Stralsund Town Hall, 1278: This magnificent facade has a strong representative intent, being higher than the three-storey town hall that it fronts.

3 Togu-do, Kyoto, 15th century: The Togu-do is built in the Shoin architectural style. Built as a private residence and subsequently used as a temple, the Togu-do contains a room for the tea ceremony, which became the archetype of all later tea rooms (chashitsu) in Japan.

4 Palace on the Grand Canal, Venice, early 15th century: The elegant palace is a typical example of the special style of the Venetian Gothic.

5 Grote Markt, Antwerp, 16th century: The status of the city of Antwerp in the 15th and 16th centuries, as one of Europe's foremost commercial and cultural centres, is demonstrated by the luxuriously designed guild halls and citizens' houses.

6 The Majolica House, Vienna, 1898, Otto Wagner: Inspired by Gottfried Semper's theory of 'dressing', Otto Wagner uses facade cladding with thin, precious materials - here in the form of tiles with floral motifs - in order to give the building an appearance that is independent of the construction.

7 The Fagus factory, Alfeld, 1911-1913, Walter Gropius and Adolf Meyer: In this building, glass is used as enclosing element, independent of the loadbearing structure. The corner is built without a column, thus emphasising the lightweight character of the transparent envelope.

8 The Seagram Building, New York, 1957, Mies van der Rohe: The bronze-coloured tower block is deemed to be the prime example of the 'skin and bones' architecture of Mies van der Rohe and still serves as an ideal prototype for skyscrapers. The facade is subdivided using slender bronze profiles, the spacing of which is reduced towards the building corners in order to emphasise the verticality of the tower block.

1

2

3

4

5

6

7

8

PLACE AND ENVIRONMENT

The individual connection with the environment, the historic, cultural, climatic and material conditions of a place require careful analysis. Only dialogue with the place itself makes the quality of architecture visible and tangible – conversely, a misunderstood reference to the place will have an effect on the popular acceptance of a building and its sense of belonging. The issues are not only those of urban space, landscape and topography, but also those of climate conditions and local resources – which influence the use of energy and technology – in addition to building control requirements.

For example, glass facades either mirror the surroundings – be they urban or rural – or allow a view into the building, depending on the angle of vision, reflection and time of day. It is possible to emphasise transparency and views into the building in order to let the building meld into the townscape or a country landscape. ↘ 1

Buildings are in a dialogue with their surroundings. They can be designed in keeping with the landscape or surroundings or in deliberate contrast to them. Owing to the material used, the turf roof houses of Iceland blend well with the landscape and replicate the hilly topography of the surroundings. On the other hand, envelopes can be integrated in a cultural context while contrasting completely with their surroundings, either by complementary colouring or an unusual use of a traditional material. ↘ 2

In today's globalised world, identity and tradition are gaining new significance. Available regional resources, knowhow relating to materials, old and new processing methods and economic means of transport are becoming increasingly important.

Social acknowledgement is also reflected in the degree of self-confidence that is evident in architecture. Traditional construction methods and modern vocabularies of form complement each other in a meaningful way. ↘ 3

A place is not only defined by the orientation of a building to account for the site boundaries and the cardinal directions, but also by the characteristics of the site itself, be it level, sloping, dipped, or even partly covered by water. The conditions on a given site can be accommodated in the design in a number of different ways. The landscape may be one of rolling hills or ragged rock; rounded or angular elements may dominate; the surroundings may be matte or feature a smooth, shiny surface, while the colours of the landscape may change over the course of the seasons. The building, in turn, may stand out from its surroundings or reflect them; it may continue the terrain or completely merge with it. The existing context can even be exploited to generate the design. In areas where buildings are highly exposed to the weather, a plinth is often used as transition between the ground surface and the building itself. In addition to its protective function, the plinth – with its material, surface finish and colour – can also serve as a formative element in the design. ↘ 4 On the other hand, the volume of a building with a fixed schedule of accommodation can be visually reduced by placing the required space partly or wholly under the natural contours of the terrain. ↘ 5, 6 Where this is required, new buildings can be integrated inconspicuously in landscape areas worth protecting or in established urban areas. Alternatively, they can enhance the surroundings if judiciously placed in a prominent position. In this case, the local topography makes additional demands on the material and construction. The design of a freestanding, exposed building must pay more attention to watertightness, airtightness and durability than a one that is sheltered by landscape features or other buildings.

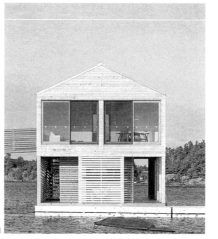

1   Tower block ensemble, Ulmenstrasse, Frankfurt am Main, 2009, Max Dudler: Two existing tower blocks were revitalised with a contemporary element facade, which is nevertheless in keeping with the Wilhelminian buildings in the neighbourhood, owing to the proportion of openings and the material chosen.

2   The Ecumenical Forum, Hamburg, 2012, Wandel Hoefer Lorch: Typical for the location, brick is used as the face material of the back-ventilated suspended facade, which nevertheless reinterprets the local style with its shape and colour scheme.

3   The Floating House, Ontario, 2008, MOS Architects: The varied properties of timber as a construction material – including the fact that it floats – were used in the construction of a holiday home; the building was assembled on land using prefabricated timber elements which were later installed on a floating pontoon at an island in the lake.

4 Timber houses in the Valais
This specific, local style of building
is a direct response to the location
(climate and topography) and materials (timber and stone). The natural
stone plinth is used to level the terrain; it also protects against snow
and moisture and serves as the
foundation for the timber structure.
The vertical arrangement of functions – plinth, stables, living space –
and hence the use of natural ventilation and heat, determines the
particular style of houses in the
region.

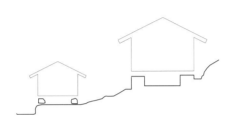

5 Visitor centre at the Hercules
monument, Kassel, 2011, Staab
Architects: The form is the result
of the location (topography, and
view of the Hercules monument).
The building follows the natural
gradient of the terrain and, by cleverly integrating various functions,
manages the differences in level
without creating excessive volume
on the slope.

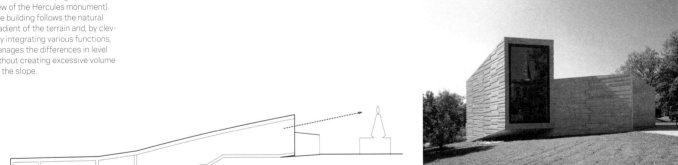

6 Extension to the Städel
Museum, Frankfurt am Main, 2012,
Schneider + Schumacher: The special feature of this locality (open
space in the inner city) is retained
by placing the building underground.
The underground structure provides the floor space required for
the exhibitions, which receive
filtered light from above while
allowing use of the roof area as a
public open space.

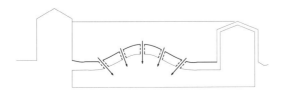

CLIMATE

Traditionally, the design of facades and roofs was and still is primarily determined by the local climate. The construction of walls and roofs developed in tandem with the respective trade skills. Materials and construction methods were used in ways that kept costs low while ensuring the longest possible service life. The shape of the building – its volume, roof pitch and eaves overhang – was a direct response to the respective weather conditions. From time immemorial the climate has been the dominating factor in the design of buildings that evolved from inherited experience. Also referred to as autochthonous building, this approach employs the naturally available local resources in a way that is appropriate for the climate and the use. In regions exposed to heavy snowfall, shallow-pitched roofs with natural stone covering (additional mass to counteract the risk of the roof lifting off and to stop snow from sliding off the roof so that its insulating properties can be used) and large eaves overhangs are common. Conversely, steeply pitched roofs reaching down close to the ground can better withstand rain and the horizontal forces generated by strong wind. ⤳ 1 In hot climate zones with little precipitation, monopitch or flat roofs usually predominate. In these areas, solar irradiation into the building is minimised by large canopies, small atria and the dense juxtaposition of buildings. Thick, solid walls with small window openings provide storage mass with a phase shift, which keeps the building cool during the day and warm during the night. ⤳ 2 Large eaves overhangs form intermediate climatic zones and prevent overheating in summer.
Numerous requirements, which can be met with more or less advanced technical and functional input, continue to influence the development and execution of the envelope. Local weather conditions on the outside should not adversely affect the cosiness and comfort of the interior. This applies not only in regions with extreme day-to-night and summer-to-winter fluctuations, or in sub-polar and -tropical zones, but also in temperate zones, as in central Europe, where the climate is subject to pronounced regional differences. Every place has a specific climate which is determined by its topography and situation. Consideration should be given not only to the differences between mountainous, inland and coastal regions, but also the differences in the microclimate, such as those between urban and rural areas and those within an urban environment. It follows that a detailed analysis of regional climate data, which are summarised in the thermal insulation standards and are obtainable in greater detail from the databases of regional weather stations, is an essential prerequisite for the design of the building envelope. ⤳ SCALE, vol. 2, Heat | Cool

While it is not possible to change the exterior conditions imposed by the choice of location, the type and functionality of the facade and roof can be influenced by the design. Infrastructure and industrial buildings are naturally subject to different comfort criteria than residential, cultural and sports buildings. ⤳ p. 28, Typology and Use
In addition to the general requirements for thermal comfort in the interior, the facade has to fulfil additional functions. Acoustic requirements, such as insulation from the noise of traffic and machinery, have to be taken into account, as have the hygienic requirements for air quality, ventilation and the prevention of air pollution from the outside. The need to reduce glare and contrast while meeting requirements for sufficient daylight influences the type and size of openings and the choice of building components for solar screening and light control. ⤳ SCALE, vol. 1, Open | Close Energy-efficient use of the facade, including energy generation and control, introduces greater complexity into the design of the envelope. The better the thermal properties of the materials of the envelope are, the less energy is required in summer for cooling and in winter for heating.
Due to globalisation, the materials and construction methods used in different countries are becoming ever more similar. With the beginning of industrialisation, new technologies and means of transport made construction less dependent on local materials, and design more independent of the local weather conditions. However, current sustainability studies have highlighted the opportunity to conserve energy and resources by using regional materials and building types to protect against heat and cold. ⤳ 3
What are the local climate conditions and how should they be dealt with? How much energy input can be expected from sunlight, and how is it possible to integrate solar screening in the design while making use of the potential energy gain? Instead of relying solely on ever more sophisticated technology to meet the increasing demands made of building envelopes, the architectural designs of the future will have to exploit appropriate materials and forms in dealing with the prevailing climate conditions. The design and implementation of building envelopes must be based on a comprehensive assessment of all the parameters and their interaction.
All these factors relating to a locality and its cultural basis indicate why, in architecture, each design task must be fully appraised anew. Similarly, tried and trusted typological, technical, or conceptual solutions should not be transferred from one project to another without close examination. Different places and different times will always give rise to very specific, original solutions.

1 Traditional farmhouse in the
Black Forest
The shape and overhang of the roof
provide protection from rain and
snow as well as plenty of space for
the storage of hay, which also insu-
lates the interior in winter, thereby
contributing to the occupants'
comfort.

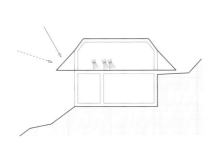

2 Traditional building structure in a
desert climate
Clay is an available local resource
and is used in solid construction. By
zoning the layout, protected areas
are created (in the shade or close
to the relatively cool ground). The
knowledge of physical phenomena
(cold air sinks) allows the utilisation
of natural cooling resources by
creating an air draught, which is
caused by the small temperature
differences in the shaded parts
of a building. This has led to a distinct type of structure known as
a 'wind tower'.

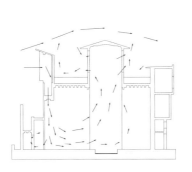

3 Office building 2226, Lustenau,
2013, Baumschlager Eberle:
Experimental office building without heating. The building has ventilation and cooling (by air), which is
actively controlled and utilised. The
material used is brick which, with
an external wall thickness of 76 cm
and a low proportion of openings
to solid wall, is used as storage
mass. This makes it possible, using
only internal heat sources such as
lighting, equipment and users, to
retain enough heat in the building
to ensure thermal comfort. In this
way the traditional construction
feature of thick masonry walls has
been modified as the basis of an
energy-conserving concept using
control technology (air).

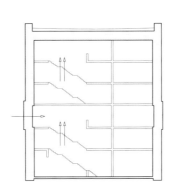

PRINCIPLES OF ENCLOSURE

Facades vividly express the interaction between construction and design, functionality and aesthetics. The loadbearing function of an envelope cannot be considered in isolation, but represents an integrated system which takes factors such as environmental context, climate and use into account. The more functions an exterior envelope has to fulfil – such as structural support, protection against the weather – and the more it is intended to express the purpose and aesthetics of the building, the more complex is the design task. Conversely, many more design options are available when the facade does not have to meet structural and functional requirements. In this context, an understanding of the unity of technology and aesthetics is the prerequisite for a good, holistically accomplished design. In the design process, the focus is on the structural system of the secondary structure, as well as on the materials and the desired appearance. Both the surface finish (from smooth to textured) and the design of the form (composition, proportion of elements and joints) have to be taken into account to the same degree as technical feasibility (in the form of production conditions, prefabrication processes and installation). At the design stage, it is necessary to establish how the material relates to the environment ⌐➤ p. 40, Ecology and Life Cycle, and also how cost efficiency, material selection and construction are affected. ⌐➤ p. 38, Economy and Process Quality The requirements for a new building are different to those for a conversion, a rehab (usually strengthening an existing structure) or a refurbishment, which are often linked with the preservation of historic buildings and represent more complex tasks with respect to the unity of aesthetics and technology. The different components of a building envelope – plinth, wall, openings, roof – have to fulfil different functions depending on their respective positions.

The plinth is the interface between the building and the ground, and can either be perceived as an independent element (e.g. in a different material or colour) or be integrated into the envelope. In addition to its functional requirements – transmission and distribution of loads from the loadbearing structure and envelope, protection against water and/or external influences and intruders, compensation for differences in the level of the terrain etc. – a plinth can also make a formal statement. A solid plinth with the height of a full storey may appear forbidding, whereas an open and transparent ground-level area has an inviting feel. On the other hand, the plinth often combines different types of enclosure. In buildings where both commercial and residential uses have to be accommodated, a different style of plinth can help with the orientation between public and private areas.

Topographic and climatic conditions determine the choice of plinth material – either based on and rising out of the ground, or detached in a different plane. Depending on its surroundings, a building can even be designed without a plinth – that is to say, a plinth without any distinct appearance – in favour of a more homogeneous envelope.

When the facade serves only as a thermal enclosure of the interior, the separation of the loadbearing function from the enclosing function ⌐➤ SCALE, vol. 3, Support | Materialise allows much more freedom in the design – be it in the visual expression of structural elements or the application of a more abstract design, be it showing the true nature of the material or mystifying it. With the transformation of the flat wall (solid construction) into a transparent enclosure of space with a system of beams and columns (skeleton construction) and cladding, the classic image of the solid wall and its visually expressed functions changes in favour of a more autonomous envelope. While in solid construction the openings are largely determined by the construction grid for structural reasons, the position of openings in skeleton construction is not determined by any particular order or geometry. ⌐➤ SCALE, vol. 1, Open | Close

The facade and the roof together form the visible envelope of a building. For this reason, the design of the envelope is ruled by universal principles. The composition of envelopes ranges from clearly distinguishable elements – plinth, wall, roof – to seamless, tent-like designs.

The envelope will always follow the shape of the building. Its appearance can be changed to suit the design approach, the context, the topography and the type of construction. For example, we are familiar with the principle of filigree facades in the Venetian Gothic, just as we know it from the Belgian art nouveau style, from historic timber construction and from modern concrete facades.

The basic principles are illustrated by the adjacent drawings and on the following pages.

1 Position of envelope
a Construction elements:
plinth, wall, opening, roof
Separation of building components,
solid construction > skeleton
construction
b Building volume + cold roof
c Building volume + warm roof
(overhang)
d Skeleton structure + envelope
(seamless) or loadbearing structure + envelope

1a  b  c  d

2 Appearance/form
a Volume with roof overhang
b Smooth/homogeneous building
volume
c Projections and recesses
d Concealed elements

2a  b  c 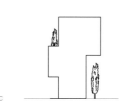 d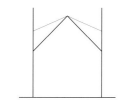

3 Design of envelope
a Solid, enclosed
b Slender, transparent
c Overlays, filter between solid
and open
d Position of openings in the
envelope

3a  b  c 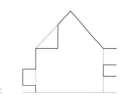 d

4 Context
a Free-standing
b Built adjoining an existing
building
c Integrated with an existing
building
d Extra volume on an existing
building

4a 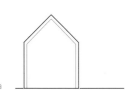 b 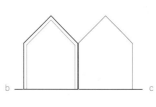 c  d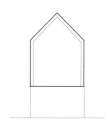

5 Topography/climate
a Buried
b Transition zone between
building and envelope
c Integration of foundations
and plinth
d Integration into an existing
envelope with a new thermal
envelope – external envelope –
internal envelope

5a  b  c  d

AESTHETICS, EXPRESSION AND SYMBOLISM

The envelope of a building is sometimes referred to as its face. It provides the building with a specific expression. In addition to the functional requirements – to protect, to keep warm and cool, ideally via specially generated and/or stored energy – a facade will always have a formal expression and a symbolic significance. The enclosing envelope is the first thing that is perceived from the outside.

'Each building, each facade is a public affair. The facade belongs to everyone, only what is behind it belongs to those who have to live with it. And for this reason, it is also clear that facades must not be a matter of cosmetics'. Manfred Sack, an architectural journalist, has defined the architect's task thus. The symbolic message of an envelope must not be used for purely decorative purposes and hence be misappropriated; instead, the shape and materials should be used to make a statement about the building's use and context, social structure and attitude. The design is not just perceived as the sum of elements and forms, but imparts symbolic expression and orientation in multi-faceted ways.

Facades have always conveyed a message. The sacral and secular images in the form of ceramic tile screens which adorn the public faces of buildings in Porto and Lisbon can hardly be bettered in terms of opulence and wealth of motif ⟶ 1 as they assert society's claim to exercise power and convey its values. This early form of 'media facade' experienced a revival with Antoni Gaudí's interpretation of the legend of St. George on ceramic tiles applied to the facade of Casa Batlló. ⟶ 2 Its latest incarnation is the printed glass facade, as used in the new Ricola factory building by architects Herzog & de Meuron. These three-dimensional compositions contribute to the expression of the building and inspire a new world of ideas; the building can function as a symbol and convey an extended message. Sacral buildings often consist of lofty, vertical structures, which allude to a higher order of existence. Public buildings with monumental rows of columns are intended to express the power of the ruler or the state. Ostentatious palaces symbolise a claim to authority, and today evoke fantasies of the world of times gone by. ⟶ 5

The form, surface texture, materials and colour ⟶ 4, 6 of a facade are the design characteristics that determine the external appearance of a building, and can be used to reinforce the symbolism. While retaining the volume, the facade can be structured and given rhythm using colour, ornament or changes of material. A smooth facade, on the other hand, can seem to have any scale. ⟶ 7, 8 Depending on the weather and the fall of light, the envelope can take on different appearances and can exploit changeable conditions to generate nuances. For example, the Centre for the Development of Local Alabaster in Teruel appears stone-faced and forbidding during the day, but at dusk it conveys an ethereal, textile feel due to the wafer-thin stone envelope.

1 Azulejo on the outside facade of a church, Porto, from the 16th century: Mosaic consisting of fired ceramic tiles, mostly square, with colourful painted decorations. A characteristic feature of the townscape on public monuments and buildings, house facades and churches, as well as on internal walls for the purpose of decoration, often composed as large-scale pictorial murals.

2 Casa Batlló, Barcelona, 1877, Antoni Gaudí: The colourful facade represents the legend of Saint George, the patron saint of Catalonia (locally called Sant Jordi); the roof represents the scales of the dragon fought by Saint George; the cross on the roof is his lance. The forged iron balconies represent skulls and the gallery on the first floor the mouth of the dragon.

3 Notre-Dame, Paris, 1163-1345: The cathedral is one of the earliest Gothic buildings in France. The well-balanced vertical and horizontal structuring of the west facade, as well as the centrally placed rose window, served as an example for many Gothic cathedrals.

4 The Schröder House, Utrecht, 1924, Gerrit Rietveld: The house is one of the most important buildings of the De Stijl movement. The cubic shape and the use of the primary colours (red, blue and yellow) in combination with white, black and grey is characteristic of the house's abstract vocabulary of form.

5 Hawa Mahal, Jaipur, 1799: The Palace of the Winds is part of a prestigious palace precinct of the Maharajas of Jaipur. It features a facade with 953 beautiful openings, with a sophisticated design providing the necessary ventilation. They also allowed the Maharaja's court ladies to look out without being seen themselves.

6 The Millard House, Pasadena, 1923, Frank Lloyd Wright: The house is an experiment in using economical concrete blocks, which are enhanced by ornamentation, thereby also expressing the versatility and beauty of concrete. Decoration and function – outside and inside – demonstrate a new commitment to the material, giving the building a modern appearance for its time.

7 The Shirokane House, Tokyo, 2013, Kiyotoshi Mori & Natsuko Kawamura, MDS: The decision to design this residence without windows is a reaction to the typically very confined situation in Tokyo and the consequently high density of development. The envelope is closed to the surroundings; daylight reaches the interior via rooflights and a roof terrace.

8 Centre for the Development of Local Alabaster, Teruel, 2011, Magén Architects: The centre focuses on the export and marketing of alabaster, which is quarried in the region. The opaque and translucent surfaces, and the many different forms of the material, function as exhibits. At night, the thinly cut facade elements give the building envelope a translucent appearance.

Symbolism
1 National Congress, Brasília, 1957–1964, Oscar Niemeyer: The building reflects the political structure of the country in an impressive way – while the Senate convenes beneath a concave dome, the House of Representatives resembles a shallow dish. Both parts of the building are connected via the ground floor and the development includes two office tower blocks.

2 Nakagin Capsule Tower, Tokyo, 1972, Kisho Kurokawa: The building is an icon of the Metabolist movement. The standardised housing units are suspended from the core and flexibly connected with each other. The principle of modular composition was also followed in the design of entire townships.

Corporate architecture
3 The Chrysler Building, New York, 1930, William Van Alen: The building was designed in the Art Déco style. The upper part of the facade features gargoyles in stainless steel that are reminiscent of the wheel covers, wings and bonnets of the vehicle brand; in addition, Chrysler wheel covers have been used to decorate the facade.

4 Best Store facade, 1970; SITE: The Post-Modern style plays with traditional concepts of the classical facade, and in this variant becomes architectural pop art.

5 BMW Munich, 1972, Karl Schwanzer: The succinct shape of the four cylinders reflects the desire of the Bavarian automotive corporation to have a directly symbolic landmark; at the same time, it derives from a new type of internal layout and the suspended construction from a central core.

Iconography
6 The Sydney Opera House, 1973, Jørn Utzon: The geometric shape – which accommodates the stages and concert halls with a gesture that is both protective and presentational – is a very memorable sculpture. It became a worldwide icon and a landmark in Sydney.

7 The Guggenheim Museum, Bilbao, 1997, Frank O. Gehry: The solid, cuboid building parts are assembled like a seemingly haphazard collage, with the external form reflecting the arrangement of the art objects in the flowing interior.

Tradition and high-tech
8 The Institut du Monde Arabe, Paris, 1987, Jean Nouvel: Traditional Arab ornamentation has been reinterpreted and given a new function in a contemporary architectural language.

9 The Centre Pompidou, Paris, 1977, Renzo Piano & Richard Rogers: The technical aesthetic of high-tech architecture was taken as the main focus of the design. The facade has become a multifunctional part of the building, providing access and accommodating the services installations, thus leaving the interior space with maximum flexibility.

In his government buildings in Brasilia, the capital city built from scratch between 1957 and 1964, Oscar Niemeyer succeeded well in combining an aesthetic effect with a symbolic claim. ⟍1 As a counter-gesture to an architecture of power, the free sculptural shapes come across as an impressive expression of democratic representation.

Architectural history has many instances where a certain design trend gave birth to a style. With the 'detachment' of the envelope from the loadbearing structure at the beginning of the twentieth century, the focus turned to the technical and material quality of the facade and its texture. There is a fine line between the necessary function and abstract aesthetics. Subsequent decades saw examples of both extremes. This is evidenced by two styles which developed in parallel and represent two opposite approaches to design: Postmodernism and the style of architecture referred to as High-tech. While Postmodernism, with its playful and sometimes witty handling of building elements and formal details, tried to escape the aesthetic dictate of functionalism and rationalism ⟍4, the High-tech style of architecture relied on the pattern language offered by the technical elements of construction. The idea is not based on an emphasis on innovative technology, but on the expression of a technology-based aesthetic. A typical example is the Centre Pompidou as a 'culture machine' in the historic centre of Paris, the exterior appearance of which is shaped by the structural elements as well as the service installations and access elements. The interior is kept clear of columns and thereby offers maximum flexibility of use. ⟍9 Some buildings can be very clearly identified by their exterior shape, so that the envelope and hence the facade acquire iconographic importance.

The identification of the public with 'their' building can give rise to symbolic nicknames such as 'The Oyster' used for Sydney Opera House ⟍6 with its spectacular shell-like structure surrounded by water on three sides. The facade of the Institut du Monde Arabe in Paris ⟍8 is a symbol of cultural provenance and a metaphor for the function of the building. The facade with its ornamental vocabulary of form is both a technical building component – the facade elements control the incoming daylight in a similar way to the iris of a camera lens – as well as a reminder of traditional Arab construction elements.

Another landmark of iconographic architecture is what has become known as the BMW Vierzylinder (four cylinders). Built in 1972 as the car manufacturer's head office and landmark, this design – which for the time was innovative – portrays the engine as a symbol and also presents the company as a brand. ⟍5 This building is thus a precursor of corporate architecture, which today is increasingly used for the purpose of marketing the identity of a company. The fact that architecture designed as a landmark can have far-reaching consequences is sometimes referred to as the Bilbao-Effect, which in a positive sense refers to the commercially successful development of tourism in a city area due to an iconographic building.

The way a building looks is not just an artistic concern, but is to a certain extent also important from the point of view of economy and ecology. The design of modern building envelopes is more than ever determined by the contemporary use of materials in accordance with their local availability, the honesty of form and composition, the aging ability of materials and the quality of the execution.

COMPOSITION AND PROPORTION

'I have never yet designed a facade' commented the American architect John Lautner who, in the 1960s, built mostly organic residences in which the interior merges seamlessly with the exterior. With regard to the complex constructions and varied forms found in contemporary architecture, this understanding of a building envelope and space seems comprehensible. When looked at closely, however, geometry, areas, lines and volumes are not just empty design features, but result from specific construction elements and how they are joined together. The determination of dimensions, joints, edges, volumes and openings as part of the design directly affects building construction and conversely, the construction requirements of the loadbearing structure feed back into the process of conceptual design. The result is a design dialogue between the abstract determination of form and the validation of its actual implementation.

The feel of a facade – and hence the intended effect of the architecture – is generated primarily through the proportions of the volume. The tenets of proportion, which aim for order among the elements making up a design, go back to Ancient Greece and are still valid today. Common to all of them is an appropriate relationship between horizontal and vertical dimensions, with regard to the type of building, its use and the user's comfort.

Independently of the geometry of the building, the overall impression is also influenced by the type and texture of the building materials. A flat finish, such as plaster or a paint coating, generates homogeneity and restraint, whereas a classic frame-based facade – a non-loadbearing glass facade with large panels and its own secondary structure – will always create linear order with its profiles and will therefore determine the appearance of the facade. The composition of facade elements, their size and hence their aesthetic expression are influenced by standardised production processes and the feasibility of on-site assembly or delivery as prefabricated units. ➘ p. 26,
Material and Texture

Flat building elements appear in numerous forms in a facade. They may be straight, curved, textured, smooth, or perforated and, depending on the material, may be used in different sizes and with different colours and finishes. Large elements usually appear like panels owing to their joints, whereas small elements are more likely to come across as a homogeneous structure, in much the same way as pixels do. Similarly, panes of glass can appear as flat areas, either 'closed' as a result of the reflection of their surroundings or as 'outlooks' in a 'closed' wall. Lines appear where flat areas are joined. The edges of volumes and openings also form lines, which form the building's contours. The lines can be made visible as edges, joint profiles, or transitions between colours. The intersection and superimposition of lines in facades can become the determining design characteristic and may need very careful planning.

Bodies are those elements in a building envelope that have depth as well as planarity. The interplay between geometry and construction – and the material – determines whether a facade is perceived more as consisting of individual areas or as a homogeneous body. In buildings, the surfaces of which are constructed in a continuous manner without joints and consisting of one material, the sculptural nature of the body can be particularly prominent.

OPENINGS

In addition to their primary task of admitting light to the interior of the building, openings in architecture are an important design tool, even though they can only be called geometric elements with a degree of reservation. They connect the interior with the exterior and interact with other design and lighting elements. The forms that they take are closely related to the socio-cultural significance of windows and doors as an interface between public space and the sheltered, private sphere. ➘ SCALE,
vol. 1, Open | Close

Historic and regional theories of proportion, amongst others:

- The golden section:
  The golden section is based on the mathematics of classical antiquity and results from the geometric definition of line segments to each other in a certain algebraic equation:
  $a/b = b/a + b$.

- Orders of columns:
  The most important system of proportion in classical antiquity, which was revived in the Renaissance.

- The theories of the Renaissance:
  Andrea Palladio: *Quattro libri dell'architettura* (Four books on architecture), Venice 1570

- Leonardo da Vinci's 'Vitruvian Man' illustrates the proportions of the human body.

- Modulor:
  A proportional system developed by Le Corbusier between 1942 and 1955.

- The Ken:
  Japanese unit of measure based on the traditional tatami mat module and used as the basis of construction, choice of material and composition.

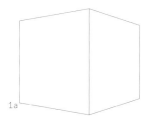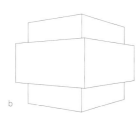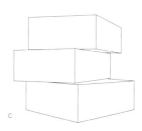

1 The cube
a Closed / open
b Cube on a receding plinth / cube with receding upper floor
c Cubes offset from each other, eventually leading to free-form design

2   Design – construction – effect
a   Homogeneous surfaces
e.g. render/paint coating, also
masonry or wood shingles
b   Subdivision of areas into elements; dimensions depend on
the material, e.g. glass panes,
panels, boards
c   Vertical subdivision
wood, glass

d   Horizontal subdivision
wood, metal, fibre-board
e   Subdivision imposed by the
panel format, various formats
f   Proportion and jointing as a
result of changes in format and
material

g   Prestigious facade,
placed in front of the actual building
to create a certain impression
h   Perspective,
use of perspective to create an
illusion and distract from the actual
dimensions
i   Free form, folding,
disruption of proportions and
composition

3   Openings – proportion –
composition
a   Facade with openings
b   Hybrid facade with individual
windows and large glazed area
c   Fully glazed facade, separate
from the loadbearing structure

4   Position of opening
a   Flush with the surface
b   Recessed with reveals
c   Surface-mounted

5   Composition
a   Without grid
b   Not following the grid lines
c   Grid camouflaged through the
interplay of transparent and translucent areas, or through changes
of material

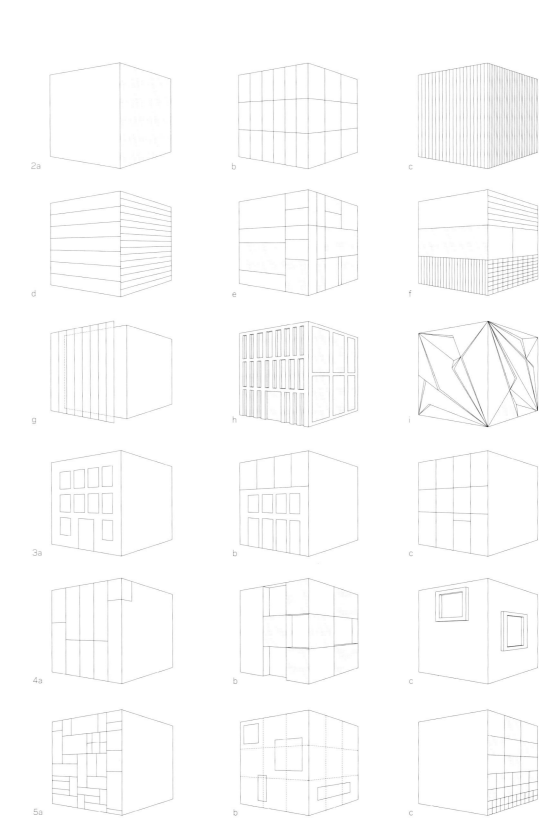

2a   b   c

d   e   f

g   h   i

3a   b   c

4a   b   c

5a   b   c

MATERIAL AND TEXTURE

Materials are perceived with all the senses. For this reason their use in the design of a facade is not just based on their structural and functional properties, but also – and primarily so – on their aesthetic and perceptual effect. Even though the surfaces of buildings are rarely touched directly or have an active impact on people's sense of smell or hearing, our sense of a building is formed by our tactile impression. We have very varying responses to timber, natural stone, and metal facades, which are determined either by its sensory qualities or, by association, the smell of the respective material in other contexts (forest, quarry etc.). Some materials are used as a compound element in building systems. The decision as to the choice of a facade material may be based either on the local building tradition and regional availability, or the intention may be to create a deliberate contrast by using a different, foreign material. The texture of the surface (smooth, rough, textured) determines the visual impression of the material, enhanced by the play of light and shadow. Thus the means available to the designer are almost limitless, and their effects can be varied further through the use of detailing, joints and colouring.

A solid brick facade can achieve an almost textile quality if a suitable brick bond, colour and proportion of openings are chosen. ↘ 4 Likewise, a construction that is in contrast to traditional regional methods of building with unworked natural stone may fit smoothly into the overall aesthetic, in spite of the foreign nature of the material. ↘ 2 The barely visible jointing of wood shingles suggests an analogy with scales or natural skin. Shingles can be used to cover free forms and also to achieve a flush joint of the materials between wall and roof. ↘ 9 The heavy and raw appearance of large-format Corten steel panels makes a building appear closed and forbidding, while the narrowness of titanium zinc panels – resulting from the manufacturing process – and their manual processing require a large number of pieces that are nonetheless simple to arrange ↘ 5, 7 The changing moods of light from day to night and from summer to winter may lend a building either a sculpturally reflective or transparently layered appearance. ↘ 6

The challenge for the architect lies in finding the right material for the design concept, in converting an idea into specific building materials, colours and surfaces. The necessity of jointing and structuring building components and their effect is enhanced by the play of light and colour. It can be perceived as harmonious, agreeable and beautiful, or dissonant and even ugly. Seemingly unbalanced proportion and disharmonies can also be used deliberately in order to give a building the desired expression. The scale and massing of a building can also be manipulated.

JOINTING

There are a number of reasons why joints appear in a facade. In the first instance, the potential production formats and the panel sizes of construction materials determine the visible material joints and joint grids. In the case of self-supporting envelopes, for example, the joint pattern is determined by the dimensions of the masonry unit (brick, natural stone) or by the joints between the shuttering boards (cast concrete walls). It makes sense to coordinate the building grid with the grid used for cladding the facade. Deviations from standard dimensions normally lead to increased cost.

The expansion and contraction of materials exposed to heat and cold create movement in the facade. This may require additional movement joints, which are either necessary for the loadbearing construction or for absorbing the change in longitudinal dimension of the facade material itself. The design of such joints represents a difficult detail with regard to weatherproofing. Details have to be designed appropriately for the material and the type of construction concerned so as to ensure that the joints are permanently sealed.

The joint is a design element used in architecture and should therefore be considered at an early stage in the design of a facade. The visible appearance of joints can also vary a great deal, depending on the material. For example, it is possible to have open joints, recessed ('shadow') joints, or joints that are almost flush with the adjoining surface.

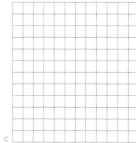
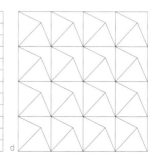

1a   b   c   d

1 Texture – principles
a Light / heavy
b Scale / grain
c Elements: homogeneous / jointed
d Light / shadow / reflection

2 The Maison Roduit, Chamoson 2005, Savioz Fabrizzi: Traditional natural stone and modern fair-faced concrete combined.

3 Housing on Giudecca, Venice, 2002, Cino Zucchi: The homogeneous finish of the render results in a flat texture, the window surrounds are coloured to provide variation.

4 Conversion and refurbishment of Munich Technical University, 2013, Hild and K: The undulating form of the suspended face brickwork is reminiscent of cloth.

5 Residence, Remerschen, 2014, Valentiny Architects: The use of weathered Corten steel produces a lively patina.

6 Library, Seattle, 2004, OMA: The self-supporting, cassette-shaped steel/glass construction functions as the envelope and reflects the surroundings.

7 The Walt Disney Concert Hall, Los Angeles, 2003, Frank O. Gehry: The order and sculptural effect of the shape are altered by the material chosen (metal).

8 Sauna building, Koblach, 2012, Bernardo Bader: The facade is subdivided by the effect of spacing the horizontal battens at different intervals.

9 The 'Mondholzhaus', Domat, 2013, Gion A. Caminada: Cladding the curved parts of the building is made simple by the use of small shingles.

10 The Silodam Container, Amsterdam, 2002, MVRDV: Each level has its own colour and identity

2

3

4

5

6

7

8

9

10

TYPOLOGY AND USE

There is a close connection between the type of a building and its facade design; this is expressed in how the inner organisation of the building harmonises with the construction and function of the facade and with its overall appearance in urban space. The type of building and its appearance can directly determine the use of a building. Construction components and services installations, as well as local building forms and details, can be expressed in the facade as important design features.

The use of a building dictates specific requirements for the building envelope; the spatial distribution of functions and the selected construction grid have a direct influence on the appearance and structure of the facade. Conversely, subdivision of the facade determines the flexibility of use. A practical facade construction grid favours the opportunities for effecting a change of use and thereby has an impact on the cost efficiency and sustainability of the building.

Buildings are designed and constructed for different types of use. The way spaces are arranged and used has an impact on the necessary openings in the facade, and hence on the building envelope. It is important to consider aspects of comfort and functionality just as much as the position and size of openings in the facade, which are required for natural light, ventilation and for the opportunity to see in or out.

With certain building functions, the facade does not always express the internal grid pattern on the outside; likewise, the design is not always intended to convey a direct expression. A strict grid inside the building may remain visible in the arrangement of windows, or it may be obscured or completely concealed by an additional facade layer. In other cases the facade functions like a filter or mask that envelopes the building and leaves the spectator uncertain of its structure.

In contrast, the form of a number of building types results almost inevitably from the use, such as infrastructure buildings or sports venues. Taking the example of a football stadium, it becomes apparent how the building type, form and facade meld into one; the number of seats, the maximum gradient of the grandstands, the roof over the spectators and the open space above the pitch all add up to a readily identifiable sports venue. This inevitable association is rarely so clear cut. In the case of a concert hall, it is possible that the building reproduces the shape of the auditorium on the outside. This is determined by the acoustics, which are affected in turn by the arrangement of the seats and the stage area. Conversely, it is possible that the auditorium remains concealed behind the envelope, to be experienced only from within. An office building readily reveals the parameters – a top priority is the level of light at each workplace. The objective is to allow enough daylight to enter the room so that the cost of artificial lighting can be minimised. At the same time, the daylight must be controllable so that computer work is possible without glare. Direct sunlight – with its associated heat gain and potential glare – is not desirable because it adds to the already substantial internal heat gain from people and electrical equipment, as well as restricting the use of the room. DIN 5035 and the Workplace Directive contain definitions of workplace lighting. Different functions have different requirements for light quality and hence have a direct impact on the design of the building envelope. For example, the all-glass facades frequently used in office buildings go against the technical requirements for light and heat. To enable their proper use, additional measures are employed such as double-skin facades, fixed and movable screening modules, blinds, screens and special glazing. For the user, a prime issue in the case of more complex systems is that of individual control. Is it possible to override the control of the screening elements manually, or is the solar screening raised or lowered by an electronic control system without the option of intervention? This can create conflicts of interest, because the automatic control system is a reliable device preventing the overheating of rooms. Users' personal preferences, such as the desire to look out or have brighter surroundings, cannot be accommodated.

In addition to admitting daylight, the facade is also responsible for thermal comfort in the building. An exterior skin with poor insulating properties results in low surface temperatures at the external walls, which can lead to technical and building physics problems as well as affecting comfort. Pronounced differences between the surface temperature of the facade and that of other room surfaces must be avoided, because the contrast in thermal radiation – as well as the resulting air movement – is perceived as uncomfortable. It is possible to compensate for cool facade surfaces by increasing the indoor air temperature, although this will have a negative effect on the total energy consumption of the building. It follows that the facade is a key interface when it comes to comfort, user-friendliness, building physics and ecology.

All these factors – in a telling and recognisable fashion – affect the appearance of building envelopes.

1 Olivetti buildings, Frankfurt am Main, 1972, Egon Eiermann: Vertical and horizontal bars provide a relief to the strict facade grid of the two tower blocks, imparting a slender, floating elegance to the solid volumes. The aesthetic quality reflects the functional requirements.

2 The European Central Bank, Frankfurt am Main, 2015, Coop Himmelb(l)au: The composition of two glass towers rises from a polygonal footprint, which is reinforced by the glass envelope of slanting, partially curved, glass surfaces. It was not possible to achieve the desired appearance and functionality with commonly available systems; for this reason a new type of facade was developed, called the 'shield hybrid facade'.

3 Library, Birmingham (UK), 2014, mecanoo architects: The new building for the library comprises three distinct parts stacked one upon the other, transparent and solid rectangular volumes clad with interlocking aluminium rings of different sizes. These symbolise the industrial past of the city and form a decorative filter that shelters the interior.

4 The Jacob and Wilhelm Grimm Centre, Berlin, 2009, Max Dudler Architects: The basic motif of the library is derived from bookshelves. The strict subdivision of the suspended stone facade expresses the use of the interior. The narrow windows are placed in front of bookshelf areas, while the wide windows provide light to workplaces.

5 Selfridges department store, Birmingham (UK), 2003, Future Systems: The 'blob' shape puts the building into context regardless of scale. Fifteen thousand aluminium plates measuring 60 cm in diameter follow the organic, sculptural shape of the building and modify its appearance depending on the angle of light.

6 Louis Vuitton store, Tokyo, 2014, Aoki Jun and Associates: The perforated front of the building has been designed with reference to the logo of the Louis Vuitton brand and makes reference to the Art Déco past of the Matsuya Ginza city quarter. During the day the external skin appears as a homogeneous surface, while at night the LED strips light up the monograms from within the facade.

ENVELOPE AND CONSTRUCTION

Every building has an envelope with an inner and an outer face which, depending on the loadbearing structure ⟶ SCALE, vol. 3, Support | Materialise, performs a number of protective functions. This may take the form of a solid, monolithic structure or of several different successive 'filter' layers, each of which has a specific function. ⟶ 4 The more recent construction methods offer greater flexibility in the loadbearing structure and hence in the design of the layout on plan. This can affect the positions of the walls and of the envelope. The separation of the loadbearing structure and the envelope goes hand in hand with the dissolution of the facade into distinct layers. Each 'filter' layer performs its own function, each building component is potentially a design element in its own right, including the columns and other loadbearing elements which are separate from the envelope. If the envelope and the loadbearing structure are one and the same, this is normally referred to as solid construction; a construction in which the envelope as the outer facade element is separated from columns and floor slabs is referred to as skeleton or frame construction. As a means of bracing, in large buildings the floor slabs are often connected with the solid building core; the thermal envelope remains nevertheless independent of the loadbearing structure.

The clear expression of structure is compromised when overlaid by the secondary construction and industrially produced elements. This type of construction method is referred to as hybrid, as it employs a variety of construction systems. Therefore the choice of construction and materials involves aesthetic, economic and ecological considerations which are directly connected with the function of the building component.

The move away from solid building components with a large mass towards high-performance filigree elements increasingly leads to greater freedom with respect to construction and conceptual design. It means that solutions can be tailored closely to each brief. Independently of whether the focus is on the recognisability of the structural elements of the construction or on conceptual aesthetics as the primary design objective, the building construction must fulfil the following requirements:
- Functionality, compliance with the principles, rules and regulations of construction;
- Freedom from defects in execution and cooperation amongst the trades, including operation and maintenance;
- High-quality design and appearance, from the installation through to the graceful aging of the facade;
- Sustainability in terms of the responsible use of resources and the energy needed for the production, use and disposal of the construction material.

As the requirements for the construction of building envelopes become more complex, more expert knowledge and experience is needed. It is not just building physics that makes high demands of the facade: all aspects of building design are involved. For this reason, good coordination and communication among the members of a qualified design team is the key requisite for the fault-free execution and function of a high-quality building envelope.

1   Apartment block in Hamburg, 1920s: The solid external wall with individual windows is typical of the Expressionist brick architecture of the 1920s.

2   Office building, Hamburg, 2011, Henning Larsen Architects: The glass facade consists of an inner envelope of timber window elements and an external mullion / transom facade with single-glazing, which makes natural ventilation possible. The solid sections are part of the solar screening system.

3   Holiday home, Salt Point, 2007, Thomas Phifer: The holiday home is shrouded in a screen of perforated stainless steel. Depending on the changes in light, the facade changes from opaque to a transparent envelope and blurs the boundaries between interior and exterior.

4 Requirements of a facade
Interface between inside and
outside
Interplay between functional requirements and design aspects.

LIGHT/COMFORT
Daylight incidence
Views to the outside
Boundary between private and public
Glare protection, light control

THERMAL COMFORT
Room climate/temperature
Constancy of temperature
Heating and cooling
Airtightness
Protection against cooling down
in winter
Ventilation of rooms, exchange of air

ACOUSTIC COMFORT
Sound insulation

SAFETY AND PROTECTION
Fire protection
Fall protection

SERVICES INSTALLATIONS
Controls – individual, central
Flexibility of use
Activation of building components
for the purpose of storing energy,
heating and cooling

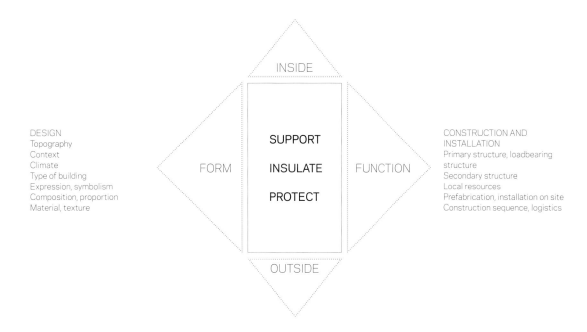

DESIGN
Topography
Context
Climate
Type of building
Expression, symbolism
Composition, proportion
Material, texture

CONSTRUCTION AND
INSTALLATION
Primary structure, loadbearing
structure
Secondary structure
Local resources
Prefabrication, installation on site
Construction sequence, logistics

INSIDE

FORM   SUPPORT   FUNCTION
        INSULATE
        PROTECT

OUTSIDE

THERMAL REQUIREMENTS
Climate envelope
Thermal and solar protection
Glare protection
Wind barrier
Protection against rain and humidity

ACOUSTIC REQUIREMENTS
Sound absorption

SECURITY AND PROTECTION
Fire protection
Fall protection
Radiation, noxious substances
Intrusion, vandalism
Sound insulation

SERVICES INSTALLATIONS
Photovoltaics, collectors
Geothermal probes, heat recovery
Solar thermal collectors

4

SOLID CONSTRUCTION

In the case of the single-skin solid wall – which performs the functions of structural support, insulation and protection in one layer – a distinction is made between 'warm' and 'cold' facades. ↘ 1

In the 'warm' facade, the thermal insulation layer is fitted directly on the loadbearing layer. When this insulation is on the outside, the outer surface must also provide protection against the weather in order to avert damage to the construction. When the insulation material is placed on the inside face of the construction, it is possible to achieve an improved energy standard without changing the exterior appearance (for example in the case of refurbishment or in historic buildings). Internal insulation must be carefully designed and its installation must be closely supervised. An important aspect of the design is the simulation of the flow of moisture over several years. Nowadays, mineral-based internal insulation systems are available with physical properties equivalent to those of external insulation.

A 'cold' facade consists of several layers which perform different functions in terms of construction and building physics. The inner skin (consisting of the loadbearing structure, the thermal insulation and the sealing layer) is separated from the outer skin (weather protection layer) by a ventilated cavity. The separation of the insulation layer from the layer facing the weather protects the critical parts of the construction, such as the base of the wall and the roof parapet, as well as areas where the insulation and sealing are offset next to openings. Exterior cladding can consist of a wide range of materials, resulting in different loads and providing different design options. In this type of construction, it is important to ensure that the points at which the exterior cladding is fastened to the loadbearing structure are detailed and installed in a way that does not permit

any vulnerability where they penetrate the insulation layer.

A solid construction is often chosen for an exterior wall as the result of a conventional attitude. Putting up buildings with brick walls and concrete floors is often deemed to be the natural solution. In most cases, this method is the most economical because the people involved in the execution do not need to have specialist knowledge. Other criteria may be longevity and retention of value. The limitation of such a construction lies in its heavy weight. This means that in buildings over 25 m high, the economic advantages dwindle while the site logistics and transport of material during the construction phase become more expensive. The greater component thickness of highly insulated masonry units results in an unfavourable proportion of footprint area to net floor area.

Solid structures can store heat over longer periods, and give it off again slowly. In solid construction, orthogonal designs are common, although it is also possible to build walls in slanting, amorphous or kinked shapes using brickwork or concrete.

Solid construction necessitates either adding elements (bricks or masonry units) or casting monolithic structures (concrete). The solid structure of the wall means that the material can be visible both externally and internally, which can provide a special experience in terms of touch and the appearance of the jointing. The weathering quality of a single-skin system can be improved by applying an additional layer such as rendering, or back-ventilated external cladding in front of insulation.

Solid construction may also take the form of a solid wall with an outer layer of facing bricks, or a cavity wall (common in Anglo-Saxon countries), which involves a ventilated cavity between the outer and inner leaves. However, the effect of suspended cladding that consists

   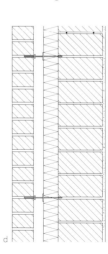

1a   b   c   d

1   Wall construction types
a   Single-skin
b   Double-skin, external insulation
c   Double-skin, internal insulation
d   Multi-skin, ventilation in front of the insulation plane

Solid construction	Single-skin	Skeleton construction

Masonry construction/face brickwork
→ p. 50

Fair-faced concrete

Log construction, visible
→ p. 58

Aerated concrete blockwork, rendered
Highly thermally insulating masonry, rendered

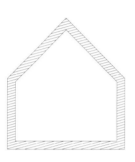

Aerated concrete blockwork, with cladding
Highly thermally insulating masonry, with cladding

Traditional timber frame construction,
timber skeleton construction,
with insulation and cladding

Timber frame construction,
with insulation and cladding
→ p. 78

External insulation layer:
Insulated concrete construction with suspended cladding of prefabricated concrete panels

Internal insulation layer:
Fair-faced concrete construction with insulation,
protective inside lining

Log construction with insulation,
protective inside lining

External insulation layer:
Steel skeleton construction with curtain wall facade
→ p. 80

Composite thermal insulation system,
with cladding
→ p. 100

Internal insulation layer:
Timber frame construction with internal insulation

Concrete skeleton construction with internal insulation
→ p. 134

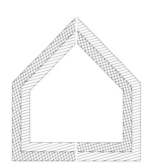

External insulation layer:
Masonry construction, single-skin, with insulation, rendered or clad

Concrete construction, single-skin, with insulation, rendered or clad

Timber panel construction, with insulation and cladding

Insulation within the construction:
Masonry construction, double-skin, with insulation, face brick or rendered
→ p. 84

Fair-faced concrete construction, double-skin, with insulation,
→ p. 54

Insulation within the construction:
Sandwich systems, with several layers, insulated, face layer
→ p. 80

Suspended back-ventilated facades,
single-skin, insulated, air gap,
envelope with exposed material
→ p. 90

Integrated insulation layer:
Membrane, integrated air gap
→ p. 98

Multi-skin

of 'solid' materials is different to that of a wall built mono-lithically. This is due to differences in the type of jointing, the junctions between building components and the visible movement joints. In traditional masonry construction, the width of windows and doors was limited because the width of arches built with masonry units over these openings was limited. Such facades usually have a balanced proportion of solid wall to opening. With the introduction of reinforced concrete elements for use as lintels over openings and in loadbearing walls, it became possible to design larger openings in solid construction too, which has led to a new aesthetic.

SKELETON CONSTRUCTION

With the disappearance of the solid wall owing to the use of new building materials such as steel, cast-iron and glass, for example in the imposing greenhouses by Joseph Paxton in the late nineteenth century, the principle of skeleton construction – already known from timber frame buildings – emerged as an alternative that promised the efficient use of material. The loadbearing function of the structure is performed by individual elements such as columns, foundations, floor slabs and plinths, thereby reducing the vertical forces and hence the quantity of material required. The separation of the building structure into loadbearing and non-loadbearing elements results in a loadbearing skeleton, which provides the designer with greater freedom in terms of layout and facade design. In this kind of construction, the thermal envelope is also the element that encloses space. While the facade elements were initially placed between columns and slabs, this technique was superseded by the construction known as a 'curtain wall', in which the facade elements are fitted full-height in front of the structure. The primary structure is moved inwards

from the edge of the building, while the secondary structure – in this case the facade and exterior enclosure – can be placed outside the building's structure. This means that, for the first time, the size of window openings is no longer limited and fenestration can be arranged in bands, as part of a grid facade, or even as full glazing mounted from the bottom up or suspended from the top. → 4

The diversity of form in contemporary architecture primarily depends on the continuing development of this construction method. The skeleton construction method does not provide storage mass in the form of walls, so this function must be performed by additional layers. The complexity of the system makes it necessary to think in terms of strict hierarchies and orders, and requires disciplined detailing, in order to be able to achieve cost-efficient production and installation. → 5 Advanced construction methods use multi-layered assemblies. Different materials and construction elements, each with special characteristics, are installed such that they can fulfil the complex requirements made of the building envelope as a unit. Facade cladding systems with back-ventilation, in which the visible facade material is separate from the insulated wall construction, have become popular. The materials used, as a consequence of their specific properties, determine the appearance of a facade, as well as its construction system and its building physics functionality. The selection of materials and the dimensioning of elements are limited by their respective properties and by the limitations associated with production and installation, be it industrial or craft-based. The external skin can be installed as back-ventilated rain-screen cladding in front of the insulated construction; typical examples are metal sheeting, fibre cement panels, wood-based panels, timber cladding and plastic panels.

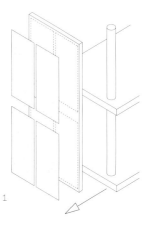

1   Functions of facade layers from inside to outside:
Vapour seal
Support
Insulation
Weather-protection layer

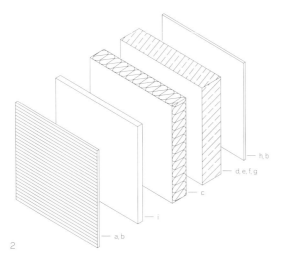

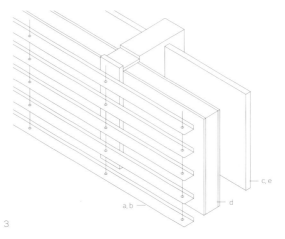

2   Typical functions of a solid external wall, which may be performed by just one material:
a   Rain protection
b   Mechanical protection
c   Thermal insulation
d   Structural integrity
e   Sound insulation
f   Fire protection
g   Thermal storage
h   Airtightness/vapour-tightness
i   Protection against humidity/ wind

3   Typical functions of a transparent glass facade:
a   Solar screening
b   Light control
c   Glare protection
d   UV-protection
e   Black-out

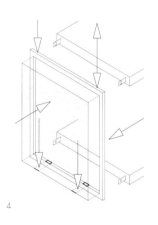

4

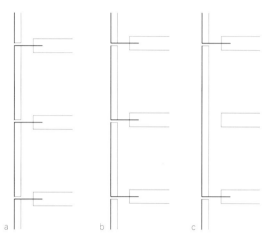

a   b   c

4 Transfer of loads

Horizontal:
Negative wind pressure
Snow loads
Strain forces resulting from
temperature fluctuations, material
expansion etc.

Vertical:
Own loads
Strain forces resulting from
temperature fluctuations, material
expansion etc.

a Suspended
b Standing
c Standing over two storeys

Cladding panels or a suspended facade may also consist of materials such as brickwork, natural stone and concrete, which historically are more associated with the solid construction method. This makes efficient use of the material and its positive mechanical properties.
→ 1, 2
Every design decision concerning the composition and proportion of such a facade is governed by the principle of the grid. This grid may have the same dimensions as the grid of the primary structure, or it may be offset with different field widths, or it may be completely independent of the main grid, forming the fit-out grid for fitting out the interior. Repeating the module dimensions helps to reduce the cost of site logistics and of manufacturing prefabricated units.

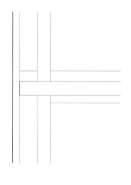 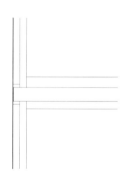 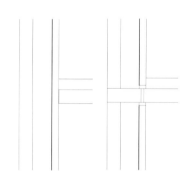

5 Position of the thermal envelope
and the associated design options
in skeleton construction

a In front of the primary structure
b Within it
c Behind it

5a 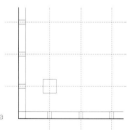   b 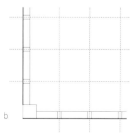   c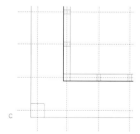

Position	Secondary structure in front of the primary structure
Advantage	Design freedom for the interior Transparent corners No thermal bridges Prevents fire flashover in the facade plane
Disadvantage	Additional fire protection required between the facade and the structural shell

Position	Facade externally flush in the plane of the primary structure
Advantage	No connection surfaces on the inside
Disadvantage	Closed facade corner Detailing of the thermal insulation of the face of the floor slab and of the primary structure Connections create thermal bridges

Position	Primary structure in front of the secondary structure
Advantage	No columns on the inside
Disadvantage	Restricts view to the outside It is necessary to decouple the floor slab thermally in the facade plane Connections create thermal bridges Higher cost

PROTECTION

Building envelopes protect people from the effects of the environment and therefore any facade construction should have a long service life. In particular this refers to the technical and building physics requirements – from the outside and from the inside – which must be fulfilled by the material and construction. For example, a simple steel sheet is capable of withstanding water and vapour pressure, but is inadequate in terms of thermal insulation. Conversely, thermal insulation layer which is not sufficiently protected against moisture ingress will become saturated with water and gradually lose its effect. However, when these two materials are combined in the form of a sandwich element, they represent a fully functional facade envelope. There are some materials that fulfil all functions with a thickness of only few centimetres (for example, insulating glazing), while other constructions need many layers in order to achieve the same result.

The two main requirements for a building envelope are, firstly, protection against damp and precipitation and, secondly, thermal protection against cold in winter and heat in summer. Respectively, thermal protection has the aim of reducing energy losses from the interior, or of preventing heat gain. This means that the envelope has an effect on the energy requirement for heating in winter and on the internal temperature or the energy demand for cooling in summer. The thermal transmittance or heat transfer coefficient (U-value, W/m^2K) of a construction defines the amount of heat that flows through a building component under defined boundary conditions (heat transfer) and is used to calculate the key energy values of a building. The smaller the thermal transmittance of a building element is, the better are its insulating properties, making it easier to save energy and reduce costs. In addition, the surface temperature of the facade on the building's interior affects the perceived comfort of the user.

The potential for better U-values lies not only in the improved physical properties of the insulation material, but also in improving the construction of facade frames and openings, as well as the glazing – using thermally insulated frames, surface coating on insulating glazing and new compound materials in the non-transparent areas. Energy is not only lost through transmission, but also through leaks and joints in the construction. These leaks can be the cause of considerable structural or material problems. Joints or cracks provide a path for moisture from the internal air to migrate into the building fabric, where in winter it may precipitate as condensate and make the fabric damp, which can potentially lead to the destruction of the components and the loadbearing structure. Furthermore, the accumulation of water in insulating layers results in a significant worsening of the insulation properties.

Considered from the outside, joints in a building envelope enable rainwater to enter directly or via capillary action, which can also lead to building defects. Joint permeability also has a direct effect on the transmission of airborne noise. The design of the detailed construction is therefore critical in order to ensure the necessary airtightness (from the inside) and wind-tightness (from the outside), and careful supervision on site is required. Airtightness can be achieved by installing special membranes, for example, whereas in solid construction a continuous layer of plaster or render is sufficient. External protection against precipitation is just as important as providing adequate thermal insulation.

Many defects in buildings result from badly matched or faulty detailing of the facade construction. Even seemingly tried-and-tested constructions, such as frame-based facades, and the respective connections with the building fabric have many potential failure points, and care must be taken in their design and on-site assembly. In wall construction, at least three layers are required to meet contemporary requirements: those for loadbearing, insulation and weather protection. In a normal masonry wall, the brick or block itself fulfils the insulating, loadbearing and sound insulation requirements. The inner plaster finish ensures the airtightness of the construction and provides the visible enclosure. The exterior layer of render protects the structure against precipitation. In such wall constructions, today's requirements for thermal insulation can be met by using masonry units with cavities filled with an insulating material or by aerated concrete blocks. Conventional masonry units can also be used if the structure is combined with an additional external layer of insulation (thermal sandwich insulation system). However, without additional measures this type of construction is less resistant to mechanical impact from the outside. Likewise, the appearance of render applied to such a sandwich system is different from that applied directly to masonry – the insulation layer will be perceived both visually and acoustically (when tapped upon). This example shows that the designer needs to weigh up the advantages of the various factors such as perception, durability, production costs, sustainability and disposal and recycling aspects. Classic defect areas – in addition to the base and the parapet/roof connection – are the joints between the building components and the points at which fastenings and services penetrate the insulation layer. Offsets in the plane of insulation and sealing materials must also be given special attention, as should the detailing of vertical and horizontal external and internal corners with respect to thermal bridging. Furthermore, the interior fit-out elements, e.g. partition wall systems, are usually in contact with the thermal envelope – something that needs to be taken into consideration in the facade design.

Diagrams of facade functions
Effects and measures

1 Solar irradiation
a Heat
b Light

2 Precipitation, snow load
a Rain
b Snow
c Ground moisture

3 Relative humidity, water vapour
a Single-layer
b Multi-skin
c Multi-layer

4 Risk of cold bridges where insulation or separation of materialsis insufficient
a Plinth
b Balcony
c Flat roof

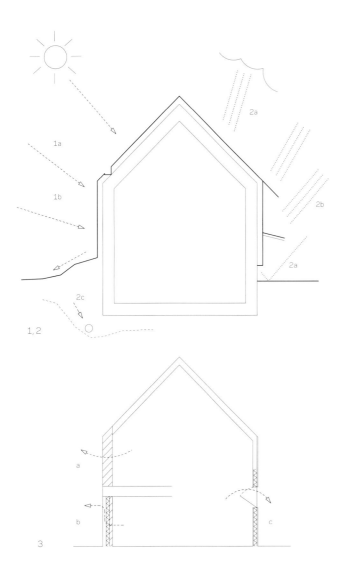

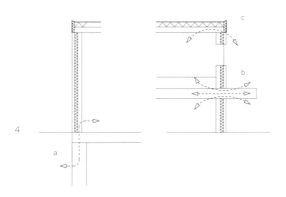

IMPACT FROM THE EXTERIOR	NECESSARY CONSTRUCTION MEASURES, such as
Solar irradiation, light	Solar screening, glare protection, light control, black-out, UV-protection (paint, material)
Solar irradiation, heat	Insulation, use of passive solar gain, reflection, surface colour
External air temperature, summer	Insulation, storage mass
External air temperature, winter	Insulation of building components, storage mass, reduction of thermal bridges, airtightness of construction
Precipitation, vapour	Protection against the ingress of water or driving rain, rain seal, leak-proof roof membrane, protection via construction elements e.g. canopy, roof overhang, plinth, fall in the terrain, drainage
Building loads, ground motion	Foundations, structural calculations, special construction methods (e.g. earthquake stability)
Snow load	Sealing measures, structural measures
Wind load	Air sealing measures, structural measures
Odour	Air seals, filtering
Noxious substances in the air	Air seals, filtering
Fire	Active and passive fire protection measures (building material class, fire resistance)
Noise	Sound insulation measures
Views in	Screening measures
Mechanical impact	Choice of material for external cladding, protection via construction elements
Soiling	Choice of material of external cladding, protection via construction elements, cleansing aids

IMPACT FROM THE INTERIOR	NECESSARY CONSTRUCTION MEASURES, such as
Air temperature winter (interior)	Insulation, expansion joint, avoiding cold bridges
Relative humidity, vapour pressure	Vapour seal, discharge of humidity, discharge of condensate, back-ventilation
Fire	Active and passive fire protection measures (building material class, fire resistance)
Noise	Sound insulation measures
Mechanical impact	Choice of interior cladding material, protection via construction elements
Soiling	Choice of interior cladding material, protection via construction elements

ECONOMY AND PROCESS QUALITY

The increasing demands made of buildings are not only apparent in the construction details, but also in the design and construction process. For some time now, the architect coordinating a large project has had additional support from specialist facade designers, air-conditioning specialist, building physics specialists and energy experts; nevertheless, basic competence in these specialist areas is still required for the purpose of their coordination. The architect operates as a coordinator and communicator and, equipped with adequate technical know-how, ensures that construction projects meet economic and commercial criteria.

In addition to the classic areas of architectural expertise, a holistic design approach also requires knowledge of the ecological and economic aspects of design, production, installation, maintenance and servicing. Extensive knowledge of new developments, technologies and available materials is also required. Strategies and assessment criteria for the correct selection of a facade solution are required at an early stage in the design in order to avoid subsequent changes which result in high costs. Similarly, it is important to be aware of changing standards and guidelines and to take into account any new technologies and system modifications. It follows that a competent design team is required to control the design process, which will make far-reaching decisions either in agreement with the building client/user or, sometimes, on its own. The level of process quality is evident in the cost planning, the control of deadlines and the quality of the building design. However, the real conceptual design process is not covered by these criteria and evaluation systems. Most intelligent facade concepts require the networking of interdisciplinary teams for their creation;

these teams will take different options into consideration and thus allow for the complexity of the tasks, evaluating different solutions in accordance with requirements and priorities. Any solution found for an individual building may not necessarily be transferable to other projects, but it can contribute to a basis and inspiration for a holistic approach to facade design.

When designing facades, the strong interdependence of the parameters of cost, quality and deadlines make it necessary to consider and evaluate different construction methods, details and materials and to find a suitable solution in agreement between the client and design team. The first step in creating the evaluation matrix – construction, material, details, cost – for design options is to define the requirements for the facade, which are normally supplied by the client or possibly the user. The objectives must be defined at an early stage and the client/user has to contribute to many decisions during the design process. For example, any subsequent change in the energy-related quality of the building envelope has a severe impact on the services installations concept.

These parameters can be influenced most effectively at an early stage in the design and development process. It is important that conceptual design quality and functionality are in harmony – within the set budget. Unrealistic cost estimates and ill-considered economies always have a negative impact on quality and the subsequent costs during the use phase. For example, a rendered facade on a tower block may reduce the initial cost of investment compared to a high-quality metal facade, but the subsequent cost involved in the maintenance/renewal of the facade at shorter intervals can very soon wipe out this advantage.

1 Relationship between integrated design, sustainability and process quality

Position	Client	User, operator	Architect	Specialist engineer	Construction industry	Property industry	Society
Requirement	Design, functionality, technology, cost-efficiency, operation, time, socio-cultural influences, economy, ecology						
Tasks	Drawing up the brief, supporting and monitoring the design and construction process	Drawing up the user requirements and processes	Analysis of location, user requirements and technical possibilities, socio-cultural influences, sustainability and ecology requirements, producing and assessing workable solutions as basis of a decision, link between all those involved in the design and production process	Analysis of technical possibilities and how they can be implemented in the construction; integration of these measures into the design	Availability of environmentally compatible raw materials, recyclability of construction materials, access to alternative energy supply	Modification of the value-creation model in favour of subsequent increase in density and revitalisation; flexibility of use concepts, change-of-use investment and location factors; sparing use of construction land/sealed surfaces	Participation models; integration of the different stakeholder groups; creating local identity for individuals and society, use models (mixed use); infrastructure and mobility concepts
Process/time factor	Design, production process, life cycle						

2 Relationships of tasks and participants in the building process, and effects on design, construction process and life cycle

POTENTIAL FOR OPTIMISATION

An important component of the optimisation of process quality is an exact definition of the task. What are the requirements that the facade of an office building has to fulfil? How transparent or opaque is the building to its surroundings? What additional loads can be absorbed by an existing building when the facade is upgraded for the purpose of energy optimisation? Should the building envelope have a flat appearance, with the openings being flush with the facade, or should the facade be structured by the grid of a construction system? What is the orientation of the building and how does this affect the use of daylight and the outlay for energy and maintenance? For example, although a south-facing facade requires solar screening and glare protection, it may, owing to passive solar gain in winter, nevertheless be an economic option, provided rigid – and hence low-maintenance – screening systems can be fitted. Appropriate solutions may be found more easily by questioning the functional requirements with an open mind and analysing the local parameters.

The selection of materials used and their processing has an influence on construction time and cost. Constructions made of materials that are simple to install – such as back-ventilated timber cladding – can be produced economically. By contrast, a back-ventilated natural stone facade is significantly more costly; the reasons are both the cost of the material itself and the fastening technology which, owing to the great weight of the stone, must consist of durable, corrosion-free material. Generally speaking, large and heavy components can only be installed with the aid of appropriate machinery (such as a

crane) and require an installation team with special know-how. Special solutions and non-standard formats almost always result in increased costs for both production and transport, and an associated extension of the construction period, unless they are produced in large numbers. In addition, the designer can influence the cost, quality and time frame of the construction by selecting a production method (prefabrication, part prefabrication or installation on site), that is suitable for the size of the project. A high degree of prefabrication will normally reduce the time required for construction on site, but extend the time required during the design phase. In contrast, assembling components on site can lead to a longer construction period, but may be more economical because local tradesmen who need shorter lead times may be available. As a rule, the use of standardised components, shorter transport distances, repeats of the same design details and simple loadbearing structures, as well as an appropriate choice of material, all result in a lower construction cost. Commissioning the completed project is likewise part of quality assurance; in this context it is important to remember that the efficiency of a system can only be assessed after completed heating and cooling seasons. The subsequent tuning of building services becomes an important component of building maintenance. The quality of the installation is a vital element in ensuring the fitness for purpose and the durability of a facade. Due to the conditions on building sites and the primarily manual construction process, the execution of the interface between envelope and loadbearing structure requires great precision and attention to detail in order to avoid future defects resulting from thermal bridges or leakage.

3 Effect of processes, costs and design freedom on building phases. Analogous to the German BNB system (BNB = assessment system for sustainable construction), see also Jones Lang LaSalle (2008)

Phase	Selection of location	Start of design phase	Start of construction	Construction period	Use period	Change of use/demolition
Processes	User requirements	Integrated design with all those involved	Selection of systems/material, production, modes of transport through to assembly on site/prefabrication	Selection of contractors through to handover	Maintenance, servicing, cleaning	Recycling or disposal
Degree of influence/costs	High degree of influence/low cost	Medium degree of influence/medium cost	Low degree of influence/high cost	Low degree of influence/maximum cost	Large cost factor depending on solution	Large cost factor depending on solution

ECOLOGY AND LIFE CYCLE

The construction industry can potentially make a big contribution to sustainable building in the sense of the careful use of land and material resources, the conservation of energy and reduction of emissions. The construction industry – including building construction, civil engineering and infrastructure – accounts for 50 % of raw material consumption worldwide. In Germany, 60 % of waste is produced by the construction industry; furthermore, in Central Europe, approx. 50 % of energy generated is used for the operation of our buildings. In view of the fact that our planet's energy and material resources are finite, it is important to select materials according to ecological criteria – from the extraction of the materials to the construction and maintenance of the building as well as its demolition, disposal and recycling.

The awareness of and sensitivity to environmental issues is increasing in our society; this should be matched by appropriate qualities in the design, use and efficient maintenance of buildings. In order to ensure this while maintaining typological and conceptual diversity in building construction, scientists have developed assessment systems and indicators for the sustainability of buildings over the last decades, which make it possible to assess and classify buildings according to standardised criteria. The best-known certificates – which can be summarised internationally under the term 'green building' – are BREEAM and LEED, developed in Great Britain and the U.S.A respectively. Assessment methods have also been developed for use in German-speaking and European countries, such as the DGNB (German quality seal for sustainable building) in Germany and the Minergie standard in Switzerland.

The key indicators of sustainability can be found in all assessment systems: ecology (building materials, water, type of site / land use, energy / technology), economy (planning processes / management, innovation and design processes, transport) and social benefits (functionality, health and wellbeing, conceptual design quality). These issues not only relate to buildings overall, but also concern the definition of the requirements for building envelopes. Apart from the energy consumption of a building, which ecological factors must be taken into account in the design of a facade? What is the influence of the service life of construction materials and assemblies on their treatment and maintenance?

PRIMARY ENERGY

An important aspect is the primary energy content (PEC) of the materials used, which describes the energy embodied in a material in its production, transport, storage, installation and disposal – also referred to as 'grey' or 'embodied energy'. It follows that materials with high primary energy content are those whose production consumes a lot of energy, such as metal, glass or plastic. Materials with low primary energy content include clay, gypsum and renewable raw materials such as timber. However, materials with low embodied energy from the production process may still have a significantly increased PEC as a result of their processing or transport requirements. When comparing facades of different materials, it becomes evident that the amount of embodied primary energy can vary significantly, e.g. a brick facade has approx. 400 KWh/m² PEC whereas a timber facade has only approx. 80 KWh/m² PEC. To put these figures into a different context: the energy embodied in the bricks used to build a single-family house is roughly equivalent to the energy used in that building over a 15-year period under normal conditions. However, the higher amount of energy in a brick facade compares less unfavourably with that of a timber facade when taking into account its longer service life, which may be two to three times as long.

Structural shell	55 %
Facade	25 %
Fitting-out	20 %
Services installations	20 %

1   Content of primary energy
in the various parts of the building

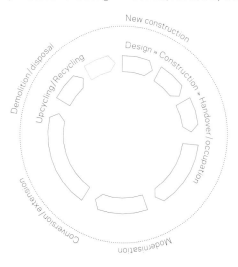

Technical factors
influencing the service life

Quality
of building materials →
Finish of construction
elements →

Maintenance
service intervals →
Proper workmanship →

Impact / wear
by users →
by weather →

New construction

Design » Construction » Handover / occupation

Demolition / disposal

Upcycling / Recycling

Conversion / extension

Modernisation

Commercial factors
influencing the service life

Profitability
← Construction costs
← Maintenance costs

← Location and surroundings

← Functionality
← Design quality

← Demographic change

← General circumstances /
income levels

2   Commercial and technical
factors influencing the life-cycle
of a building.

3 Selection of certificates/
assessment categories

LEED (USA):
Careful use of resources (land/
mineral resources), water efficiency
Energy and atmosphere
Materials and resources
Interior space quality
Innovation and design process

BREEAM (Great Britain):
Management
Energy, water
Land resource consumption and
ecology
Health and well-being
Transport, material
Pollution

DGNB (German quality seal for
sustainable building):
Ecology, economy
Social and functional aspects
Technology, processes, location

BNB (assessment system for
sustainable building), contains
assessment criteria for the
construction of German government buildings:
Ecology, economy
Social and functional aspects
Technology, processes, location

4 Technical service life of building
components (according to manufacturers' information) ➚ **Appendix,
p. 156**

5 Cleaning intervals for different
facade materials (according to
manufacturers' information)

LIFE-CYCLE COST/ECO-BALANCE

Frequently the cost of a building is assessed on the basis of construction costs only, although clearly there are additional costs that arise after completion of the building for maintenance, servicing and upkeep. Over the long term, these exceed the production costs. Currently, calculations for the cost efficiency of projected buildings work on the basis that, of the total cost, 20 to 25 % are investment costs and 75 to 80 % are costs resulting from the operation of the building. When the whole life cycle of a building is taken into account, the scope is broadened to include not only the construction cost and the operating, maintenance and value-preservation costs, but also the costs of demolition and disposal. ➚ 2

The notions of life-cycle cost (LCC) and eco-balance (LCA – life-cycle assessment) were originally developed for industrially manufactured products. When transferred to the construction industry, they were differentiated into two frames of reference. The first concerns the technical service life of the essential building components: How long does a building last? The second concerns the usability of the building: What duration of commercial use can be expected? The term 'technical service life' refers to the period over which the building, including its installations, is available before it is demolished. ➚ 4

The duration of the commercial use of a building is subject both to its fitness for a given purpose and to the economics of real estate investment. Factors such as the pay-back of construction costs, patterns of demand, the development of the location, and functional and aesthetic design qualities can have a significant impact on the commercial viability of a building during its service life and can even lead to its premature demolition. The holistic assessment of life cycles makes clear the direct interdependence of ecology and economy. The shorter the service life of a product and the more frequently a component has to be replaced during the commercial lifetime of a building, the higher the energy consumption (PEC) and the greater the burden on the environment; the costs of removing, disposing of and replacing components rise, and this too affects the eco-balance.

MAINTENANCE

The choice of building materials is also affected by the required frequency of servicing and maintenance, because the subsequent costs of these far exceed the construction cost of the building components. On the other hand, proper maintenance of the facade contributes to its longevity. Facade glazing, windows and exterior doors require quarterly cleaning, whereas coated metal facades have an average cleaning cycle of two to three years. By comparison, natural stone and untreated solid timber are very long-lived. ➚ 5

Accessibility is crucial to cleaning and maintaining facades. Good detailing can protect facade elements and thus prolong their service life. Higher buildings with large glazed areas require either shading ledges/gratings that can be walked on for maintenance, or lift platforms/cages. Additional hydrophobic coatings, as well as roof projections, can significantly extend cleaning intervals e.g. for glass. When assessing anticipated soiling, local conditions must be taken into account; for example, the expected cleaning intervals in an industrial area with high emissions, or near busy roads, are significantly shorter than those in a quiet, residential suburb.

Building component/layer	av. service life, years
External wall, loadbearing – concrete exposed to weather	70
External wall, loadbearing – brick, calcium silicate brick	120
External wall, non-loadbearing – softwood, exposed to weather	45
External wall, non-loadbearing – hardwood, exposed to weather	70
Exterior paint coating – impregnation on wood	15
Exterior render – cement-based, lime-cement-based	40
External render – thermal insulation sandwich system	30
Cladding on substructure – natural stone	80
Cladding on substructure – aluminium	45
Substructure – stainless steel	45
Substructure – timber	30

Facade material	Cleaning cycle/years
Aluminium cladding	2
Zinc sheet cladding	3
Enamelled steel sheet cladding	1
Glass	0.25
Natural stone	20
Prefabricated concrete elements	12
Clinker brick	20
Solid wood, fully coated	5
Solid wood, untreated	20
Fibre-cement tiles, coated, small format	10
Fibre-cement board, coated, large format	2

REFURBISHMENT, WASTE AND RECYCLING

REFURBISHMENT

In addition to the new construction of buildings involving the design of building envelopes that meet contemporary technical requirements, a large proportion of the construction volume to be expected in Europe will involve the refurbishment and renovation of existing buildings. There are many ways of dealing with existing buildings, ranging from simple reinstatement in which only the necessary repairs are carried out, through to energy upgrades and structural conversion work with the aim of improving the quality of the building by increasing its functional flexibility. A holistic assessment using the life-cycle model as a tool can be useful for determining a decision in this respect. → p. 40, Ecology and Life Cycle

The refurbishment and renovation of buildings can be economically and ecologically interesting alternatives to demolition and new construction. This is not only a question of better energy efficiency through upgrades and new installations to improve sustainability, but also one of structural measures.

An advantage here is the fact that the building can be retained, for example in inner city locations where new buildings would require new approvals, which may be subject to conditions relating to density, height and the distance from other buildings. The infrastructure, identity and services of city quarters can thus be retained while carefully developing the building stock to accommodate new functions and uses. Retaining the substance of buildings reduces the cost of construction; for example, if the facade of an existing office building has elementary defects because of an unfavourable grid dimension and the restricted ingress of daylight, this can be remedied by replacing the facade. The adaptation to a more economical facade grid improves efficiency and functional flexibility and thus makes the building more attractive to prospective tenants.

In addition it is possible that, beyond the purely technical functionality, the image of the building is improved. For example, the conversion of a residential post-war tower block in Paris demonstrates intelligent intervention involving changes to the basic structure. → 1 By contrast, the adaptation of the facade of a residential tower block, owned by the Munich students' union, to contemporary requirements with respect to energy standards and fire safety demonstrates how refurbishment is possible without losing the expressive character of a building. → 2

Requirements specific to the function of a building also play a role, for example it may be necessary to change the structure of a building in order to adapt it to a new function. Typical examples are defunct industrial and office buildings which are converted to residential or cultural use, or the use of historic buildings as hotels and restaurants. These conversions, fit-outs and extensions can be made distinct from the original fabric and thereby use the facade to confidently demonstrate the changes that have taken place. Alternatively, they can enter into a restrained dialogue with the existing style or take it further in much the same spirit.

Where a historic facade consists of natural stone, bricks or timber framing, it is important to ensure that the original character of the building is not lost. Likewise, mouldings, window and door reveals and other valuable historic embellishments may be of a quality that warrants preservation. Proper professional refurbishment requires knowledge of historic materials and traditional building methods. The decision in favour of one or the other design approach is arrived at through consideration of the respective design task, the user, the importance of the building itself, the built surroundings and – last but not least – with the agreement of the authorities and listed building department.

1 The Bois le Prêtre tower, Paris, 2011, Frédéric Druot with Lacaton & Vassal: A 17-storey apartment block - built by Raymond Lopez in 1958-61 – was extended by a prefabricated module suspended in front of the facade for the purpose of zoning and increasing the available living space. In addition, movable solar screening panels were fitted to conserve and store energy in the modules.

1

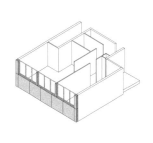
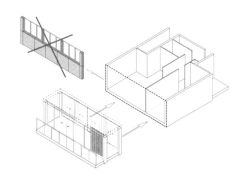

Refurbishment

2 Student housing in the Olympic Village in Munich, refurbishment 2012, Knerer Lang: A new curtain facade was developed as part of the overall refurbishment. A lightweight concrete frame system has been placed in front of the existing, newly insulated facade. The previous GRP panels underneath the windows have been replaced by solid panels with aluminium cladding, in combination with a new window element.
a   Prior to refurbishment
b   Following refurbishment

3 Office building on the Neue Balan campus, 2012, Oliv Architects: The energy upgrade of the existing facade was used to increase the grid dimension of the facade in order to improve the efficiency of the layout and thus to create more attractive lease properties in the new campus.
a   Prior to refurbishment
b   Following refurbishment

New building with recycled materials/recycling of building parts

4 The Welpeloo Residence, Enschede, 2012, Superuse Architecture: Sixty percent of the building consists of locally available recycled materials or materials intended for other purposes. The timber used in the facade was reclaimed from old cable drums while the glass elements are made of offcuts obtained from a nearby glass factory.

5 The 'Lesezeichen Salbke' open-air library, Magdeburg, 2009, KARO* Architects: This structure re-uses facade elements from the Horten department store in Hamm, which was built in 1966 and demolished in 2007.

2a

b

3a

b

4

5

WASTE AND RECYCLING

Many materials are already part of a closed cycle, which means that they are not declared as waste, but are processed into a secondary raw material, or used as fuel for the generation of energy. Bricks are crushed to make recycling concrete, glass is processed to produce insulation material, and the mineral material from demolished walls is used to make ballast for roads. The intention is to create cycles of this kind for all building materials in the future.

The direct re-use of building materials is rare, because in many instances it is not possible to provide the required long-term guarantees. Only products of high artistic or historical value qualify for direct re-use. The use of second-hand materials in the repair or refurbishment of historic buildings is common; a good example is the re-use of old oak timber for the repair of historic timber framing or roof structures. The re-use of weather-resistant second-hand timber from old barns and farmhouses for facade cladding is also increasingly popular. Recycling with unorthodox materials such as industrial offcuts or scrap to form complete buildings ⟶ 4 and the re-use of expressive facade elements in a new function ⟶ 5 gives the effect of old, familiar materials with a new and interesting feel. Whether a second-hand component can be re-used depends on a number of factors. Clearly, easy removal and good durability of the material increase the chances of the product's re-usability. Another important aspect is how easy it is to separate different materials. Composite materials such as aluminium panels with foam infill are highly questionable in this context, as is thermal insulation bonded to a carrier material. It would be easy to recycle the metal profiles of a frame-based facade if the type of alloy were known and had been manufactured with a view to being recycled. This type of recycling should be made possible by the respective industry. The facade thus becomes an ecological interface, because the selection of building materials and of insulation, as well as the subsequent expenditure, all affect the energy balance and, at the same time, the choice of material determines the basic materials that are later available to waste management.

OUTLOOK

In recent decades, the construction and technology of building envelopes has undergone rapid development. What started off as a simple transparent screen of animal skins, or a solid, monolithic wall with window openings that were limited in size, has developed into a complex component. The building envelope – facade and roof – should not be understood as an independent technical component with all its individual elements, but as an integral part of the design, as the interface between the interior and the exterior, as that part of the building which represents its 'face'. Irrespective of the technical construction of a facade, the performance aspects are becoming more important: the catalytic properties, acoustic properties, energy generation, information transfer etc. There are no limits to its development. Research projects on material properties and compound materials, as well as the knowledge gained from biology and the natural raw material resources, are yielding ever new findings. Adaptable climate envelopes – also referred to as intelligent facades – change configuration independently in a rapid reaction to the changes from day to night and from summer to winter.

In the field of thermal insulation, technical progress lies in the optimisation of material properties. The growing demand for facade surfaces that can be supplied in transparent and opaque variants and the need to make use of existing solar irradiation has led to innovations such as transparent thermal insulation (TTI). Translucent filler materials or an aerogel developed for space travel generate the opaque effect and function as good thermal insulators. A facade can also be utilised for the active exploitation of solar energy, functioning as an energy generation and storage system.

PCM modules (PCM = phase-change material) provide latent storage mass – in the form of hydrated salt or wax – and store solar energy which otherwise would lead to overheating. They can give off the heat via phase change during the cooler night hours as part of a closed charging and discharging cycle. The term 'building-integrated photovoltaics' refers to photovoltaic elements that have been installed as an integral part of a facade, fulfilling functional, energy-related and aesthetic criteria. The aesthetic requirement and the desire to integrate solar cells and collectors into the building envelope as a fully comprehensive system call for new facade solutions.
At the same time, new production methods enable different dimensions and more compact component assemblies. Surface coating on insulating glazing or the integration of light control systems in the gas-filled interpane cavity regulate the provision of daylight or shading. Liquid crystals and electrochromic glazing mechanically change their aggregate state and colouring in favour of transparency or opaqueness.
Cleverly designed material layers can significantly reduce the energy consumption of a building. In the case of a closed cavity facade (CCF), the air gap between the inner insulating glazing and the outer single glazing is completely sealed. The constant passage of dry, clean air through it prevents the formation of condensate and increases the thermal and sound insulation properties of the elements. In addition it is possible to integrate solar screening, information systems, or lighting, for example, in the cavity. New properties of materials are being discovered with the help of computer-aided modelling and simulation, and through the analysis of Nature and its structures.
The resulting composite materials and construction principles (e.g. the opening and closing of the petals of a flower) are applied to facades to create intelligent shading systems which react to changes in the climate without complex programming. Many of these experimental facades, which are currently being developed as pilot projects in research institutions, have yet to be tested for their practical feasibility.
'Fit for the future' does not necessarily mean high-tech. The focus on eco-balance, service life and fitness for purpose has also led to the development of facades with low technical input which make careful use of resources or use renewable materials. One example is Ricola's new herb warehouse in Laufen, which includes an 80 metre-long solid clay facade that was constructed on site. The building manages completely without air-conditioning. The clay envelope, which has been left unplastered on the inside, is sufficient to regulate the heat and humidity within the building. The high-bay store built for Alnatura in Lorsch features a full timber construction sunk into the cooling earth, which reduces the need for air-conditioning. In the case of office buildings, glass facades are being superseded by solid perforated facades, thus avoiding the need for high-tech installations; an example is the office building 2226 in Lustenau, which has a facade of brickwork that is 76 cm thick. This in turn consists of a 38 cm inner skin of loadbearing bricks with vertical perforations and 38 cm of insulating bricks with a greater proportion of internal air cavities. Here too, this material has made it possible to omit a large part of the air-conditioning installations normally used in office buildings. Because of the thickness of the wall, it was possible to use the masonry units without a thermal sandwich insulation system.

1   Office building, Rotkreuz, 2011, Burkhart und Partner: The efficient loadbearing structure and the innovative facade concept are the dominating characteristics of this office tower block. The 'closed cavity' facade consists of individually enclosed elements providing good thermal insulation, maximum transparency and good sound insulation; the cleaning costs are low, the solar screening is maintenance free and the installation time was short.

2   The Alnatura high-bay store, Lorsch, 2014, BFK Architects: The ecological principles of the organic food chain were incorporated in the construction of its new high-bay store, which is currently the largest of its kind to be built of timber. The use of approx. 2,000 tonnes of PEFC-certified timber is not the only innovation; the design also dispenses with mechanical ventilation and artificial cooling by utilising simple physical effects and natural earth cooling.

3   Apartment block for IBA, Hamburg, 2013, zillerplus Architects and Town Planners: Photovoltaic and solar thermal panels are used as balcony railings and roof parapets in an integrated design concept. The facade element with plant growth provides thermal protection in summer, and a curtain of PCM (phase-change material) withdraws excess heat from the interior during the day and releases it at night.

4   Office building 2226, Lustenau, 2013, Baumschlager Eberle: The building does not need any heating system, relying solely on the heat generated by the users and emitted by the technical infrastructure in the building. The external walls consist of an inner, 38 cm thick leaf of loadbearing perforated bricks and another 38 cm thick leaf of insulating bricks with a larger proportion of perforations.

5   The Ricola herb warehouse, Laufen, 2014, Herzog de Meuron: Locally available natural mineral material – clay from the Laufen valley – was used for the new herb warehouse. The facade blocks were produced from clay in a new process in a temporarily constructed production building, and then installed as prefabricated elements on the site. The temperature and humidity inside the building are self-regulating.

1

2

3

4

5

ENCLOSE | BUILD
SELF-SUPPORTING ENVELOPES

INTRODUCTION

The term 'self-supporting envelope' is used here to refer to building envelopes that consist of a solid material, such as masonry or timber, which forms both the external wall and the loadbearing structure. This type of construction is one of the traditional building methods, as are the skeleton construction systems used in timber framing. The typological distinction between self-supporting envelopes and detached, suspended facade elements developed during the 19th century as the result of new design ideas, materials and technologies, as well as increasingly complex requirements and building standards. The latter, in particular, mean that exposed solid constructions present us with new challenges when they have to be dealt with as part of the repair or conversion of existing buildings. In this situation, issues of thermal insulation, building physics and weather protection have to be resolved while maintaining the architectural quality. The ease of building with solid construction methods contributes to their continued popularity, primarily in residential developments. Self-supporting envelopes and wall constructions in masonry, concrete, or timber continue to be widely used, but the traditional construction materials often require some form of strengthening to allow their continued use. Historic buildings were often constructed using whatever material was available locally; one might say that they grew out of their surroundings. This very direct interaction and the properties of the material concerned led to a very natural and regional style. ⟶ 1

Today, the choice of building material is almost arbitrary everywhere; nevertheless, the existence of historic buildings creates regional references which can either be ignored or deliberately replicated in the conceptual design of new buildings. Solid constructions are subdivided into two categories, reflecting their structure and function: those of single-skin and multi-skin external walls. Single-skin constructions are further subdivided into single and multiple-layer systems, the latter of which perform the functions of structural support, insulation and weather protection in different layers of appropriate size and sequence. As a rule, single-skin materials consist of one single material, such as natural stone or concrete. The vigorous, homogeneous expression of such materials can give a building the desired appearance. ⟶ 3a, b

However, when it comes to the current requirements, single-skin buildings are mostly no longer entirely suitable in respect of thermal insulation, moisture protection and sound insulation. By contrast, multi-skin constructions consist of a homogeneous loadbearing layer and additional elements which perform specific functions, such as the external render which provides weather protection. ⟶ 3c, d

Multi-skin constructions consist of several skins, which are either firmly connected to each other or self-supporting. As a rule, loads are supported by the inner skin while the exterior skin – with or without an air gap – has to satisfy the building physics requirements. ⟶ 4 One example of multi-skin wall construction is a loadbearing masonry wall with an outer skin of facing brick and a cavity containing a moisture-resistant thermal insulation layer. Another example is a solid timber construction consisting of log planks or cross-laminated timber panels, in which the insulation layer is placed between the vertical supports and the air- and vapour-tightness is achieved

1

2

1 Historic residential building in Florence, 17th century: The external walls consist of continuous solid brickwork with a thickness of up to 52 cm. Openings give the wall a compositional rhythm.

2 Apartment building in Munich, 2014, zillerplus Architects and Town Planners. Increasing the density of the inner city with a building in timber construction; nail-laminated board has been used for the external walls.

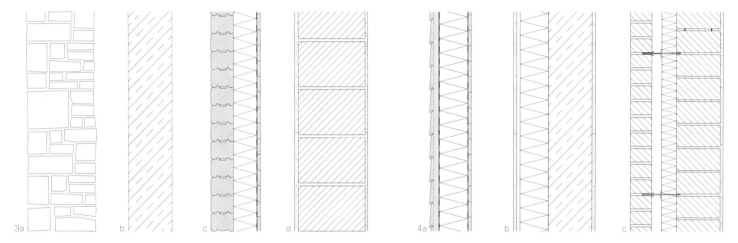

3 Single-skin solid wall
construction
a   Single-skin – natural stone
b   Single-skin – fair-faced concrete
c   Multiple-skin – log construction,
insulated, with interior lining
d   Multiple-skin – masonry, with
exterior render / interior plaster

4 Multiple-skin solid wall
construction
a   Multiple-skin lightweight construction consisting of laminated
wood panels with insulating layer
between the panels, external
breather paper and cladding
b   Multiple-skin solid construction,
loadbearing layer, insulation and
weatherproof render
c   Multiple-skin solid construction,
loadbearing layer, insulation, air gap
and facing

by separate layers. The material for construction of the external wall is selected in accordance with criteria of style, function and availability. Depending on the material – masonry, concrete, or timber – different loadbearing capacities and building physics properties have to be considered.

A common aspect of all solid wall constructions that function as protective building envelopes is that, in addition to the loadbearing function (the material's own weight and that of other building components, as well as imposed loads) and the bracing function, building physics requirements also have to be fulfilled. In addition to thermal insulation, air-tightness and sound insulation, these include weathering from solar radiation, rain and frost. Crucial to the weatherproofing of facades is their protection against driving rain. The term 'driving rain' refers to wind-driven precipitation which impacts horizontally on exterior surfaces. This can lead to water penetrating the exterior wall due to the capillary properties of the building material, gravity and wind pressure. In solid types of wall construction it is important that the amount of water penetration is kept to a minimum – additionally supported by hydrophobic treatment – but also that any water that has penetrated the fabric can rapidly dry out again. Among the traditional materials in solid construction that comply with this requirement are bricks and log planks. Another common construction principle involves a loadbearing skin and an external weathering skin, separated by an air gap. In this construction the internal, loadbearing skin is protected because the outer skin, like an umbrella, keeps rainwater away from it. ➔ 4c In addition to protection against driving rain, a facade must provide adequate thermal insulation and air-tightness. For

this reason, loadbearing structures without a facing layer either feature an insulation element at their core, or internal insulation – alternatively they may be uninsulated but have significantly thicker components.

Solid constructions consisting of a special material such as highly insulating bricks, aerated concrete blocks and insulating concrete, fulfil the thermal insulation requirements but (with the exception of the insulating concrete) cannot be left unfinished: they have to be rendered / plastered on both faces. In the case of insulating concrete, the insulation is applied to the core of the structure, leaving a concrete surface exposed both inside and out. Face masonry – whether of natural stone or bricks – is exposed to moisture, both rising from the ground and from rain, which enters the capillaries of the structure. Another problem associated with the masonry of existing buildings that have little or no insulation is that the surface temperature of external walls may be quite low on the inside and lead to the formation of condensate.

Today, the most frequently used self-supporting construction, taking cost efficiency into account, is a solid masonry wall consisting of fired or unfired masonry units in combination with an external thermal sandwich insulation system.

From a design point of view, it is important to ensure – for example, when carrying out repair work – that the special features of an existing facade, such as recesses and other decorative elements, are not covered over but replicated in an appropriate manner. This applies in particular to buildings listed as historic monuments or those in a conservation area. Ultimately however, the question arises as to whether a thermal insulation sandwich system should not be classed as a separate suspended facade.

MASONRY

Masonry in its various forms has been shaping the appearance of our towns and landscapes since their creation. Initially, natural stone was used 'as found'; it was not until the Bronze Age, when better tools became available, that the processing of stones developed. In parallel, the first clay bricks were made, which initially were left unfired. Solid masonry represents an archetypal construction method, the jointing principle of which even children playfully discover. The layering of units and permanent fastening with the help of the respective binding agent creates loadbearing systems referred to as 'bonds'. The structural properties of masonry include high compressive strength in combination with low tensile and flexural strength. Even though the material is available today as an industrial mass product, and automated production processes are available, masonry structures are almost exclusively built using manual techniques according to craft rules. The properties of the masonry unit, its colour and structure, its shape and surface and the method of jointing give each masonry facade an individual appearance. The craft-based and technical possibilities for making openings add further variation in terms of the latter's shape and size.

The term 'masonry' refers to any building component constructed using natural or man-made masonry units. 'Natural stone' refers to sedimentary rock such as limestone and sandstone, or igneous rock such as gneiss, granite and porphyry. The category of man-made masonry units includes bricks (air-dried or fired, made of clay or brick-earth), calcium silicate units and all blocks made of one or more different base materials.

MAN-MADE MASONRY UNITS

Bricks consist of a fired ceramic building material and can be subdivided into solid and perforated bricks. Solid bricks are the oldest type of small-format brick. They include face bricks and clinker. These are both very durable facade materials and are preferred in many regions in Europe. The appearance and colour of bricks is largely determined by the local raw material and the method and temperature of the firing. The firing and the material not only affect the strength of the unit, but also its surface and texture. For example, if the clay contains a high proportion of iron, this will turn to iron oxide during firing and give the bricks an orange-red to red colour. The colour can be varied by adding other metals to the clay mixture. For normal brick firing, a temperature of between approx. 800 and 1000° is required; from approx. 1200° the clay starts to melt (sintering). This will produce bricks with few capillaries and better hydrophobic properties. In addition, the surface is more varied, with the colouring varying from red to blue through to black and even green. The low water absorption ensures that these bricks have better frost-resistance. It is almost impossible to control the colouring of the bricks in different firings, even with modern furnaces. Sorting the bricks several times results in comparable batches.

The category of unfired man-made masonry units includes calcium silicate units, lightweight concrete blocks, concrete blocks and aerated concrete blocks. Calcium silicate units have a high raw density, which results in good sound insulation and high strength. They can be used for face masonry. Such walls are usually finished with coloured slurry or a paint coating that leaves the structure of the masonry bond visible. The finishing coat provides extra protection to the surface of the wall and the contrast between the dark joint and the almost-white masonry unit is eliminated. Large-format calcium silicate units – referred to as precision blocks – are cost-efficient to lay. However, they are not designed for use as a face material but are normally either rendered or clad.

NATURAL STONE

Natural stone is used in accordance with its geological origin and its associated individual properties. It requires great manual skill to build high, structurally sound walls using stone that is unworked or merely split. Walls built of natural stone, whether 'dry-stone' or jointed with mortar, are perceived nowadays as an archaic form of construction. For millennia, such stones were generally used in places close to where they were found. Natural stone was always the material used for prestigious buildings such as places of worship, temples, churches and castles. Since Vitruvius, the less natural stonework exhibits the traces of processing, the greater its artistic worth has been considered. Today natural stone as a solid building material is only used in exceptional cases, except for the repair of historic buildings. The material is mostly used in the form of suspended slabs with back-ventilation. ⟶ p. 86, Natural Stone

FORMATS AND BONDS

Irrespective of whether the bricks themselves are air-dried or fired, the forms that have developed all over the world are usually rectangular or square on plan and of a size and thickness that allows easy handling on the construction site. Where bricks are used as face material, these formats determine the appearance of the facade – the production process is thus visually expressed.

Standardisation and serial production made bricks a ubiquitously available construction material throughout the Roman Empire. Present-day brick dimensions are based on a dimensional unit which is derived by dividing the standard measure of length by 8 (metric: 1 m/8 = 12.5 cm; imperial: 1 yard/8 = 41/2 inches). The classic

1   Types of masonry material
a   Face brick – hand-made
b   Face brick – machine-made
c   Calcium silicate block
d   Autoclaved aerated concrete block
e   Natural stone, shown as quarried block/polished panel

2 Formats and dimensions of masonry units to DIN 4172 – Modular Coordination in Building Construction
a DF (thin format)
b NF (standard format)
c 2 DF (thin format)
d 8 DF (thin format)

3 Course dimensions and header / stretcher bonds
a Header course
b Stretcher course
c Perpendicular joint (10 mm)
d Horizontal joint (10 to 12 mm)
e Face of header (brick + joint = 12.5 cm)

The dimensions and construction of masonry buildings are defined in Eurocode 6, which comprises the standards DIN EN 1996-1-1 to 3 and the respective national appendices (in Germany, this is applicable as an alternative to DIN 1053-1).

4 Brick/block bonds
a Stretcher bond – all courses are laid as stretchers, with the bricks being offset by 1/2 to a 1/4 length from course to course.
b Header bond – all courses are laid as headers with bricks being offset by 1/2 width from course to course.
c English bond – header and stretcher courses are laid alternately. The perpendicular joints of all stretcher courses are vertically in line.
d Flemish bond – header and stretcher courses are laid alternately, with every other stretcher course offset by 1/2 length from the previous one.

5 Examples of decorative bonds

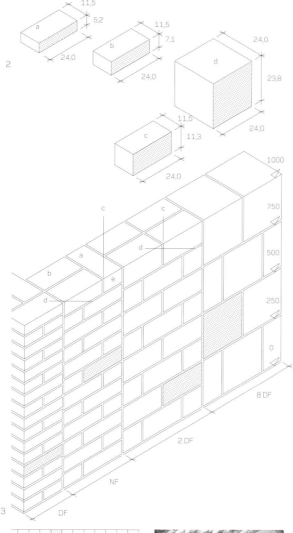

brick format also determines the vertical dimension of the units. For the thin format (German DF), this is calculated as a multiple of the nominal brick height plus the thickness of the horizontal joint as follows (metric: thin format = 52 mm plus 1 horizontal joint × 4 layers = 250 mm; imperial: 65 mm plus 1 horizontal joint × 4 layers = 300 mm). For the standard format (German NF) it is calculated as follows (metric: standard format = 71 mm plus 1 horizontal joint × 3 layers = 250 mm; imperial: 73 mm plus 1 horizontal joint × 3 layers = 250 mm). ➔ 2
The selection of brick format is determined by design aspects, cost efficiency and the work process. The smaller formats are usually better suited for use as face brickwork, piers, lintels and for walls that are curved on plan. By contrast, the larger formats are primarily intended for more efficient work processes and are particularly economical for use in internal and external walls with large areas. In addition to the size and colour of the brick, it is the way in which courses are laid – the bond – that determines the appearance of face brickwork. The two basic courses of brickwork are the header course (with the end of the brick showing) and the stretcher course (with the side of the brick showing). ➔ 3
By arranging the courses in different ways or offset from each other, different bonds are created, such as the header bond in which only the heads of the bricks are visible, or the English bond in which a header course follows a stretcher course. ➔ 4
Beyond these basic examples of bonds, a wide range of other bonds exist. In addition, the architectural effect can be enhanced by projecting or receding courses, which have a sculptural effect on the facade. Brick bonds lead to a strict, almost mathematical system of rules for the design and construction of facades. The art lies in straightforward, natural arrangements and jointing in harmony with the overall appearance. ➔ 5

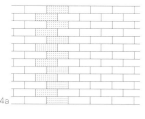
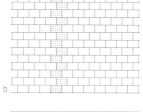

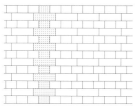
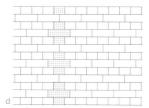

4a   b   5   c   d

JOINTS

In addition to the masonry units, it is the joints that give character to masonry. A distinction is made between horizontal joints – the horizontal connection between the upper and lower faces of the brick courses – and the perpendicular joints, the vertical joints between the heads of the bricks. The type of mortar and thickness of the horizontal joint, as well as the ratio between joint width and joint depth, all depend on the format of the masonry unit used. For common brick formats (e.g. DF or NF), the mortar thickness in horizontal joints is approx. 12 mm (imperial: 10 mm) of standard mortar whereas precision blocks such as those of calcium silicate, aerated concrete or cement-based material are bonded using thin-bed mortar (approx. 2 mm thick). The design of the joints is important both for their effect and, primarily, for their durability. ➔ 1 Similarly to the masonry units it holds together, the joint material has to fulfil demanding requirements with regard to air-tightness, protection against driving rain and durability. The greater thermal conductivity of the joint material compared to the masonry units must be considered in the energy balance, as it is a potential thermal bridge.

The simplest and most economic joint face is created with a 'flush joint', in which the gap between masonry units is fully filled with mortar and any protruding material is struck off flush with the trowel. The colour of the mortar determines the colour of the joint, the wall mortar being the joint mortar. Where the joints are fully filled subsequently, the mortar is removed to a depth of at least 1.5 cm and the facade is pointed up, filling the empty part of the joint with a facing mortar in a separate work process. In this way it is easier to control the intended visual effect, since it is easier to inspect the colour of the mortar and to achieve different forms of joint facing.

SURFACE STRUCTURE

The external layer of material works as weather protection as well as performing an aesthetic function. The appearance of the facade can be significantly influenced by either emphasising the joints and the joint pattern or understating them, with the design options ranging from sober functionalism to ornamental whimsy. With respect to the colour scheme of facades, the following rule of thumb applies: the darker the colour of the joint, the more radiant the appearance of the masonry unit. Another design option is the use of what is known as a decorative bond. A special expression can be achieved by using an irregular pattern, a special pattern or ornamentation that has been designed in detail and specified in a laying plan. In addition, the colour scheme of the bricks used can be modified either by sorting the batches delivered, or by mixing additives into the joint mortar. A plain rendered area can be textured by using different rendering methods and materials, as well as by adding granulate or pigment to the mortar.

OPENINGS

In solid, self-supporting masonry, the size and shape of openings is limited for structural reasons, also affecting the potential number of windows. In the past, horizontal supports between uprights were built with brick arches, whereas today they are created using concealed lintels of steel or reinforced concrete. ➔ SCALE, vol. 1, Open | Close The craft-based, classic methods of building openings in masonry depend on the material, with openings forming

1 Different options for finishing joints
a Concave joint
b Flush joint
c Weather joint
d Repointed joint, the joint has been raked out and filled with new mortar
e Struck joint, providing poor protection against water ingress

2 Refurbishment of factory building, Munich, 2004, Allmann Sattler Wappner Architects: The listed rear building dating from 1893 has been fully refurbished. The special effect of the masonry with face bricks in the historic format of 25 cm × 12 cm × 6.5 cm is created by applying a lime wash finish.

3 House extension, Aachen, 2011 Amunt Architects: The brick facade of the existing building is keyed into the extension wall consisting of light-weight pumice / concrete blocks, which – with a thickness of 24 cm and good thermal insulation properties – reduce transmission heat loss. This contemporary approach plays off the different colouring of the new and old masonry against the compact form of the new building. 1 + 1 = 1.

an important design element that can become an ornament in the facade.

SOLID MASONRY

Today, solid masonry structures with solid bricks or clinkers as face brickwork can only be used for unheated utility buildings. Face brickwork structures which comply with the current requirements for thermal insulation consist of highly insulated masonry units made of porous clay or aerated concrete. The masonry courses are bonded with a polymer-modified mortar and the perpendicular joints are tongue-and-grooved. This means that the exterior walls have to be rendered/plastered on the outside and inside in order to ensure air-tightness and protection against rainwater. Lintels, wall connections and the support of floor slabs require detailed design, since specially shaped units are required in order to minimise thermal bridging and to comply with the requirements for sound insulation and structural integrity. With this type of construction and appropriate wall thicknesses, it is possible to achieve good U-values without having to forego the advantages of a solid construction. When it is intended to achieve the visual effect of face brickwork, it is also possible to consider a special skin of face brickwork, in which the masonry looks very similar to a solid masonry wall, but has the advantage of complying with the requirements for thermal insulation and protection against the weather. ➘ p. 82 ff, Face Brickwork and Brick Panels
Special attention needs to be paid to the selection of the render/plaster systems, which must be suitable for the material properties of the masonry unit used and which are part of the entire wall system.

4   Section through masonry wall construction, scale 1:20:

a   Wall construction:
Clinker face brick, 140 mm
Narrow gap, thermal insulation, 115 mm
Loadbearing masonry, 240 mm
Internal plaster, 20 mm

b   Roof construction:
Layer of gravel, 50 mm
Double layer of bituminous sealing membrane
Insulation with a fall, 200 to 300 mm
Bituminous vapour barrier
Reinforced concrete slab, 160 mm, with plaster finish, 15 mm

c   Construction of ground/ upper floors:
Solid wood planks, 23 mm
Floating screed, 40 mm
Separating layer
Impact sound insulation, 30 mm
Reinforced concrete floor slab, 150 mm

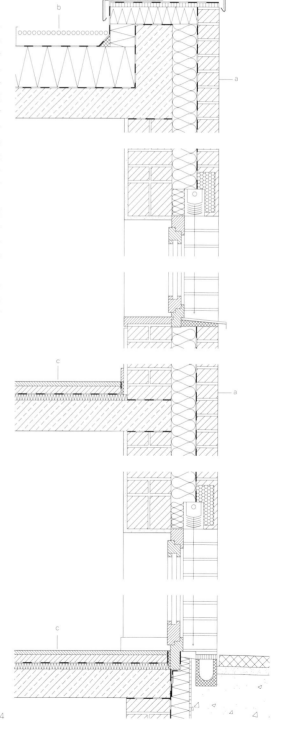

4

CONCRETE

Concrete is a construction material that consists of a mixture of cement, water and mineral aggregate. It cures and takes the shape of the formwork holding it. Knowledge of this material and its properties has existed since the second century BC: it was called *opus caementitium* by the Romans.

It was not until the end of the 19th century, when steel began to be used for reinforcing concrete, that this material was able to support greater structural loads and hence became widely used in building construction, even creating a specific construction style. In its uncured state, concrete can easily be shaped and is therefore very suitable for the sculptural design of facades involving large spans. The material, which is constantly undergoing further development, is very cost-efficient and offers great design flexibility with regard to shape, treatment and surface finish, making it a very popular material. Concrete can be adapted to meet many different requirements whether they relate to structural strength, durability, building physics, fire protection or specific user needs. Designs should avoid subjecting it to changes in shape due to temperature fluctuations, and to the ingress of water, both of which have a negative impact on the properties of concrete.

Concrete is either mixed on the construction site – referred to as 'in situ concrete' – or transported to the site in ready-mixed liquid form, which is then pumped directly into the formwork and compacted. It is also possible to supply the material to the construction site in the form of a prefabricated or semi-prefabricated element, which is placed by crane.

In view of current requirements regarding thermal insulation and for the avoidance of thermal bridges, it is not possible to have monolithic exterior walls unless they are very thick, even if insulating concrete is used. For this reason, concrete building envelopes are normally built using a two-skin construction with core insulation or suspended, prefabricated, concrete facade panels. It is also possible to build solid concrete walls with interior insulation; in this case (and in contrast to exterior core insulation) it is important to minimise any thermal bridging via components that connect with the exterior skin of the wall (i.e. floor slabs and interior walls).

PRODUCTION

In addition to the basic ingredients, i.e. cement, aggregate and water, it is possible to use various supplementary cementing materials and chemical admixtures to modify the properties of the concrete. Adding materials such as stone dust or pigments affects the colour of the concrete, while glass fibres or plastic fibres improve its loadbearing capacity. Concrete additives are only used in small quantities, but they change the chemical and physical effect of certain properties of the fresh, uncured concrete, without it losing its durability and without the steel losing its corrosion protection. For example, plasticiser changes the workability of concrete. The strength of concrete and its consistency during processing depend on the proportion of its constituting components. The choice of stone dust and the size of grain affect the appearance and strength of the material, as do the quantity of additives and the compatibility of different additives. The quality of concrete is affected by the water / cement ratio (w/c ratio). The strength of concrete is reduced when it contains too much water. The consistency of concrete, which here refers to its stiffness, depends on the purpose it is to be used for. For the purpose of laying concrete, it is important to ensure that it can be put

1 Constituents of concrete
(see DIN EN 206 Concrete)

Cement
– CEM I: Portland cement
– CEM II: Portland composite cement
– CEM III: blast-furnace cement
– CEM IV: pozzolanic cement
– CEM V: composite cement

Aggregate (types)
– fine, naturally rounded (sand / crushed stone fines)
– mixed grain (gravel / stone chips)
– coarse, broken grain (coarse gravel, crushed stone)

Water
– gauging water
– surface moisture

Concrete admixtures
used to change the properties
Fine mineral material:
– stone dust
– fly ash, ground tuff, trass or silicate
Organic substances:
– synthetic resin emulsions
Others:
– colour pigments
– fibres (steel, glass, or plastic)

Concrete admixtures
for modifying the physical and / or chemical properties, such as:
– workability
– curing behaviour
– hardening
– durability
in the form of plasticisers, retarding agents, accelerators, stabilisers and waterproofing agents.

2 Unité d'Habitation, Marseilles 1947–1952, Le Corbusier: The coarse, rough finish of the untreated concrete is elevated to an aesthetic feature. The béton-brut is treated like stone and benefits from the contrast with the surfaces of the other materials, such as steel and glass, and the colours used on the loggias and sill panels. The concrete was installed without any insulation, owing to the mild local climate and the lack of energy-saving regulations at the time.

3 L 40, Berlin, 2010, Roger Bundschuh, Cosima von Bonin: The forms are accentuated by the envelope of black face concrete without joints. The solid facade consists of three layers – a loadbearing inner layer of in-situ concrete, core insulation and an outer skin of lightweight concrete with black pigment.

2

3

CONCRETE TYPES	DESCRIBED in TERMS of THE MANUFACTURING PROCESS, INSTALLATION METHOD AND PROPERTIES
Top concrete	Concrete which is added subsequently to an existing concrete layer, e.g. in order to make up the level or to improve the loadbearing capacity.
Prefabricated concrete elements	Concrete, reinforced concrete, or pre-stressed concrete components prefabricated in a factory, which are installed on site fully cured.
Insulating concrete	Special form of lightweight concrete with foam glass instead of stone aggregate to give it good insulation properties.
Fibre concrete	Concrete with an admixture of fibres (steel, glass, or plastic) in order to improve the mechanical and structural properties.
High-performance concrete	Concrete with high compressive strength, achieved by minimising the water/cement ratio; this is used for compound structures and special structures of minimal dimensions.
Lightweight concrete, autoclaved aerated concrete	The weight of this concrete is reduced by omitting stone aggregate and aerating the concrete. Low thermal conductivity.
Standard concrete	Concrete which is compacted by vibration and achieves its final compressive strength after 28 days; av. strength class C25/30; may include various additives.
In-situ concrete	Concrete made and used on site; it is compacted and cures in the formwork. The concrete can be strengthened with reinforcement steel in order to improve its structural performance.
Recycling concrete	Concrete in which the stone aggregate consists of recycled concrete and crushed masonry.
Reinforced concrete	Compound material of concrete and steel. The partial strengthening (reinforcement) of concrete results from combining its high compressive strength with the high tensile strength of steel.
Rammed concrete	Concrete without reinforcement, which is compacted in layers by ramming (or tamping) instead of vibration.
Fair-faced concrete	Concrete with specific requirements for its visible surface. The surface texture can be modified by using special formwork surfaces, surface treatment and additives such as colour pigments.
Ready-mix concrete	This concrete is mixed at a central location and transported to the site.

4

4 Concrete terms

5 Joint details
The width of the joint and the thickness of the jointing material depend on the size of the elements: the expected movement due to thermal factors must be absorbed in the joint. Such joints are usually 15 to 20 mm wide. > DIN 18540
a Joint sealer (joint sealing compound and foam strip)
b Joint with plastic compression profile
c Dummy joint, design element

6 Consistency check

7 Installing a formwork anchor

8 This climbing formwork consists of large shuttering panels which are pulled upwards at regular intervals once the concrete has cured.

9 Formwork system for loadbearing walls; large formwork elements that are placed in sections using a crane

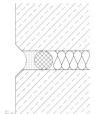

5a b c

6 7

8 9

in place and compacted without difficulty; possible consistencies range from very stiff to very free-flowing and include self-compacting concrete (SCC). When pouring concrete into the formwork, it is important to ensure that the mixture does not separate. It should be compacted evenly to prevent air inclusions. Similarly, a constant external temperature is important during installation, preferably between +5 °C and +30 °C, otherwise suitable measures must be taken to maintain the material's workability, e.g. cooling and the addition of water when the ambient temperature is too high. The required compressive strength is normally reached after 28 days of curing. In order to give the concrete its form it is poured into hollow formwork (shuttering). This consists of a formwork system (dependent on – or independent of – the building, made of timber, steel or plastic) to which sheathing is fixed (form face creates surface texture). Shuttering ties consisting of threaded bars with screw anchors in a conduit are used to prevent the hollow formwork being pushed apart. The anchor holes remain visible after curing, and are closed with a plug after curing. For this reason, the arrangement of the anchors should be considered as early as the design stage.

JOINTS
When building with fair-faced concrete, attention must be paid to joints on account of their visibility, be they shuttering joints, day-work/construction joints, required expansion joints, or dummy joints designed for appearances. The design of the joints is a critical aspect, whether it is intended to give the building component a smooth appearance, or impose, for example, a grid pattern. Narrow joints with little or no surface gap convey the impression of a smooth surface whereas broad joints with a pronounced surface gap emphasise the impression of individual panels due to the effect of the shadow. In addition to appearances, the format of concrete panels and even concrete components must take into account technical requirements relating to production; the size of panels is restricted by their weight and the options for transporting them.

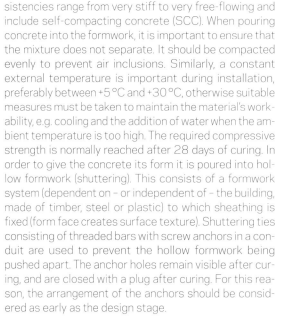

FAIR-FACED CONCRETE

Fair-faced concrete refers to concrete components with a surface that remains visible; their appearance is normally determined by the texture of the form face. Fair-faced concrete is defined according to a range of classes. → 1

The quality of fair-faced concrete can be assessed objectively with the help of DIN 18217 'Concrete surfaces and formwork surface' or SIA 118/262 'General conditions of concrete construction'.

FORMWORK SURFACE – TEXTURE

The surface of concrete elements can be modified using various methods of texturing the surface as described below. One of the means of doing this is the shuttering, the inner surface of which is particularly important as it is the negative form of the concrete component it is meant to create. When the shell construction is designed, a formwork plan is an important design element, defining the geometry of the formwork and the desired joint pattern.

Once the concrete has cured and the formwork or shuttering has been removed, its profile and texture can be seen on the surface of the concrete element. The appearance can be affected by the choice of different formwork materials, different sizes of shuttering panel and the layout of the fixing points. The quality of the surface appearance is subdivided into fair-faced concrete classes on the basis of criteria for the formwork skin, the expansion joints and joints in the formwork, porosity, evenness of colour and smoothness of the surface. In view of the fact that the requirements are very exacting, it is important that all those involved in the design process are consulted in good time and that the tender documents include a specific description of the design. Similarly, it is a good idea to produce sample surfaces to define the texture and quality of the finish. The successful completion of a specified finish and the quality of fair-faced concrete depend on a number of factors, such as the quality of the concrete mix and additives, the processing (soiling, leakiness of the formwork, incorrect compaction or release agent) and the effects of the weather (external temperature, precipitation).

When choosing formwork/shuttering material, it is important to ensure that it does not trigger a chemical reaction with the concrete during the curing process. For this reason, preferred materials include timber and wood-based materials, steel or plastic. When timber shuttering is used, e.g. rough-sawn timber boards, the material must be soaked in water first so that it does not start swelling when the concrete is poured in, as this would withdraw too much water from the concrete and would result in sanding of the surface after curing. Shuttering panels

consisting of wood-based materials with different types of plastic coating are a popular choice. The use of such panels produces very smooth surfaces; the texture of the facade is determined by the pattern of the panels (i.e. the joints) and the fixing anchors. The tighter the formwork is, the better it prevents the run-off of the cement slurry when the concrete is placed and compacted. This reduces unwanted defects in the colour, surface pattern and texture. Release agent is applied to the formwork before the concrete is placed and ensures that the formwork can be easily released from the component after curing. Nevertheless, the removal of the formwork can be a difficult, labour-intensive process – similar to the design and construction of the formwork, for example in the case of complicated shapes with several curved surfaces. Of special significance in concrete components are the edges. These are usually formed with a chamfer (which is created by inserting a small triangular batten into the formwork) in order to avoid damage to the edge during the construction process or at a later date.

Should any breakage occur to a sharp edge, i.e. one without any chamfer, this can only be repaired manually. The points of repair are usually visible due to differences in colour, which may become more obvious as the material ages.

1 Fair-faced concrete classes
These define the requirements for the surface, the formwork pattern and the edges.
1: low level of requirements: cellar walls or areas primarily used for industrial purposes
2: normal level of requirements: stairwells, retaining walls
3: special requirements: facades in building construction
4: non-standard special requirements: prestigious components in building construction

2 Comparison of properties of standard and lightweight concrete

3 Visitor information centre at the Messel mine, 2010, Landau + Kindelbacher: The solid reinforced concrete building is constructed of in-situ concrete with a fair-faced concrete finish inside and outside, forming a double-skin external wall with core insulation, the work being divided into 87 sections. The texture of the walls was created by constructing the formwork with a skin of planed, tongue-and-groove boards, with an irregular arrangement of the board joints.
Concrete class C25/30 to C45/55, fair-faced concrete class 2

4 Gropius' new Meisterhaus, Dessau, 2014, Bruno Fioretti Marquez Architects: Contemporary reconstruction on the existing foundations. The external walls are built of light-coloured lightweight concrete with low thermal conductivity so as to minimise the weight on the historic foundations and avoid the need for additional insulation. The natural stone aggregate was replaced by expanded clay globules and lightweight sand in order to reduce the weight of the shell construction further.
Concrete class LC 12/13, fair-faced concrete class 4

2

	Standard concrete	Lightweight concrete
Dry bulk density	2000-2600 kg/m³	350-2000 kg/m³
Compressive strength	5-55 N/mm²	2-6 N/mm²
Strength classes	C8/10 to C50/55	LC8/9 to LC50/55
Thermal conductivity	1.51-2.3 W/mK	from 0.11 W/mK

3

4

5 Surface, textures
a Showing the shuttering panels and anchor points
b Surface resulting from rough-sawn shuttering
c Visible result of the laying process, e.g. tamping
d Relief created by inserting moulds into the formwork

6 Surface, colours
a Colouring achieved with colour pigments and pulverised stone
b Imprinted surface / 3D print

7 Detail of section through fair-faced concrete wall with core insulation, scale 1:20

a Wall construction:
Reinforced / in situ concrete, 250 mm as weather protection
Thermal insulation, 120 mm
Reinforced / in situ concrete, 250 mm as loadbearing layer

b Roof construction:
Concrete slabs laid in sand, 150 mm
Bituminous sealing membrane, 10 mm
Thermal insulation, 200 mm
Bituminous membrane as a secondary seal, 5 mm
Lattice girder plank with added concrete, 260 mm

c Floor construction:
Hardened screed, 20 mm
Cement screed with underfloor heating, 80 mm
Bituminous sealing membrane
Impact sound insulation, 40 mm
Fair-faced concrete floor slab, 280 mm

If it is intended that the facade has a more pronounced, high-relief texture, it is possible to process the surface of the cured concrete mechanically or chemically, or to use concrete matrices to create a special effect. These matrices come in serially produced patterns but may also be tailor-mades. A special application of matrices is photo-engraving, in which a photographic image is transferred to a sheet material using a CNC milling machine in order to create the relief which then models the fair-faced concrete surface; another option is the direct application of photographic prints to prefabricated concrete panels for the purpose of facade decoration.

COLOURING

The colour of concrete is affected by the selection of the cement and aggregates. In order to achieve as homogeneous a colour as possible, the mixture (cement, aggregate size and added materials) and the water/cement ratio should be as consistent as possible. In addition, all material supplies should come from the same cement factory or aggregate supplier. Classic mixtures are likely to have a dark-grey to light-grey colour. Raw materials with low iron oxide content make it possible to produce white Portland cement, which in turn produces very pale grey concrete surfaces. It is also possible to add pigments to the concrete mixture to achieve a certain colour scheme. Oxide pigments can give the following colours:
– white: titanium oxide
– red, yellow, brown, black: iron oxide
– green: oxides of cobalt, nickel, zinc, titanium and aluminium
– blue: oxides of cobalt, aluminium and chrome
– yellow: oxides of titanium, chrome, nickel and antimony

The colouring of concrete is durable and weathers well, although the intensity usually diminishes somewhat during the first years of service.

5a

c

6a

b

d

b

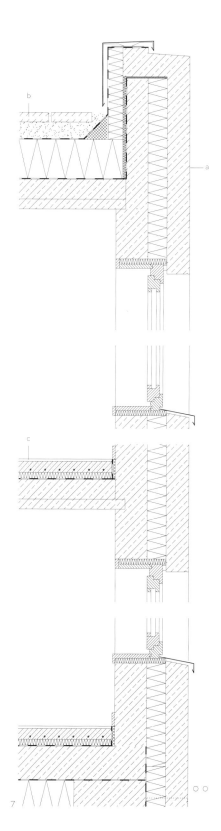
7

TIMBER

Alongside clay and natural stone, timber is one of the oldest building materials and is of paramount importance throughout the world due to its excellent structural properties and wide regional availability as a renewable raw material. Similarly to clay, timber contributes to an agreeable indoor climate because – in addition to its moisture-regulating capacity – its lower thermal conductivity allows its surface temperature to remain similar to that of the air in the room. When designing timber-based structures, it is important to take into account the change in volume due to shrinkage and swelling of this natural material, and the additional fire protection measures required. Careful selection of the material and skilful handling, working and installation are important when choosing timber as a construction system. In solid wall construction, a distinction is made between different construction methods. One of the oldest methods of building with timber is log construction – also known as 'strickbau' in the Alpine region – along with the use of piles for stilt houses. In these systems entire logs are prepared and stacked, and the structure is made rigid by the jointing details at the corners (called 'verstricken' in the Alpine region). ➘ 1 A characteristic feature of this construction is the projection of the logs at the corner joints, which is a geometric and structural necessity. The round logs, which have been stripped of their bark, usually remain visible externally and thus determine the appearance of the building. With the help of different profiling techniques, for example by making special grooves and inserting profiles to create a secure bearing, the logs are prepared for true horizontal and structurally sound stacking. In this way the construction can be carried out without additional fasteners. Today, additional thermal insulation is added in the core of the wall, as well as an air-tightness membrane, in order to comply with current thermal insulation and air-tightness requirements. In contrast to modern timber frame construction, log construction has to comply with strict specifications in construction and design in order to meet the necessary standard of workmanship. Settlement of several centimetres has to be taken into account, as do the openings in the facade, which are determined in their arrangement and size by the 'module' of the log. Traditionally, these buildings feature relatively large closed areas and small window openings in landscape format. The obvious material jointing and its dimensional conditions contribute to the special, archaic attraction of such buildings. The dimensions take into account the naturally available length of logs which, for spans without posts, are approx. 4 to 5 m. The layout design is based on the rectangular positioning of the internal walls. Timber construction systems using planks glued together are a modern form of solid timber construction. In contrast to logs, these panel-type elements – which are referred to as nail-laminated and cross-laminated board – consist of largely dry and non-shrinking layers which are glued together straight, across or cross-wise, or nailed or even doweled, and which are either produced as solid units or include a cavity. ➘ 5, 6 The advantageous properties of these components are their reduced cross-section, low weight, high strength and dimensional stability. The option to manufacture such components as prefabricated elements facilitates installation on site. Since the size of panels is not subject to a specific dimensional system, only the manufacturer's specific sizes have to be taken into account. The timber material itself is often concealed, because the loadbearing elements are covered by an external layer of insulation to afford the necessary thermal protection and may also feature a separate cladding on the inside. In contrast to the classic log-built buildings, openings of any size and shape can be cut into these modern elements. This means that the facades no longer have to adhere to the strict order of log construction and allow more and larger openings, with greater flexibility in the interior layout.

1a

b

1   Corner joints
a   Traditional round logs
Structurally effective connection by notching the logs on one side
b   Square-sided logs
Structurally effective connection by dovetailing both contact surfaces along both axes

2

3

2   Historic log building in Grisons
The natural stone plinth serves as foundation wall, to even out the terrain and to protect the timber structure above it from snow and humidity

3   Timber buildings in Vrin, Gion A. Caminada: Traditional methods that have been given a technical upgrade to produce this contemporary expression of the 'strickbau' method, a Swiss variant of log construction that is typical of Vrin.

4 Forms of solid timber wall construction
a Round logs with flat contact surfaces and fillet joints
b Rectangular section logs with tongue and groove
c Rectangular section logs with ridge and groove
d Log wall with thermal insulation
e Prefabricated units of laminated solid timber plus thermal insulation

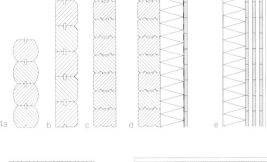

4a   b   c   d   e

5 Different kinds of vertical timber lamination
a with square arrises
b chamfered
c profile with cable groove

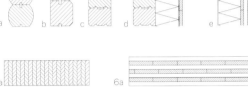

5a   6a

6 Different kinds of timber cross-lamination
a alternate layers of cross-lamination
b cross-lamination with some layers in parallel with adjoining layers
c cross-lamination with cavities between layers

b   b

c   c

7 The Schattenbox residence, Eichgraben, 2008, Superlab - Dold and Hasenauer OG: The fully prefabricated cross-laminated timber units consist of solid timber sections. The cross-lamination of the different layers of the units results in good dimensional stability and structural strength.

8 Cross-section through a log building, scale 1:20

Wall construction:
Log construction, loadbearing, 120mm
Thermal insulation on grid of battens as substructure, 120mm
Vapour check
Thermal insulation between battens as installation plane, 40mm
Double layer of plasterboard, 25mm

Roof construction:
Roof tiles
Battens/counter-battens
Rafters with thermal insulation, 180mm
Vapour check
Thermal insulation with battens as installation plane, 40mm
Double layer of plasterboard, 25mm

7

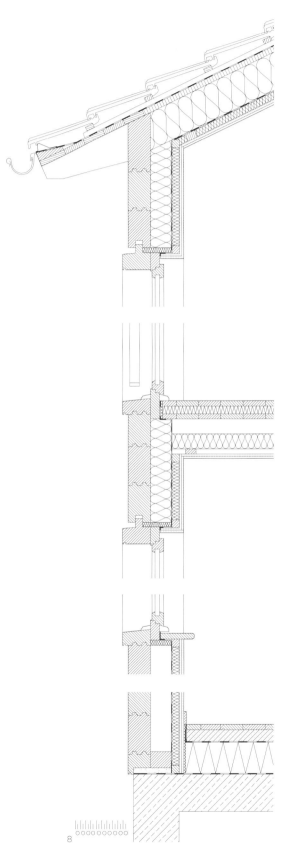

8

ENCLOSE | BUILD
NON SELF-SUPPORTING ENVELOPES

CHAPTER 3

INTRODUCTION

The desire for larger openings that provide more daylight and ventilation, while at the same time providing protection against the weather and changes in the climate, drives the search for new materials. Similarly, the need for larger spans and economic structures, which is a feature of the industrial age, has led to modern construction systems. Industrial methods of producing and finishing materials such as steel, glass, metal and reinforced concrete broaden the formal and technical possibilities of architecture. Industrialisation has made it possible to overcome the material heaviness of this construction system. Comparatively slender cast-iron and iron structures – initially used for smaller bridges and later for daring feats of engineering – make large spans possible. Frames with rigid nodes and frame construction constitute a secondary loadbearing structure which supplements solid construction components and opens the door to layouts with greater flexibility of use – independent of the facade and its openings. The Crystal Palace, which was designed by Sir Joseph Paxton on the occasion of the World Exhibition in London in 1851, is considered a milestone in the quest to alleviate the heaviness of the building envelope. Prefabricated from modular iron and glass components and constructed in a short period of time, the building represents the beginning of the glass/steel architecture of modern high-rise building construction. ⇘ 1 The first facades involving this type of lightweight construction with a high proportion of glass were designed for industrial buildings. In order to improve working conditions in factories and thereby improve the performance of the workers, glazed building envelopes were developed as an interface between interior and exterior, admitting more daylight and sunshine and allowing an increased air exchange. In consequence of this, they surrendered their loadbearing function. ⇘ 2 Ludwig Mies van der Rohe, an important proponent of the Modern movement, promoted the separation of the architectural elements according to their functions into loadbearing and non-loadbearing elements, consisting of different materials and structures. For a competition for a high-rise building in Berlin in 1921, he produced a design that expressed his vision of 'skin and bones architecture', in which the transparent glass skin encloses the loadbearing structure, which itself consists only of columns and floor slabs.

Farnsworth House, which is a later design, is considered a prototype of all modern glazed buildings. The loadbearing structure consists of a slender steel skeleton construction and the frames of the facade, with its large glazing panels, are attached to the steel columns with angle profiles. This principle of enclosing a building, in which the facade encloses the primary structure like a curtain (hence the term 'curtain wall facade'), allows flexible use of the layout, which can be zoned at will, independently of the facade. The industrial production of prefabricated elements meant that lightweight slender facade elements soon became a viable alternative to solid building envelopes. Today, curtain wall facades make an important contribution to the economical construction of buildings, particularly office and administration buildings. ⇘ 3, 4 The expressive term 'curtain wall facade' stands for a range of technically differentiated construction systems.

1 The 'Crystal Palace', Great Exhibition, London, 1851, Sir Joseph Paxton: In spite of its ornamental embellishment, the bold glass iron construction – with the streamlined and slender loadbearing structure providing an uncluttered interior – represents the transition to modern architecture.

2 Steiff factory, Giengen, 1893: The double-skin facade consisting of translucent glass panes is considered to be the first curtain wall in industrial building. The outer facade has been suspended in front of the construction, while the inner one stands between the columns.

3 Bauhaus Dessau, 1926, Walter Gropius: The glass facade suspended in front of the loadbearing skeleton structure determines the appearance of the workshop wing and reveals the structural elements. The glazing at the building corners reinforces the lightweight impression.

4 The Farnsworth House, 1951, Ludwig Mies van der Rohe: The external walls consist of large-format glass panes, connecting the cubic interior with the outdoor space.

For example, there is a fundamental difference in the construction of a curtain wall facade and that of a suspended facade with back ventilation. A curtain wall facade functions as a 'warm facade' without back ventilation – either in single-skin form as a mullion/transom facade or element facade, or as a double-skin facade.

The lightweight, non-loadbearing external wall is suspended from the loadbearing structure as an independent package, either floor by floor or spanning several floors. ↘ p. 66 ff By contrast, a suspended back-ventilated facade is termed a 'cold facade', which has an air space that separates the protected insulation layer from the external weathering layer. The cladding of the exterior skin is independent of the loadbearing structure but firmly attached via a substructure. ↘ p. 82 ff

In both systems many requirements have to be met by slender building components in a small space. These are complex items in terms of their construction, delivery and installation. For this reason it makes sense to involve specialist designers, system manufacturers and construction companies in the design at an early stage.

CURTAIN WALL FACADES

A curtain wall facade is a lightweight, non-loadbearing envelope which is attached to the loadbearing structure of the building using a substructure. The term 'curtain wall facade' covers the mullion/transom construction method, the element facade and the double-skin facade. A distinction is made between systems using individual framing elements and facade elements, which are attached to a skeleton structure. Both systems consist of a frame construction using storey-high mullions and horizontal transoms to produce entire shear-resistant elements. The spaces created by the framing are filled with a range of different materials with a bracing function – transparent glazed elements or opaque panels – and functional elements, such as openable windows and doors, ventilation elements, solar screening and glare-protection elements.

The framing is primarily constructed using steel and aluminium profiles, and occasionally also timber profiles. Sandwich elements consist of an insulating core with covering layers of plastic, glass, metal or reinforced concrete. There is a relatively wide choice when choosing the grid pattern of the facade, because the loads are transferred – either suspended or from the ground up – separately from the main loadbearing structure. The connection points of the facade to the primary system must have fixed points as well as sliding ones, in order to be able to absorb any movement from the loadbearing structure, and they must be three-dimensionally adjustable so that tolerances in the construction can be accommodated.

The difference between a mullion/transom facade and an element facade consists in the degree of prefabrication. This also affects how the elements are joined, which parts of the profiles are exposed to view, and the sealing planes. Particular attention must be paid to the joint between the elements. While the mullion/transom facade, installed on site, still allows a certain freedom in the facade design and the adaptation of the sealing system, as well as in the finishing pressure plates, the installation of the individual elements of an element facade relies on the fixings being precisely aligned to the shell structure. The elements are placed on brackets (or the elements below) and are laterally pushed together. In this way, one installed element secures the next one, which is then attached to the primary system at the free ends. In this system the visible width of profiles at the joints is larger. The system is particularly attractive for large construction sites and high-rise buildings owing to prefabrication and pre-assembly of the glazing and the integration of any services installations, as well as the short installation time and potentially the possibility of working without scaffolding. A limiting factor is the restricted design freedom, since individual requirements can only be accommodated to a very limited extent due to the serial production of the system.

5 Curtain wall facade (suspended)

6 Mullion/transom facade
built from bottom up or suspended
Semi-finished products are assembled on site

7 Facade system
of prefabricated units

8 Double-skin facade
Building services are integrated in
the respective facade system

5

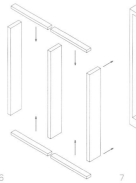
6

7

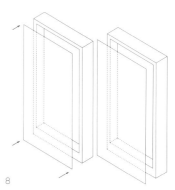
8

SUSPENDED BACK-VENTILATED FACADE

Suspended back-ventilated facades (DIN 18516-1) are based on the principle of double-skin construction. A loadbearing inner layer takes on the structural and sealing functions of the facade, while the outer layer, like an umbrella, protects the structure against the impact of the weather. ⤳1 The weather skin is never watertight; it may even be designed with open joints, depending on the material. Any penetrating water will normally run down the back of the outer skin. The base of these structures and any connections to openings in the facade must allow the water to drain off in order to prevent damage from the ingress of water into the building fabric. An air space is formed between the skins, in which – like in a chimney – air flowing in from below rises, thereby discharging any penetrating condensate through evaporation at the top. This system can be used with a wide variety of cladding materials, and thus allows great freedom in the design of the facade. Compared to single-skin cladding that is attached directly to the exterior envelope, back-ventilated double-skin construction systems have the advantage that the materials can independently shrink and swell, as well as contract or expand according to fluctuations in temperature. With the correct detailing, it is possible to use non-diffusive materials, such as metal, without any negative building physics effect on the inner loadbearing part of the wall.

Depending on the material of the external skin, the substructure can consist of timber battens and profiles, lightweight metal profiles, or stainless steel elements. In order to avoid stress from lack of free movement, the substructure must be able to accommodate movement in all directions. A temperature range of between –20 °C and +80 °C must be taken into account. Substructure systems should be permanently protected against corrosion; this should include any damaging effects from adjacent building materials (crevice/contact corrosion). Nowadays, depending on the function of the building, back-ventilated facades are fitted with an insulation layer on the outside of the inner skin. The thermal weak point of the system is the point of attachment of the envelope to the loadbearing building component.

In view of the fact that the exterior envelope of a double-skin system is separate from the structural system of the building, it is important to pay attention to the relationship between the interior and exterior. While the pattern of joints only has an indirect relationship with the loadbearing part of the structure, the two elements nevertheless have to be designed to complement each other. The size and arrangement of openings is limited owing to the structural limitations of the loadbearing structure. Individual windows are just as possible as fenestration bands or a combination of suspended opaque facade elements with large glazed facade panels. An important part of the detailed design is the position of the window in relation to the insulation plane and the construction of the reveals, particularly with respect to back-ventilation and the ingress of moisture.

Today, back-ventilated double-skin construction systems are used for a wide range of buildings. One reason for this is the diversity in conceptual design based on the various materials available, such as ceramics, natural stone, reconstituted stone, metal, timber, fibre-cement panels and plastic. Many suspended systems can be used for both wall cladding and roof cladding.

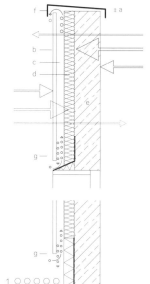

1   Schematic of suspended, back-ventilated facade.
a   Height of coping a with fall
b   External skin = weather skin
c   Air gap, back-ventilation
d   Insulation
e   Loadbearing structure
f   Drip edge; its overhang depends on the building height
< 8 m = a ≥ 5 cm
< 20 m = a ≥ 8 cm
> 20 m = a ≥ 10 cm
g   Water discharge

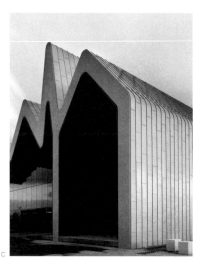

2   Examples of suspended, back-ventilated facades:

a   Student housing at Campus Westend, Frankfurt am Main, 2008, Karl + Probst Architects: The large-format fibre-cement panels provide a structure to the facade.

b   The Brandhorst Museum, Munich, 2009, Sauerbruch Hutton: Ceramic bars with differently coloured glazing suspended in front of the wall let the building appear solid or airy, depending on the mood created by the changes in daylight.

c   The Riverside Museum, Glasgow, 2011, Zaha Hadid Architects: The complex geometry of the building envelope is enhanced by the material and orientation of the titanium zinc sheets.

SUSPENDED FACADE PERFORMANCE REQUIREMENTS

Owing to the complexity of the layered construction and the basic loads of the inner and outer systems, the suspended components are subject to exacting performance requirements.

STRUCTURAL SYSTEM

Suspended facades are exposed to various loads:
- wind load (pos. and neg. pressure – horizontally)
- snow loads in the case of non-vertical facades (acting vertically, and on a sloping structure also horizontally)
- imposed loads (preventing falls – horizontally)
- restraint loads (from changes in shape due to thermal expansion and sources of shrinkage – multidirectional)
- impact loads (vehicles, intrusion – horizontally)

A suspended facade is differentiated into the secondary system (mullions, transoms, frames, glazing bars) and the tertiary system (supported infill panels or cladding). When exposed to loads, facades are subject to deformation at their bearing, i.e. elastic deformation (deflection) and plastic deformation (creep), in addition to which there may be restraint loads (due to thermal expansion/contraction, or swelling/shrinkage). Where deformation is restricted, this results in stress. Such stress must not exceed the strength of the building components which must be separated by expansion joints. The primary loadbearing system is often built with greater production tolerances than the facade components. Jointed facade anchors (bearings) that allow a degree of movement can prevent the facade being affected by loads produced by changes in the primary structure. Rigid bearings in the element can help to restrict deformation of the facade, but this requires material of adequate strength and thickness.

THERMAL INSULATION

When the suspended facade also fulfils the thermal insulation function of a building envelope, the following aspects have to be taken into account:
- avoiding or minimising thermal bridges
- limiting transmission heat loss by using components with high thermal resistance (insulation, insulating glazing)
- avoiding heat loss through air exchange by using airtight construction systems on the inside and windproof connections on the outside, e.g. by applying continuous pressure on sealing profiles.

It is important to ensure that the facade has sufficient thermal resistance to maintain comfortable indoor temperatures. Large glazed areas in particular permit extensive thermal radiation loss on cold days and nights, and can therefore be perceived as uncomfortably cool. Their inside surface cools down the adjacent air and causes draughts. If adequate thermal resistance cannot be provided, temporary insulation (e.g. roller shutters in front of glazing panels) and convective heating of the external wall (radiators, floor convectors) are required. Solar heat gain during the heating period, by using glazing or transparent thermal insulation, is just as good for the overall energy balance as the reduction of thermal gain outside the heating period by using solar screening.

PROTECTION AGAINST DIFFUSION AND CONDENSATION

Joints between facade elements must be airtight, which can be achieved by applying pressure with the glazing bars on the sealing profiles (which must have sufficient deformation capacity) and by keeping the deflection of the assembly under wind load to an acceptable level. Components that are externally airtight prevent penetration by cold air and hence condensation in the building fabric, as well as penetration by rainwater or driving snow. When the entire building component is airtight, it prevents the loss of warm air to the outside due to negative wind pressure and hence heat loss. Components that are sealed against the ingress of water (under pressure) protect the fabric from driving rain. Where external skins and joints are designed not to be watertight, any penetrating water enters an air gap from where it is conducted back outside; the gap should be pressure-equalised to render any flow of air insignificant. Special openings are provided to ensure pressure equalisation and water discharge. The inside face of an external wall should be kept warm enough to avoid condensation at the surface and thus mould growth. Where the construction makes this impossible, condensate channels are provided to control the discharge of water. The seals of glazing panels and window casements cannot always prevent the penetration of humid air. The resulting condensate collects in rebates or profiles and is led outside.

FIRE AND LIGHTNING PROTECTION

The fire safety concept must include the facade. In some classes of building, if there is a risk of flashover via the facade, this must have adequate fire-resistance (E30 to E90) and residual stability. This should be settled early in the design stage as it limits the choice of structure and material. Alternatively, flashover can be hindered by using non-combustible components in the facade (e.g. canopies or horizontal ledges, projecting walls, or wall panels beneath windows in a material such as reinforced concrete. These influence the transparency or opacity of the design. Connections and fastening devices attached to the loadbearing system must be non-combustible. Falling facade elements should not pose a threat to rescuers and occupants in a fire.

MULLION / TRANSOM FACADE

The curtain wall principle gained ground internationally in the 1960s owing to the maximum transparency of this type of facade and its technical possibilities. The separation of the loadbearing structure from the envelope, and the desire for an apparently seamless transition between the interior and exterior (as designed in buildings by SOM Skidmore Owings Merrill, HPP Hentrich-Petschnigg & Partner, and earlier by Egon Eiermann) encouraged the development of slender construction profiles that made it possible to enclose interiors with glass elements only. Today, slender glass facades are a firm part of the repertoire of contemporary architecture, and are being continually developed with respect to material properties, energy efficiency and sustainability. The most common facade system is the mullion/transom construction system.

The principle of separating the load of the facade from the primary structure of the building by using a secondary structure consisting of mullions, transoms and infill panels allows great freedom in the design of the facade, as this can be structured flexibly and independently of the building layout, including solar screening and services. The pronounced grid pattern of the exterior envelope imposed by the visible secondary structure needs special attention in terms of conceptual and detailed design. ➘ p. 20 Economic solutions are facilitated by the availability of comparatively large infill elements of varying widths, profiles of varying dimensions, a range of different construction materials (e.g. steel, aluminium or timber profiles) and modular construction. Installation on site is carried out either with prefabricated elements or with the individual facade components. Mullion/transom systems can be used in vertical and sloping facades, as well as in roof construction.

CONSTRUCTION ELEMENTS

The construction consists of vertical mullions that are attached to the primary loadbearing structure. They are commonly either supported on or suspended from the edges of the floor slabs, thereby transferring the dead loads and any loads from positive or negative wind pressure. Horizontal transoms connect the vertical load-transferring mullions, to which they are fixed either with bolts, by welding or using a push-fit system.

In order to be able to withstand wind load, mullions and transoms must have an adequate resistance moment, which is why they often consist of rectangular box sections with appropriate depth. These sections may consist of coated steel, stainless steel or anodised aluminium, and more rarely of timber, veneered plywood or plastic. Steel profiles are always used to reinforce plastic profiles and sometimes, in the case of greater loads, to reinforce aluminium profiles.

Metal and plastic facades work with profile widths of between 50 and 60 mm and profile depths of between 50 and 190 mm; where a greater depth is required, a frame profile is bolted onto a rectangular hollow section. It is common to use the vertical mullions for the transfer of loads, which is why they carry more weight and have a greater depth than the horizontal transoms. For example, they are attached to the floor slabs or structural beams/lintels with a fastening method designed to resist tensile stress. The spacing of mullions is usually between 60 and 150 cm and is aligned with the dimensions of the fitting out grid. The facade anchors must be capable of absorbing tolerances and deformation, and must be designed to accommodate any thermal expansion of the secondary structure. ➘ 4

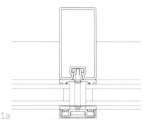
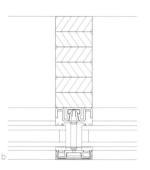

1 Profile schematics

a Aluminium profile with thermal separation
b Timber section with thermal separation and system profile

2 AachenMünchner Versicherung, Aachen, 2010, kadawittfeld-architektur: The facade facing the boulevard connects the main entrance with the different, staggered, building volumes via a slender storey-height mullion/transom construction with structural glazing. The 2.70 m grid with two layers of insulating glazing and some curved glass panes provides maximum transparency.

3 The Folkwang Library in Essen, 2014, Max Dudler. Light is a sensitive issue in library buildings and requires detailed attention. Direct intensive light must be avoided. The insulating glazing unit of a conventional mullion/transom facade is given a polychromatic photographic imprint on the side.

4   Schematic structure of a
mullion/transom facade

a   Primary structure – floor slab,
columns etc.
b   Facade mullion – vertical
c   Mullion holders
d   Facade transom – horizontal
e   Infill unit
transparent, e.g. fixed glazing or
opening unit
opaque, e.g. solid panel
f   Glare/solar screening
g   Pressure plate and screws

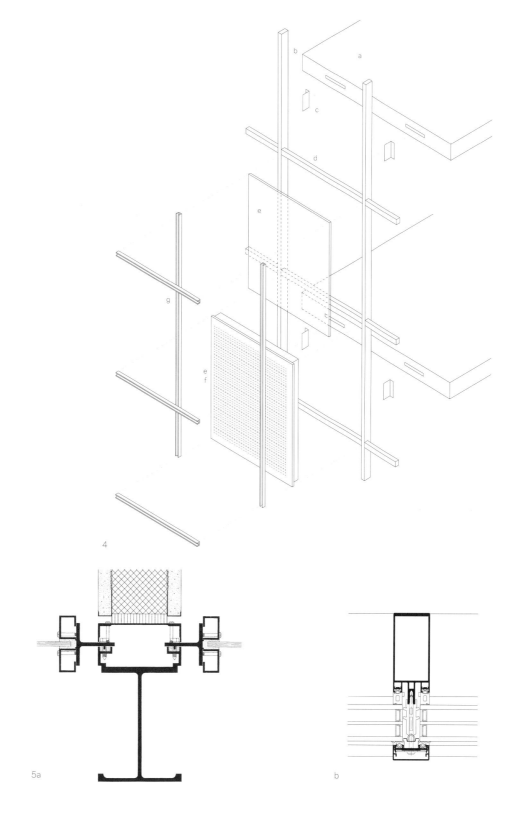

4

5   Comparison of historic and
contemporary facade details

a   The Seagram Building, New York,
1958, Ludwig Mies van der Rohe
and Philip Johnson
Horizontal section, scale 1:5
b   Present-day mullion/transom
facade: additional requirements
have led to ever more complex
designs.
Horizontal section through mullion,
scale 1:5

5a

b

INFILL PANELS

Infill panels may consist of a range of different materials, be they transparent or opaque. If infill panels of different thicknesses are used, the difference can usually be accommodated by the skeleton construction system. As well as insulating glazing, common infill elements are panels with a covering layer of metal, plastic or (enamelled) glass, and a core of mineral wool or polyurethane foam. Various opening elements can be integrated in all systems. Vertical and horizontal pressure plates that hold the infill elements are attached to the framing and exert even, linear pressure on the infill elements and the substructure. Elastic sealing profiles (made of neoprene, ethylene propylene diene monomer (EPDM), PVC containing plasticiser) or silicone are inserted in the joints of the infill elements with the mullions/transoms and the pressure plates, and held fixed. This means that the construction consists of two sealing planes – the external cladding layer is watertight and the inner layer is vapour-proof.

If the size of the infill element is not large enough to close the opening of the shell construction – i.e. several elements are needed with a joint – or it has limited structural capability, horizontal transoms (bars) have to be inserted to ensure adequate stiffness and to transfer the weight to the vertical mullions. The use of transoms prevents movement due to thermal expansion, which means that expansion joints are required; these may show in the elevation of the facade and therefore need to be taken into consideration in the design.

DESIGN CONSIDERATIONS

Infill elements consisting of insulating glazing or panels represent the actual building envelope and have a major impact on the appearance. This envelope provides air-tightness, wind protection, sound insulation, protection against driving rain, and thermal insulation. In the design of the joints, the following need to be taken into account:
– Thermal separation
Thermal separation is achieved by inserting plastic strips or profiles into the metal profiles, or by separating the construction to form an inner loadbearing skin and an outer pressure plate, whereby the insulating layer is only penetrated where the bolts are fitted; it is also possible to screw the bolts into a plastic profile. The heat flow at the screw-in points should be minimised in any case.

– Resistance to driving rain and condensate
Due to unavoidable geometric failure points in the seals, it is possible that humid air from the inside and driving rain from the outside penetrate the joint. Any condensate and rainwater must be collected in the profile and conducted to the outside in a controlled way; water vapour

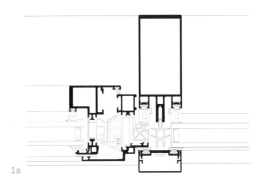

1a

is discharged by ventilation (double joint seal), as otherwise there would be positive vapour pressure in the profile and vapour could penetrate into glazing and other panels via the edge seal.

Several systems are available for sealing the joints and fastening the infill panels:
– Glazing putty
Owing to its adhesive and cohesive properties, putty is waterproof and malleable, but it tends to become brittle when exposed to UV light, so it has to be protected with a coating. These days it is only used for the refurbishment of historic building components.

– Pressure plates with sealing profiles
The most common system for mullion/transom facades uses a pressure plate that is screwed either into the frame profile or into a thermally separating plastic batten mounted on the outside. This batten presses on inserted rubber seals and is protected against the weather by a clipped-on covering strip. The covering strip can have various shapes, depending on the design intention.

– Structural glazing
In order to achieve a flush appearance in glass facades with as little of the profiles' surface showing as possible, 'structural glazing' facades have been developed, in which glass panes are held in place by structural sealant rather than mechanically. In such systems the glass panes are not clamped against the substructure, but are held with adhesive sealant. In Germany, it is a legal requirement for these glass panes also to be secured with concealed screw connections. The external joints are approx. 20 mm wide and are sealed with a permanently elastic compound. The adhesive bond is designed to transfer wind forces only; the dead weight of the structure is transferred by fixing the glazing to small brackets or pads in order to ensure that, in the case of failure of the adhesive bond the glass panes cannot fall down (particularly important with high buildings).

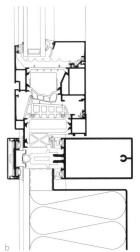

2

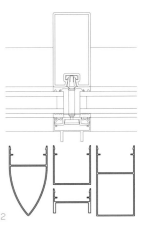

3

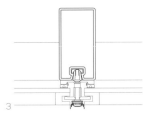

1 Principle of opening element connection
a Horizontal section
b Vertical section

2 Different types of pressure plate
Pressure plates transfer forces between the frame and the infill panels; these plates come in a variety of depths and shapes, and cover the construction.

3 Principle of structural glazing

4 Load transfer in a curtain wall facade
The facade components can either be suspended from the top or built up from the bottom. When they are suspended (fixed at the top), the components of the facade are subject to tensile stress from their own weight, while components built up from the bottom (standing) are subject to compression stress and have to be secured against buckling. For this reason, facades suspended from the top can be designed with slenderer profiles.
a Standing
b Suspended

5 Salewa headquarters, Bolzano, 2012, Cino Zucchi + Park associati
Imposing all-glass facade using a structural glazing system. A continuous surface is created on the outside by using profiles that can only be seen on the inside; on the outside only the glass surfaces with slender shadow joints are visible.

6 Schematic connection to primary structure, scale 1:20
a Mullion profile
b Transom profile
c Adjustable connection at the top with height adjustment
d Fixed connection at base
e Insulating glazing unit
f Insulation panel and seal of joint with the floor slab

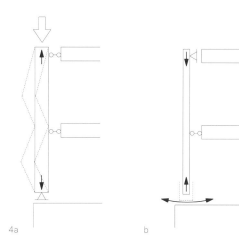

4a   b

5

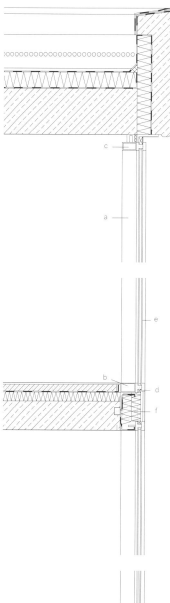

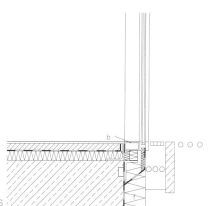

6

GLASS AND GLAZING ELEMENTS

Glass is neither combustible nor flammable; it is transparent, has a homogeneous, smooth surface that can easily be cleaned and is resistant to chemical reactions. Glass is water-repellent and does not change its shape when exposed to fluctuations in temperature. Glass has high compressive strength, but low tensile strength. The infill panels in mullion/transom construction systems may consist of insulating glazing elements, optionally filled with transparent thermal insulation or light-diffusion inserts. Element facades or double-skin facades may also feature back ventilation; this makes it possible to install photovoltaic (PV) elements, solar thermal panels or printed/enamelled glass panels, at the back of which very high temperatures may occur. The desire for a glass construction system that functions not only as bracing, but also as a primary structure, is reflected in architectural designs of great transparency and lightness, which appropriately display the special characteristics of glass. This development has led to a number of modern glass construction systems that transfer their dead weight via glass columns, glass beams and glass fins. This has become possible owing to the optimisation of the material properties of glass for structural applications, for example by using semi-tempered glass panels or laminated safety glass for transferring loads within the plane of the glass. For reasons of safety and loadbearing capacity, glass facades are often constructed using laminated safety glass. This is produced using toughened safety glass and semi-tempered glass, which are bonded together in several layers including elastic tear-resistant polymer films. Should the glass fracture, the fragments are held in place by the film. Today, some types of laminated glass that are bonded using casting resin are also classed as laminated safety glass for the purpose of building control approval.

FASTENING METHODS
A range of different systems can be used for fastening glass panes and transferring the loads:

– Fastening using pressure plates
In a construction with pressure plates, the loads in the plane of the glass panes are transferred to brackets at the lower edge of the glass. Pressure plates with elastic padding absorb the loads perpendicular to the glass panes. In addition, the lateral and top edges are secured with pressure plates to prevent deformation. The unrestrained corners of the glass are free of stress. ⌐ 4

– Bearing on pins
In this system, panes of laminated safety glass are supported from steel brackets, with the panes overlapping like scales. Owing to the system's poor resistance to

driving rain, it is only used for back-ventilated or low-specification facades, depending on the use and function of the building. While the glass panes are supported by brackets (pins) at the bottom, at the top edge they lean inwards and are held by the bearings; the bottom support is not continuous but at points. Where wind forces have to be taken into account, laminated safety glass ($3 \times$ TSG) is required. Wind forces are transferred through friction or by counter-bearings. The edges of the glass panes are completely free of stress. ⌐ 5

– Disc fastening system
This system is suitable for insulation glazing; the edges of the glass panels are free of stress. In a pre-stressed fastening system with discs, a hole is inserted at precise points and a polymer bushing is inserted, through which the anchor bolt is pushed. This avoids tension peaks due to imperfections. Conical pressure plates (countersink holders) can also be fitted flush with the surface. The load transfer can take place by pre-tensioning the seal and glass pane via the bolt fixing through friction and through shear stress at the flank of the hole. Alternatively, it is possible to use undercut anchors; however, this system results in very high stresses around the hole.

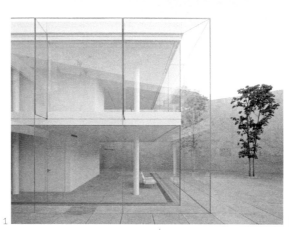

1 Office building, Zamora, 2012, Alberto Campo Baeza: The continuous two-layer envelope made of laminated safety glass panes with a horizontal glass edge to the roof is joined with silicone joints and rails recessed in the ground. Laminated safety glass fins provide rigidity to the joints of the glass panels on the upper floor.

2 Herz Jesu church, Munich, 2000, Allmann Sattler Wappner Architects: Core elements of the glass facade are the horizontal and vertical glass fins, which perform a loadbearing function and have been bonded to U-shaped stainless steel profiles for the transfer of loads. Extensive experimental and theoretical investigation was required to furnish proof of the loadbearing capacity.

3 Breaking patterns of glass
Thermally pre-stressed glass panes are classified either as semi-tempered glass or toughened safety glass. The latter crumbles into small, almost spherical parts, while the former breaks into large radial shards. Semi-tempered glass is used where the broken shards will remain in the frame or cannot fall out (to avoid injury).

a Toughened safety glass
b Semi-tempered glass

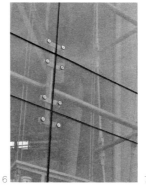

4 Kattendijkdok Westkaai, residential towers, Belgium, 2009, Diener & Diener Architects: The load of the structural facade glazing in the direction of the pane ('in plane') is transferred to brackets using pressure plates at the lower edge of the glass. Pressure plates with elastic padding transfer any loads that are perpendicular to the pane ('out of plane'). In addition, the lateral and top edges are secured with pressure plates to prevent deformation. This means that the free corners of the glass are free of stress.

5 Kunsthaus Bregenz, 1997, Peter Zumthor: Laminated safety glass is supported by steel brackets at various points at the base. Where the glass panes are supported by pins, they slant inwards at the top edge against the bearing. They overlap in the manner of scales. Wind forces are transferred through friction, which requires heavy glass panes made of laminated safety glass (3 × toughened glass), or by counter-bearings. The edges of the glass panes are completely free of tension. Owing to its poor resistance to driving rain, this system can only be used for back-ventilated facades or those with low weatherproofing requirements.

6 Stadttor Düsseldorf, 1997, Overdieck Petzinka and Partners: Corridor facade with external single-glazing anchored at points. The pre-stressed fastening system with discs requires drill holes that are precisely positioned and tailored for the insertion of polymer bushings through which the anchor bolt is pushed. This avoids tension peaks due to imperfections. Conical pressure plates (countersink holders) can also be fitted flush with the surface. For the purpose of fastening glass panes in holes subject to shear at the reveals, the screw is cast in plastic in the hole in order to ensure an even transfer of forces.

7 Helsinki Music Hall, 2011, Laiho-Pulkkinen-Raunio Architects: For the purpose of reinforcement, glass fins are attached to the facade using point anchors and bonding.

– Point fastening using bolts
These point fastenings result in local stress peaks in the glass with high loads, which is why the preferred method is to use drilled point fastening devices. The means of transferring loads from the glass pane to the secondary loadbearing system must be capable of accommodating thermal and wind-related deformation. This is achieved by having one fixed point and three anchor points that allow movement.

Systems that use point fastening methods require laminated safety glass or semi-tempered glass, because if one pane fails, the adjacent panes or other building components have to absorb the resulting forces. Glass beams (glass fins) and also glass needles can be used to provide stiffness against negative wind pressure. Joints are sealed with a permanently elastic compound. Where insulating glass panels are used, an additional inner rubber profile helps to equalise vapour pressure and discharge water. In the case of insulation glazing without a frame, a means of draining water from the rebate joint must be provided, the sealing system must have sufficient mechanical strength and the edge seal must be UV-resistant. ⟶ 6

– Fastening system using adhesive bonding
It is also possible to bond holding discs to the glass using elastic adhesive; this bond is capable of absorbing small rotational movements. A separate construction is required to prevent glass panes from falling should any of the holding discs fail. ⟶ 7

SECONDARY LOADBEARING SYSTEMS
Glazing with point fastening systems can either be supported by a range of loadbearing systems or it can be part of a secondary system. The following secondary loadbearing systems are available:

– Frame systems consisting of profile tubes
These consist of a number of profile tubes that are joined to form a grid frame similar to a mullion/transom system. Frame systems are very stiff, so any deformation has to be accommodated by the anchor fastenings.

– Cable networks
Flat or curved space frames consist of cables with compression struts inserted between them. This system requires two cable systems, one for negative and one for positive wind pressure. In spite of the pre-tensioning, significant deformation takes place.

– Vertical cable facades
These consist of vertical cables or tensile bars suspended from the top, allowing a very slender loadbearing system. The pane fastenings are attached to the cables and transfer the weight of the glass and wind forces. One version of this system is the glass curtain in which the glass panes – utilising pre-tensioning – make up the tensile elements. The glass panes are attached at four points.

This type of glass element facade is highly complex and requires cooperation with consulting engineers early in the design stage. Designs using this system do not readily fall into any standard structural category and therefore usually require individual consent from the building control authorities, unless the necessary evidence of structural integrity is available for an approved system.

ELEMENT FACADE

Element facades consist of storey-high elements forming complete room enclosures. They are an efficient alternative to a classic mullion/transom construction in situations where a homogeneous facade surface, such as that of a tower block, has to be installed without scaffolding in a short period of time, or where a facade has to be installed in a restricted space as part of a revitalisation project. Each module contains the necessary components of a building envelope, including the rigid loadbearing frames, transparent glazing (either fixed or openable), opaque panels, ventilation elements and the part covering the edge of floor slabs, in the form of a single- or double-skin system. In contrast to conventional mullion/transom construction, prefabrication allows the profiles of the opening elements to be slimmer, which means that the visible profile width is reduced. In addition, prefabrication at the factory means that solar screening elements can also be fitted.

The functional requirements for the building envelope affect the design of the facade. Depending on the way in which opening and ventilation elements are integrated (full-panel size/with a separate frame in the centre of the element/in small-format horizontal bands/alternating with closed elements), the design of the facade varies, resulting in different aesthetic effects. The jointing of prefabricated elements on site involves extensive logistics and requires exact detailing of the design of the construction and expansion joints; an important aspect of this facade system is the fact that the shell construction has to be completed to minimal tolerances.

INSTALLATION

The individual elements are installed storey by storey in front of the shell construction plane using precisely aligned fixing plates, either fixed rigidly or with a movement tolerance, and are aligned in all three dimensions within the available tolerances. Following the installation of the facade, the interior fit-out can start without any delay. The usual width of the prefabricated elements ranges from approx. 120 cm to 250 cm, the elements being manufactured to suit the axes of the grid system. Lightweight timber constructions can be produced covering several axes, up to a width of 6 m; narrow metal panels can be produced up to 14 m long. If the elements are taller than the full-storey height, they have to be transported flat (up to 250 cm wide) owing to road transport regulations. Prior to installation they have to be erected by crane. As individual elements are installed side by side, the visible width of the edge profiles is combined. The standard width of the mullion (twice the edge width of a single element) is approx. 80 mm. The covering function can be performed by a pressure plate (which is also preassembled in two half shells) or by the detailing of the structural glazing system.

SEALING

The elements are joined using special overlapping connection joints – horizontally with continuous sealing rails and vertically with push-fit seals. A distinction is made between, on the one hand, the joints within the element which, similar to those in the mullion/transom facade, are

1, 4 Office building, Münster, 2011, Vervoorts & Schindler Architects: The facade elements were prefabricated and inserted as functional units. The solar screening has been integrated in the elements to create a flush surface, thus retaining a harmonious exterior when the screening is closed.

2 The connection points of the facade to the primary system must have fixed points as well as sliding ones, which must be three-dimensionally adjustable so that tolerances in the construction can be accommodated.

3 Schematic of element facade
a Floor slab
b Facade element
c Element connector
d Glazing

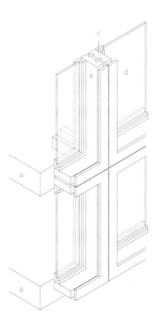

1

2

3

sealed using permanently elastic compound or pre-compressed sealing strips, and on the other hand, the joints between the elements. The latter are closed with pressure plate seals unless the geometry of the joint and the installation sequence make it possible to insert the seal during installation.

The joints between the elements must be capable of absorbing all of the thermal deformation of the components which, due to the larger size of the elements, is greater than that of mullion/transom elements. Constructions with elements fastened in this way can be installed to a facade length of 50 m and still absorb the resulting expansion in the joints. In spite of the ability to absorb deformation, the joint between the elements must remain watertight and airtight. The selection of the panel material and the design of the profiles have to take into account building physics requirements for the facade, such as thermal and sound insulation, fire protection and effective solar screening independent of the weather, as well as safety requirements. The most commonly used profiles consist of extruded aluminium sections with thermal separation; however, it is also possible to produce special profiles from a variety of materials, such as structural bronze.

5   The Prime Tower, Zurich, 2011, Gigon Guyer: Elements such as the automatically operated large parallel opening windows of up to 400 kg are integrated in the element facade.

6   Schematic facade section, scale 1:20
a   Floor slab
b   Facade element
c   Element holder with fixed and sliding points
d   Element connection

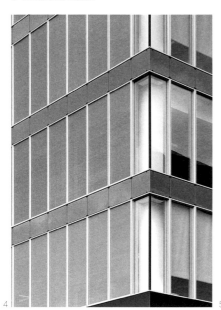

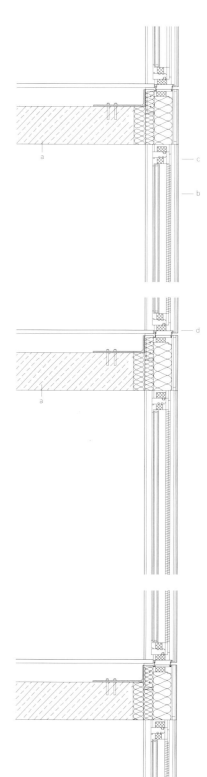

DOUBLE-SKIN FACADE

The principle of the double-skin facade (as opposed to the single-skin element facade) is based on a development of the historical box-type window in which, sometimes seasonally, a secondary window is fitted in order to achieve a climate buffer between the two. Today, double-skin facades consist of two planes – an outer glazed skin which protects against the weather, and an inner thermally insulating construction plane which can be configured to suit the various functional requirements (solar screening, protection against glare, thermal and sound insulation, natural ventilation and provision of daylight). Between the two skins is an air-filled space that functions as a thermal buffer zone. One of the objectives in the development of this facade system was to achieve natural ventilation of the interior, rather than having to use air conditioning, and thus to improve the quality of the interior climate. The space between the two skins can be accessed via ventilation openings, installed either in the outer or the inner skin – a solution that is also possible in very tall buildings. Another advantage is that solar irradiation can be utilised for seasonal heat storage and natural thermal convection in order to encourage a steady flow of air. Double-skinned facades, appropriately designed to meet structural building physics requirements, can be particularly suitable for tall buildings exposed to strong wind loads and requiring extensive sound insulation. However, in view of the additional cost of a double-skin facade, designers may want to consider whether it is necessary on all sides of the building. Where double-skin facades are used on two sides of the building only, special attention must be paid to the transition between the different types of facade construction. A distinction is made between different types of double-skin facade, depending on the different types of ventilation.

MECHANICALLY VENTILATED FACADES
These facades consist of a closed external envelope of insulating glazing and an internal facade of single glazing, which can be opened for the purpose of cleaning and maintenance. The difference to other systems is the mechanical air movement, in which warm preconditioned air is directed through the air space and discharged above the roof. An advantage of this system is the good sound insulation, while the energy consumed is a negative aspect.

SECOND-SKIN FACADES
In this system, a lightweight second layer without horizontal or vertical compartmentalisation is placed in front of the actual facade, enveloping the entire building and creating a layer of air as a buffer in front of the facade.

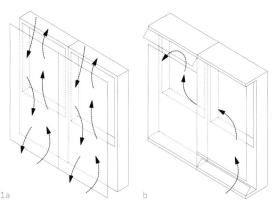
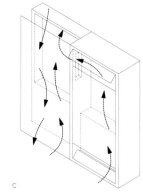

1a   b   c

This buffer zone is also used for ventilation. In winter, this zone can be closed to the outside and used for storing solar irradiation, while in summer the openings in the outer layer can be opened to prevent overheating. The intermediate space of the buffer zone may be quite narrow, or it may have considerable depth, thus creating a new, enclosed space of its own. An advantage is good external sound insulation; a disadvantage is the transfer of sound within the building via the surrounding air space. A development of this system is the closed cavity facade (CCF), in which the space between the inner and outer facade skins is lightly pressurised and fully encapsulated. Dry, clean air is injected, which prevents the formation of condensate and soiling. The cavity can accommodate solar screening and light-directing elements. In contrast to the mechanically ventilated facade, the second-skin facade relies on natural thermal convection.

CORRIDOR FACADE AND SHAFT BOX FACADE
Another variant is the corridor facade, in which the air is injected separately for each storey. The inlet and outlet air openings are arranged in an offset manner in order to prevent any thermal overlay of the air flow. The resulting corridor is also used as a cleaning platform. An advantage is that each storey is individually protected against overheating. The construction of the shaft box facade (a further variant) is based on alternating box-type windows with ventilation shafts. Owing to the stack effect, air is sucked into the shafts at low level, heats up and flows past the box openings, thereby providing a comfortable room climate. Due to the low proportion of openings, the sound insulation of this facade is good. However, the natural stack effect decreases with increasing height, so that this type of facade is unsuitable for tall buildings.

1   Schematics of double-skin facades
a   Facade with second skin
b   Corridor facade
c   Shaft box type facade

2 Süddeutscher Verlag tower, Munich, 2008, GKK+Architekten Prof. Swantje Kühn, Oliver Kühn: According to calculations by the architects and engineers, the building is expected to save 80 % of the primary energy that would normally be used during operation, and hence reduce operating costs by up to 35 % compared to comparable conventional buildings. This result is due to the double-skin facades with decentralised facade ventilation devices, the individual control of ventilation, solar screening and temperature in each office, and the use of the ground storage systems for heating/cooling according to the season.

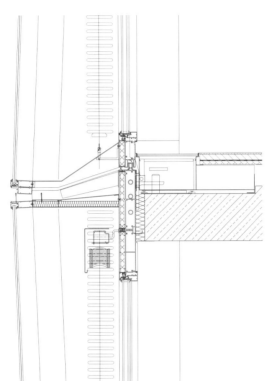

3 Allianz headquarters, Zurich, 2014, Wiel Arets Architects
A development of the 'closed cavity' facade, with self-contained, highly insulating box-type window elements, the cavity of which is used for conducting dried air. In contrast to double-skin facades with openings to the outside air, this system prevents the ingress of dirt or dust into the box element and also prevents condensate forming in the facade gap. This means that the glass surfaces facing the gap do not have to be cleaned. Curtains with a highly reflective aluminium coating are used as integrated solar and glare screening.

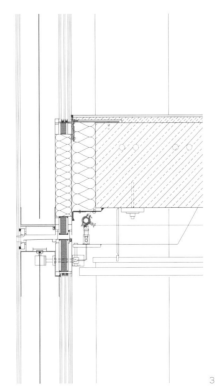

ELEMENT FACADE – CONCRETE

Element facades made of concrete consist of individual prefabricated elements that are installed and joined on the construction site, forming a secondary structural system. They are distinct from single- and multi-skin prefabricated concrete units which, like sandwich construction units, form part of the primary structural system. Prefabricated concrete elements consist of several layers: the loadbearing layer, a thermal insulation layer and a face layer. It is also possible to include an air gap in the construction of the elements. The large-format prefabricated elements – which consist of reinforced concrete or lightweight concrete with a dense structure – can be produced up to a length of approx. 5 to 6 m to cover the full height of a storey. The size of elements is limited by their weight (< 10 t) for the purpose of transport and site movement and by the installation situation, and has to be determined to suit the respective project.

CONSTRUCTION AND JOINTING
The concrete elements are attached to the primary loadbearing system in two basic ways: either suspended via specially shaped lugs, or attached via anchors. In the latter case, they are anchored to the structural system with stainless steel components that are fixed to the prefabricated element, making an unrestrained joint that can be adjusted. If the installation were to be via a rigid attachment with high-strength mortar or welded steel anchors, this would lead to stresses resulting from the expansion of the facade element (primarily thermal) or from movement of the primary system (deflection, creep). ⌐ 1, 2
In order to accommodate the movement of panels, the facade requires joints, the size of which is determined by the geometry of the structural system or colour of the facade, since dark components expand more, as do components with thermal insulation on the inside.
The joints are designed to resist the penetration of driving rain by virtue of the joint geometry or a combination of sealing systems: they may be closed with sealing profiles that are either inserted subsequently or cast into the elements; after mounting they may be sealed with permanently elastic compound. ⌐ 3
Thermally insulated facades are constructed by adding an inner skin with thermal insulation and face panels, e.g. gypsum planks. Freestanding inner skins are insulated either with mineral wool or expanded polystyrene and are protected by a vapour check layer on the inside surface; alternatively, the insulation consists of foam glass that has been bonded and skimmed with cold bitumen. Since in this case the inner skin moves with the facade, it has to be connected to the structural system with appropriate joints. Windows and other built-in components that are tied to the inner skin must be connected to the facade with joints that allow adequate movement. Conversely, a

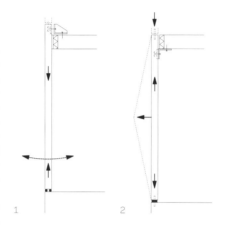

1

2

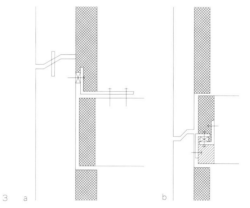

3 a

b

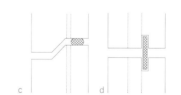

c

d

4

1 Suspended prefabricated components are subject to tensile stress only, which affects the type of reinforcement. For this reason they usually only suffer shrinkage cracks, and transfer all impacting forces to the primary system, which must be capable of absorbing them.

2 Prefabricated components that are attached at the back transfer vertical loads (primarily own weight, rarely the load from ledges) to the elements below. The primary system absorbs the horizontal forces (wind, earthquake). These elements must be stronger owing to their exposure to compression and the risk of buckling.

3 The anchoring points between the facade and the primary system represent thermal bridges, the effect of which can be reduced by inserting plastic separating layers. The fixing substrate should have sufficient thermal storage mass to reduce any cooling effect.

a, b The geometry of the horizontal joint sections is such that any penetrating water is discharged to the outside. An internal rubber seal can be used to provide additional protection and airtightness.
c Vertical
d Horizontal

4 Store front for Art and Architecture NYC, 1992, Steven Holl / Vito Acconci, facade renewal in 2009: The new facade is made of glass-fibre concrete and can be opened in different ways, depending on the season and the exhibition. The store front mediates freely between the exterior and interior; it creates open connections or limits them and offers visitors changing spatial experiences.

5 Horizontal section, scale 1:20
a Glass-fibre concrete panel
b Thermal separating element
c Wall bracket
d Thermal insulation
e Connection element
f Vertical profile
g Ventilation gap

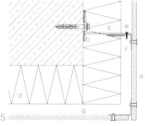

5

6 School in Marburg, 2010,
Hess Talhof Kusmierz: The external
skin consists primarily of prefabricated concrete elements. As a special reference to the location, these
concrete elements feature a relief
surface which originates from a
negative imprint of the existing
facade of the nearby town hall. The
matrices for the manufacture of the
concrete elements were produced
using the washed concrete method.

7 Utrecht University library (UBU),
2005, Wiel Arets: The walls and
facades of the building feature a
textured surface. The facade
panels were prefabricated using
B35 concrete.

8 Museum of Architectural
Drawings, Berlin, 2013, SPEECH,
nps tchoban voss: Historic drawings were used to produce the
facade reliefs; they were applied
as a matrix (a negative of the motif)
to the system formwork. The joints
and edges were sealed with silicone. The motifs take the position
of the necessary holding anchors
into account, concealing them.

9 Paul Sabatier University,
Toulouse, 2010, Espagno & Milani:
The facade of the university has
been designed using a photographic engraving method in which
the image information is transferred to elastic matrices using a
computer-assisted process. This
process facilitates an aesthetic –
yet economic – application of
images to a concrete surface.

component that is built into a prefabricated facade element requires flexible joints with the inner skin.

MATERIAL AND SURFACE
Prefabricated concrete elements can be finished with
very delicate surface textures – in the form of fair-faced,
textured or washed concrete. As these elements are prefabricated at a factory a more consistent quality can be
achieved than with production on site. Both normal concrete and high-density lightweight concrete are suitable
for a fair-faced finish. Surface treatment using mechanical
processes such as dressing, (fine) washing, sandblasting,
etching or burning is easier with prefabricated elements
and likely to be more consistent. By inserting a frost-
resistant covering layer of ceramics, natural stone, glass
shards or similar materials into the formwork, it is possible to produce compound elements with reinforced concrete as the structural part. A prerequisite for this type
of construction is a permanent bond between the layers,
as well as adequate coverage of the concrete. The use
of formwork matrices and computer-aided production
make it possible to create any kind of patterned surface
(even images), whose appearance can change greatly,
depending on the angle of solar incidence and the view-
ing angle. By contrast to in-situ concrete components,
prefabricated elements are thinner and are easier to produce in slender or sculptural shapes owing to the controlled production process.
Concrete elements require detailed design and planning,
covering aspects such as transport, installation, bearing
details and jointing of the elements. In addition to the surface finish, the geometry of the joints is an important
design element. Since this is also affected by structural
requirements, development of the facade grid also needs
to take certain aspects of manufacturing and installation
into account.

7

8

6

9

ELEMENT FACADE – TIMBER

Timber element facades have been developed from traditional timber construction and are produced either as prefabricated units in a timber frame or as panels with structural skins consisting of solid wooden board. Both systems are based on the same construction principle, the only difference being the format of the semi-finished product. The advantages of building with elements are obvious – owing to the low weight and the high degree of prefabrication, buildings can be constructed economically and quickly. In the first method, that of timber frame construction, timber sections are joined to make a frame, which is then braced by attaching at least one covering layer of a wood-based board material (e.g. chipboard, OSB board with a thickness of 12 to 18 mm). The cavity (i.e. the frame plane) is filled with thermal insulation. ⌐ 1, 2 Timber panels, the second method, consist of cross-laminated board with a layer of external thermal insulation. These panels have adequate structural stiffness without additional measures. Openings are inserted by cutting. The thermal insulation is attached using counter-battens and sometimes also dowelling. Timber elements can be supplied with a fully finished surface – with or without back-ventilation – in various forms: structured timber cladding, a thermal sandwich insulation system, face brickwork, or metal cladding. In contrast to log construction ⌐ p. 58 it is possible to produce not only plane but also curved surfaces with timber frame construction. In addition, the system provides greater design freedom with respect to the layout and the placement of openings. The windows are fitted in the plane of the thermal insulation layer. Any openings that do not fall within the construction grid can be accommodated. The size of the prefabricated elements depends on transport restrictions and installation options (sequence of delivery). Taking into account the aspects of sustainability, life cycle and the optimum use of materials in prefabrication, this construction method is not only suitable for horizontal and vertical extensions or infill buildings, but also generally for multi-storey timber construction.

CONSTRUCTION AND JOINTING

The timber frames are constructed using solid timber that has been graded according to strength, dimensional stability and maximum moisture content, such as solid timber (up to 5 m length) or specially graded solid construction timber. With the latter, sections that are longer than standard solid timber (up to 14 m) can be produced by joining sections using finger jointing.

The common width of frame sections is 60 mm; the depth depends on the necessary insulation layer and the height of the frame element. Where a depth in excess of 12 cm is needed, several rectangular sections are glued together to form double or treble profiles. In order to reduce heat loss and material consumption, it is common nowadays to use I-beams or box beams instead, or to attach additional thermal insulation to the outer face of the panel. In order to avoid thermal bridges, the thermal insulation layer should be at least 6 to 10 cm thick and continuous in front of the primary system, with brackets only reaching half way into the insulation. With cross-laminated board the thermal insulation is fitted in front of the loadbearing element. This means that the boards can bear on their full bearing surface without creating thermal bridges. Since timber components are subject to minimal thermal expansion only, the connecting joints may be very narrow. Weak points in the system exist where the airtight layers are penetrated.

Owing to the low shear strength of the material, tensile forces are difficult to transmit to timber sections unless substantial steel connectors are used to make the connection. For this reason, timber frame elements are not installed suspended, but rather placed on a bearing and thus subjected to pressure from their own weight. The risk of buckling can be reduced with the help of intermediate bearings. Timber frames have a minimum bearing width of 12 to 15 cm and are placed on ledges of the primary system or on angle brackets.

1   Timber frame construction details

2   Layers
a   Facade cladding
b   Wind sealing plane
c   Insulation and structural plane
d   Air sealing plane
e   Interior fit-out

3   Grid dimension + corner detail
The construction grid is coordinated with the width of cladding panels so that offcuts can be kept to a minimum.
1.25 m   e = 625 mm
2.50 m   e = 833 mm

4   Residence in Munich, 2014, zillerplus Architects and Town Planners: Increasing the density of the inner city with a building in timber construction. Following prefabrication at the factory, erection on site was completed within 5 weeks.

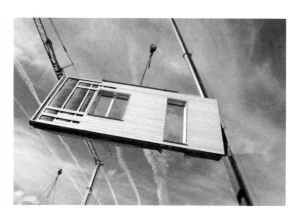

5 Schematic section of timber
frame construction
Scale 1:20

Wall construction
Vertical siding, 25/60 mm
Battens/counter-battens
24/28 mm
Breather paper
Insulation, 145 mm
Vapour check/barrier, 12 mm
Battens/counter-battens
24/28 mm
Wood lining, 18 mm

6 Construction options
a Non-vapour permeable, with
back-ventilated facade (classic)
b Vapour permeable timber frame
construction with back-ventilated
facade

7 Overlap of vapour check with
adhesive tape
a One-sided
b Double-sided

8 Airtight detailing at cladding
joints
a Adhesive tape
b Skim coat

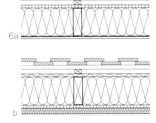

6a

b

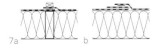

7a   b

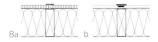

8a   b

In multi-storey buildings, the installation can be carried
out using various construction principles, which differ in
the jointing of the building components. In platform framing, the intermediate deck rests directly on the frame of
the wall and the next wall above is placed on to the edge
of the deck. In terms of building physics, this results in a
weak point at the level of the intermediate deck. A positive aspect is the fact that the elements are storey-high,
which facilitates transport via heavy goods vehicles.
In balloon framing, the vertical timber sections of the
external wall are continuous from the floor to the roof,
thus creating an insulation layer free from thermal
bridges, as well as an air-tight envelope. In this construction the intermediate deck rests on beams/bearers that
are attached to – or joined with – the vertical members
of the external wall. When mounting prefabricated elements, care should be taken that the joins are structurally effective and that the elements are anchored as they
are put up, so that the period of instability is minimised.
Timber components must be protected from moisture.
To protect the elements from driving rain, back-ventilated
cladding of low weight is installed on the external face of
the boarding and the thermal insulation behind that is
protected by a barrier material (also called breather paper) consisting of thin diffusive sheet or vapour-permeable medium-dense wood fibreboard. ↘ 6 In order to prevent the damaging formation of condensate within the
assembly, diffusive (back-ventilated) wall constructions
must be sealed airtight on the interior face. The lining material forms the convection barrier; where elements and/
or building components join, they have to be sealed airtight with tape; alternatively, connecting joints can be
sealed with pre-compressed sealing tape. Adhesive tape
must be attached with pressure to produce a permanent
mechanical seal. ↘ 7, 8
If diffusion to the outside is restricted (e.g. sandwich insulation systems) vapour checks must be applied to the
inner face. The vapour check of timber frame components can be protected from damage by a lining of gypsum or wood-based board. This creates a gap in front of
the vapour check, which can be used as an installation
zone and is usually filled with porous insulation (generally
mineral wool). Alternatively, the insulation can be wood
wool slabs with a factory-applied one-sided coating of
cement mortar (one-sided non-porous finish) or wood
wool slabs that are fitted with dowels and rendered on
site. The mineral layer (cement-based render, plasterboard) has poor thermal insulation, but it combines with
the thermally efficient wood wool slab to form an effective system. Element facades in timber can be clad externally with various materials. If consistency is desired,
the structural timber elements can be clad with a wood-
based material. ↘ p. 96

5

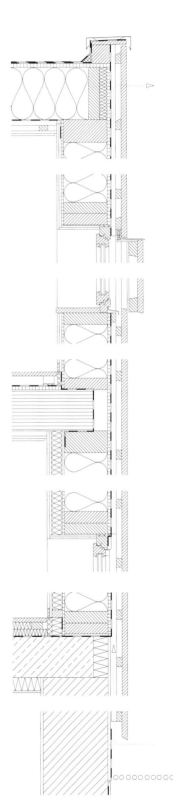

SANDWICH SYSTEMS

When industrialisation began to make an impact on the construction industry at the beginning of the twentieth century, modular sandwich construction elements started to become commercially viable when produced in high numbers. These systems are in common use today in industrial as well as residential buildings. Since industrial construction methods tend to lead to aesthetically monotonous results, serially produced elements are increasingly being covered by individually designed finishes ⟶ 1. The basic composition of insulating sandwich panels includes two layers – a structural layer on the inside and a thin external cladding layer consisting of various rain-proof and frost-proof covering materials – as well as an internal core of thermal insulation. Owing to the rigid bonding between the layers (either with adhesive or a building foam), the sandwich panel is considered to be a single-skin construction element. Metal sandwich panels achieve their structural strength as a result of this compound construction. Production is carried out using a continuous automated conveyor system (in the case of large numbers) or in piecework in smaller workshops.

1

Sandwich panels are defined according to the main materials used. On the one hand there are panels with a weight of 10 to 20 kg/m² with a thin plastic/metal covering layer and a thick core consisting of e.g. extruded foam, and on the other there are panels with a weight of 150 to 300 kg/m² or > 300 kg/m² in which the structural part consists of reinforced concrete, which is insulated with a thermal insulation layer and protected by a cladding layer.
The stiffness of the system makes it possible to use the panels without framing. The shear-resistant bonding enables them to transfer wind forces and self-weight, and limits the deformation of the cladding skin, which would cause stresses in both layers. This means that the bonding must be flexible enough to ensure that the covering skin only suffers cracks – if any – in the micron range, otherwise driving rain can penetrate and the panels will not be frost-proof. Although metal skins are impermeable to vapour and are waterproof inside and out, water vapour can nevertheless penetrate via the thicker inner concrete layer and it must be possible for this to be discharged to the outside. For this reason, the thermal insulation must be resistant to damage from moisture. The junctions between the elements themselves are sealed with double joint sealers in all systems. An air-tight inner tape limits the ingress of water vapour and humid air, and an outer drainage chamber with appropriate joint geometry, or an air-tight diffusive outer seal, ensures that any water can drain off and that the joint is continually vented. Sandwich elements are usually storey-high and are placed into the openings of the primary structure. This means that both the insulation and the covering skin can be contin-

uous in front of the primary system and thermal bridges can be avoided. The geometry of the projecting covering skin determines the position of the element joints. The elements' own weight is transferred via the structural layer while horizontal forces are transferred via more substantial connections than usual or via anchoring to the intermediate floors of the building. The functionality of the system depends on the careful detailing of the joints – both inside and out. Elements into which moisture has penetrated must be replaced.

CONCRETE SANDWICH ELEMENTS

As a rule, concrete sandwich elements consist of standard reinforced concrete. In order to minimise the work of installation, elements are usually storey-high and approx. 5 to 6 m long. From the point of view of cost-effectiveness, one should consider that small elements mean more joints and are therefore more costly to produce, whereas large elements require a stronger primary structure. Since the inner layer consists of concrete approx. 15 to 20 cm thick, it can provide good fire protection (fire resistance of 90 minutes); in addition, the substantial thermal mass of the material helps to reduce overheating in summer. The covering layer stores part of the ambient heat and thereby reduces the amount of thermal radiation reaching the interior. The stresses and deformations resulting from changes in temperature must be absorbed in the joints between the elements. In the exterior layer, the reinforcement should be covered by concrete of a depth that is sufficient with regard to the texture of the surface and the harshness of the environment.

1 Olympic Village, Munich, 1972, 2010 Werner Wirsing, bogevischs buero: Instead of refurbishment, it was decided to rebuild the student housing (1,052 terraced houses in miniature format) in the former Olympic Village in sandwich construction. The original project had been built from prefabricated concrete units.

2 With concrete sandwich elements, the loadbearing layer must be at least twice as thick as the 7–10 cm thick covering layer in order to be able to absorb the quantity of water vapour that penetrates through diffusion and to allow the element to dry out sufficiently. The connection between the layers relies on (stainless) steel thrust anchors; the insulation must be pressure and moisture resistant, the usual choice is expanded polystyrene.

2

3 Cloth factory, Berlin, 2014, nps tchoban voss: The building envelope was to be refurbished, but the existing structural fabric could only support minor additional loads. By using lightweight, extremely smooth aluminium sandwich elements with high structural strength, the weight of the new facade was kept to a minimum. The design of the facade pays homage to cloth as a material, as the panelling has been printed with a pattern that runs around the building like thread on a weaving loom.

4 The layers of metal sandwich elements (metal panels) are bonded to create a shear-resistant connection. The polyurethane foam that is applied as thermal insulation also bonds directly with the metal. Any mineral wool insulation needed for fire resistance is attached with adhesive. The rigidity of the system is limited by the strength of the insulation.

5 Schematic section through metal panel
a Horizontal
b Vertical

6 Schematic section through concrete sandwich element
a Horizontal
b Vertical

aa Loadbearing layer
bb Thermal insulation
cc Joint
dd Grouting
ee Sealing tape, sealing profile

3

4

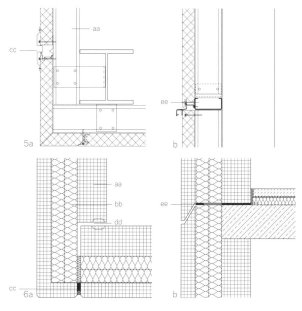

METAL PANELS

Metal sandwich elements are lighter in weight and are used for large spans in order to save material and reduce load. Metal panels are usually produced from strip galvanised steel sheeting with a coloured coating; occasionally also from aluminium or stainless steel.

The elements are 60 to 100 cm wide and up to approx. 14 m long, which determines the number of joints. In order to improve the stiffness of the panels, it is possible to use metal sheeting with profiling in the longitudinal direction.

Metal panels are attached to the loadbearing structure using metal brackets that are part of the system. The fixing distance depends on the prevailing wind forces and the resistance moment of the panels. In order to prevent damage to the thin fixing sheets or panel sheets when exposed to the suction force of wind, the size of the elements or the spacing of fixings is adjusted appropriately. Any projecting building component such as parapet panels requires a bracing substructure. To protect the elements from the ingress of moisture, the two meeting edges along the longitudinal joint are profiled, while the lateral joint is butted. Similar to internal and external corners, lateral joints should be covered with profiled metal sheet sections, for example; they are also prone to deformation and require a stiff substructure.

Windows and other infill components are attached to the substructure and not to the panels, so they have to be connected with sufficient tolerance while ensuring airtightness and providing protection against driving rain. When selecting the covering layer and insulation material, as well as the type of bonding and connection joint, the required fire resistance class must be taken into account. A special feature of metal panels is plastic deformation of the metal, which creates a camber for greater stiffness, for example in the case of different internal and external temperatures, owing to the greater longitudinal expansion on the warm side. This effect can be detected in glancing light. The deformation must be taken into account when designing the connection details. Owing to their rapid installation, relatively low weight and standardised fixing details, metal sandwich facades are a cost-effective solution, especially when the elements can be attached directly to the primary system. The placing of joints and windows – in particular, the detail of the lateral joints – has an effect on the design and the structural system, and must be carefully considered.

SUSPENDED FACADE – FACE BRICKWORK

In their appearance, outside layers consisting of face brickwork are similar to solid brickwork. Traditional double-skin construction – which has the purpose of combining the different qualities of masonry, i.e. water-resistant clinker bricks as weather protection and masonry units as a loadbearing layer – has been developed further to meet increased requirements regarding thermal insulation and weather protection, and is widely used in regions where brick construction is a traditional feature. As with face brickwork, special requirements apply to the design of the exterior surface and the joint pattern. Nevertheless, face brickwork too opens up a wide range of design options. The space between the outer and inner layers can be used to integrate sliding elements, window frames, and light fittings. The material of the facade can consist of masonry units with different colours, which can be arranged to form patterns similar to marquetry work. Likewise, it is possible to create differences in depth to provide a more pronounced texture to a facade. Face brickwork is part of a two-skin system in which the other skin consists of masonry or reinforced concrete. This inner skin provides an impervious closure and transfers the vertical and horizontal loads. The outer skin (face brickwork) determines the visual appearance and provides protection against the weather. In order to ensure adequate back ventilation, the minimum distance between the two skins must be 40 mm, while the maximum distance must not exceed 200 mm. A basic distinction is made between: double-skin external walls with an air gap; double-skin external walls with an air gap and thermal insulation; double-skin external walls with core insulation, and double-skin external walls with a coating of render as a barrier layer (detail for exceptional cases). → 2

MATERIAL

Brick is the summary term for single masonry units consisting of clay, sand and lime, or a concrete material that are hardened by a firing or air-drying process.

Bricks for brick cladding are used as protection against the weather and therefore have to meet certain requirements which are specified in DIN EN 771-1 and DIN V 105-100, one of them being frost resistance. The standards include the following definitions:

- Face bricks are high-density (HD) bricks produced industrially in various textures and colours, either as solid bricks or with perforations.
- Hand-formed bricks are produced without perforations and feature an heterogeneous surface.
- Clinker bricks are HD bricks fired at high temperatures so that the surface sinters: melting the material and forming a vitreous, glazed finish.
- Ceramic clinker bricks are HD bricks formed from high-quality clay that, in the firing process, sinters into a high-density material.

Special bricks are manufactured in various shapes to produce specific design effects for facades or other building components.

The colour and surface texture of face bricks can be affected by the chemical reaction of the components contained in the raw material and by changes of temperature during the firing process. An important factor that affects the colour of the material is the amount of oxygen input during the firing process, with more oxygen resulting in reddish shades and less oxygen in blue/black hues. In addition to the differences resulting from industrial or manual production, the texture can be varied further by mechanical processing or patterns in the moulds.

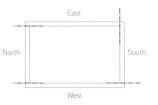

1

1 Vertical expansion joints should be arranged at the corners of the building and – in the case of a standing cladding layer – at different levels, as well as at lintels and underneath windows. In the case of large, continuous masonry surfaces, expansion joints should be provided every 8 to 12 m, depending on the type of masonry unit.

2 Double-skin systems:
a Double-skin external wall with air gap
b Double-skin external wall with air gap and thermal insulation
c Double-skin external wall with core insulation
d Double-skin external wall with layer of render

aa Depth of anchor penetration ≥ 50 mm
bb Face brickwork
cc Wire wall ties with drip disc
dd Air gap ≥ 40 mm
ee Loadbearing wall
ff Internal plaster
gg Core insulation, max. 150 mm gap
hh Plaster layer
ii Narrow gap (10 to 20 mm)

Owing to the joints in the brickwork, face brick layers are not waterproof. This means that water draining details must be provided behind the face brick. In any case, the insulation used should be permanently hydrophobic.

3 Sealing at the base to DIN 1053-1

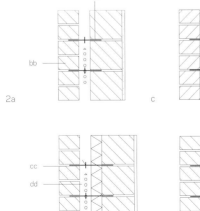

2a

b

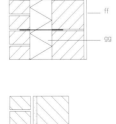

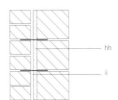

c

d

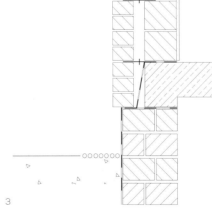

3

4

5

Owing to the thermal expansion of the material, it is important to include expansion joints in the construction. As a rule of thumb, expansion joints with a width of 10 to 15 mm have to be provided in brick facades at about 12 m spacing, and have to be closed with a suitable permanently elastic sealing material. The arrangement of joints should be considered at the design stage, as they can be used to underscore the functions of the building or, conversely, be placed such that they are not very conspicuous. Openings that are arranged in strict vertical alignment make it easier to accommodate expansion joints, while meandering joints in random bond brickwork are less conspicuous. ➘ 1

CONSTRUCTION
In order to transfer the weight of the exterior skin to the loadbearing wall, it is necessary to provide brackets or support ledges, which must support the full width of the brick. Common details involve projections at intermediate floor level, or corrosion-resistant steel sections that are either dowelled to the concrete, or cast in it. Projecting continuous horizontal concrete bearings can result in a visually interesting facade structure. In order to achieve the necessary thermal insulation performance, such bearings require careful and usually complex detailing. ➘ 4, 5

The vertical distance between such bearings is about 12 m for skins with a brick width of up to 11.5 cm. Owing to its structural strength, exterior brick cladding of this thickness has become established in practice. Brick cladding of a lesser thickness (approved thickness is ⩾ 9 cm) may only installed up to a height of 20 m above ground and must be supported at 6-metre intervals. The cladding skin is connected to the loadbearing inner skin using non-rusting Z- or L-shaped wire ties to prevent any buckling or tilting. This form of anchoring is also used to transfer wind loads, whereby the anchors must be capable of withstanding both positive and negative pressure in the form of compressive and tensile forces respectively. These ties should be spaced at max. 50 cm vertically and max. 75 cm horizontally. Additional fixing points must be provided at all edges, building corners, openings and along expansion joints, as well as at the top end of the exterior cladding skin (DIN 1053-1). The construction details must be formed in a way that allows moisture to be discharged (drip edges etc.).
The inner skin and intermediate floors must be sealed against moisture at the base of the gap between the two skins. Any moisture penetrating the brick cladding will thereby be conducted to the outside, away from the building. For this reason, the sealing component in the gap must be installed with a fall towards the outside. ➘ 3

4   Steel brackets support the weight of the face brickwork and transmit it to the loadbearing structure via dowels or anchor rails cast into the concrete. The bearing plate and design of the anchor bracket can vary, depending on the load to be supported.

5   Anchors through the air gap secure the face brickwork against buckling and transmit any horizontal wind forces to the loadbearing structure.

6   Munich Technical University, 2012, Hild & K: The main building of the Munich Technical University was built using a reinforced concrete skeleton system in 1959. The refurbishment required a redesign of the facade, the construction of which was completed with clinker face brick.
The vertical pillars are shaped in undulations which are vertically offset. This sculptural design is intended to express the non-loadbearing function of the wall. In view of the fact that some of these undulations project up to 700 mm from the facade surface, special support brackets and anchors with a greater diameter and with lengths of between 450 and 820 mm had to be used (standard anchors are only approved for distances of up to 200 mm).

6

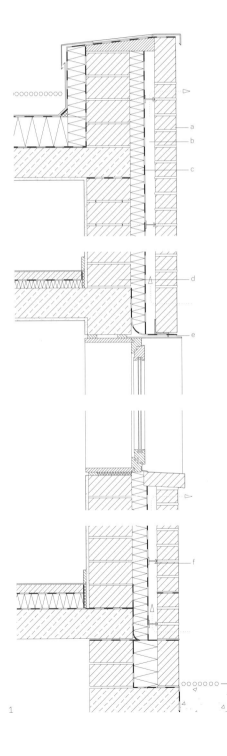

Above openings in the external brickwork – such as windows or doors – the wall is supported with anchor brackets or steel bearing sections. With the help of modern bearing systems, openings in brick-clad walls are easy to produce. For this reason it is also technically possible to build walls with large horizontal openings, or even fenestration bands, in contrast to traditional brickwork, in which the format of the openings is vertical, with the load from above supported by full or segmental arches. The means of supporting the load, such as lintels, can be used as a design element. In constructions with an air gap, ventilation openings must be inserted at the base and top of the cavity as well as at any intermediate bearings, in the form of open perpendicular joints. In a two-storey building with brick cladding using 52 mm thick bricks, the vents provided at the face, top and lower edges of any bearing structures should be placed at approximately every other perpendicular joint of the external skin.

1 Schematic section through face brickwork, scale 1:20
a Face brickwork, 115 mm
b Air gap, 40 mm
c Thermal insulation, 140 mm
d Loadbearing masonry, 240 mm
e Steel section lintel
f Wire wall tie

2 Extension to the Melanchthonhaus, Wittenberg, 2013, Dietzsch & Weber Architects: The front of the three-storey extension is aligned with the existing neighbouring buildings with the windows arranged at the same height as those in the Melanchthonhaus and adjoining gate building. The facade of the extension consists of stock clinker brickwork with a rough, matt surface in various shades of grey; these were was assembled on site to create the composition. The sculptural effect of the building is emphasised by recesses for the openings; the elevation appears as one monolithic element without the traditional zoning of plinth, main facade and roof.

3 Ravensburg Museum of Fine Art, 2013, Lederer Ragnarsdóttir Oei: At first sight, the new building appears familiar on account of its dialogue with its urban environment and the material qualities of the brick masonry. The outer skin consists of recycled bricks. The roof has been constructed of prefabricated brick vaults, which span the interior space without intermediate support.
The bricks were recovered from the demolition of a Belgian monastery and, having been recycled, underscore the importance of sustainability in building construction.

SUSPENDED FACADE – BRICK PANELS

4 Schematic section through brick panel facade, scale 1:20
a Brick panel, 30 mm
b Panel holder
c Aluminium support section, horizontal
d Aluminium support section, vertical
e Fixed/sliding point
f Thermal insulation
g Wall construction

5 Corner details of suspended brick elements
a with metal profiles
b mitre cut

6 New office building, Gooiland, 2011, Koen van Velsen: The new building responds to its rural context through its traditional outline form. A geometric structure with a lightweight feel is created with the help of earth-coloured brick facade panels that are produced from earthenware to match the roof. The use of panels with either two or three dummy joints generates a playful surface.

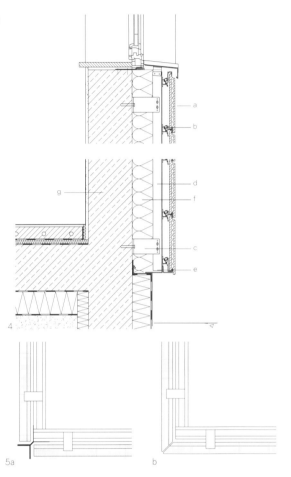

It was not possible to manufacture of brick panel facades until modern firing and production techniques had been developed. Fired and relatively large cavity panels made of clay-type material have been used for facades since the 1980s. Common formats of panels are 150 to 300 mm in width and 300 to 500 mm in length, with a thickness of approx. 30 mm. With advances in production technology, it is now possible to produce elements with a length of up to 3000 mm. In order to optimise the substructure, the panels are usually installed horizontally, although there are also vertical systems on the market. Brick cladding panels in standard formats are a cost-efficient alternative to face brick or natural stone facades. Since this modular prefabricated material has good durability characteristics, it would appear to be suitable for facades with large surface areas, both in new construction and refurbishment work.

CONSTRUCTION

The facade system basically comprises four components: brick panels, panel holders, a horizontal support section and vertical joint profiles. The basic vertical section consists of a standard section. The brick panels are designed such that the upper panel has a nosing that overlaps the one below. The panel holders feature a clip system that allows the panels to be installed on the bearing section without using tools. Brick panels are offered in similar colours to those of roof tiles, ranging from red through to yellow and grey shades. In addition, it is possible to texture the surfaces (brushed or grooved). For larger areas, it is commercially viable to produce special solutions with respect to format and surface finish. Normally, the facades are subdivided in accordance with the selected module sizes. For this reason, the dimensions of the construction, i.e. column grids, storey heights and the dimensions of openings, should be harmonised with the size of the panels at the design stage.

In the case of refurbishments, it may be opportune to vary the width of panels to compensate for different heights. In order to accommodate different lengths of panel, it is possible to cut the panels or produce them in special sizes. The corners of buildings are mastered by fixing a steel section along them, or using specially shaped panels to form a mitred corner. → 5

Similarly, the details of junctions at openings, such as reveals and windowsills, can be resolved using metal components or specially shaped brick components. Another interesting option for the design of facades is offered by special components made of the same raw material as the brick panels, such as louvres and solar screening systems.

SUSPENDED FACADE – NATURAL STONE

Owing to its durability, natural stone is an obvious choice as a facade material, particularly for prestigious buildings. The characteristic pattern of the stone used and its surface finish determine the appearance of the facade. In addition, thanks to its low primary energy content, its long service life and its good recyclability, natural stone is an environmentally friendly building material.

MATERIAL
Natural stone is grouped by its provenance:
– Igneous rock (plutonic and volcanic rock)
– Sedimentary rock
– Metamorphic rock

The igneous rock types, such as granite and basalt, are significantly harder than sedimentary rock (sandstone and limestone). Between these two in terms of hardness are the metamorphic rocks, such as gneiss, crystalline marble and slate. Facade stone is selected for its appearance (colour and texture) and for its respective material properties, such as compressive strength, water absorption, breakout resistance, weight and thermal expansion. Differences in the rock's colour and structure, as well as inclusions, are the result of geological processes.

For this reason, and in order to take variations in texture and colour into account – as well as patination – it is important to inspect larger samples of the material when making any selection. Depending on the hardness and condition, natural stone surfaces are finished in a number of ways, including sawing, embossing, dressing, bush-hammering, charring, smoothing, grinding and polishing, as well as leaving the surface unworked after quarrying. ⌐2 These means of processing, which were originally wholly manual, can now almost all be carried out with machine tools. If the material is used in a uniform way at parapets, reveals, cill panels and in the plinth area, it creates an overall monolithic impression, which can be reinforced by positioning the material in one plane with

closed joints. Open joints and mouldings or offsets in the stone have the opposite effect and can provide a facade with rhythmic subdivisions or give it an animated surface texture.

When designing such a facade, the maximum size of the panels must be taken into account, which depends on the type of stone and is limited by the size of blocks available. As a rule, large-format panels (upwards of approx. 1.5 m) are significantly more expensive than small ones. In addition to the higher price of the material, fitting the panels on site is more costly because large panels cannot be installed manually owing to the greater weight. The proportions of the panels are also important. For example, if panels are cut in a format in which the ratio of width to height is narrower than 1:4, there is an increased risk of breakage during transport and installation on site. In addition, the design of a facade needs to coordinate the size and arrangement of the panels with the dimensions of the openings in the facade. This involves design decisions such as whether to opt for horizontal or vertical formats, which can echo or even emphasise the shape of the building and its openings. Furthermore, details for the connection to other building components and for the building corners have to be developed. It is also possible to accentuate certain parts of the facade, such as the plinth or the window reveals, by using a different material thickness, or a special profiling or surface texture. If the fixing points are to be provided as part of the shell construction, the facade plan needs to be produced in parallel with the detailed design of the shell construction. A common method is to produce panel position drawings as elevations for all facades, including the planned anchor points. Furthermore, it is important to determine the anchoring points for any scaffolding, because the anchor bushes remain in the facade so that new scaffolding can be erected without causing any damage to the structure.

1 House M, Grünwald, 2009, Titus Bernhard Architects: The back-ventilated suspended facade uses gneiss that has been sawn and broken across the strata; it has been installed with contact joints, with the rough surface facing outwards. The visible concrete floor slab has been prestressed to create a camber in order to bear the loads resulting from the cantilever.

2 Surface treatments
a Rough hewn
b Brushed
c Picked
d Tooled
e Sandblasted
f Unworked

3 Carrara marble quarry

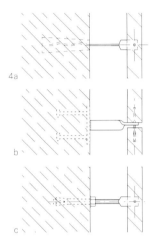

4a

b

c

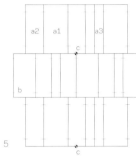

a2 a1 a3

c

b

c

5

4 Anchors for natural stone
a   undercut anchor
b   anchor welding plate cast in
concrete
c   dowel retaining anchor

5   Example of a facade layout plan
a   Panel, number and position
b   Anchor position with dimension
details for placing the anchor pins
c   Indication of scaffolding anchoring points

6   Schematic section through wall
with natural stone cladding, scale
1:20

a   Wall construction
Natural stone, 40 mm
Air gap, 40 mm
Insulation, 160 mm
with hydrophobic treatment
Reinforced concrete wall, 240 mm
Internal plaster, 15 mm
b   Dowel retaining anchor
c   Roof upstand clad with natural
stone, with a bonded drip
d   Special loadbearing brackets

CONSTRUCTION

Most modern natural stone facades are installed as suspended cladding panels. In exceptional cases they can
be built from the ground up instead, provided the material is thick enough. → p. 84 The structural components
supporting suspended cladding usually consist of concrete, steel, or masonry. In order to connect the stone
facade to the loadbearing structure, it is necessary to
use an anchoring system or an appropriate substructure.
This may consist of stainless steel, aluminium, or corro-
sion-protected steel. Depending on the format, the stone
panels can be supported either in the horizontal joints or
in the vertical. The ideal spacing of the anchors on each
side is at 1/5 of the panel length from each end. Both
open and closed joints are possible. When the joints are
closed, the forces from negative wind pressure at the
building corners and roof junctions are likely to be higher.
This must be taken into account when calculating the anchor points necessary to resist wind suction factors. The
structural stability of natural stone facades has to be calculated and documented in all cases. Anchors are available in the form of dowelled, welded, or mortar-embedded systems and should preferably be made of stainless
steel. The selection depends on the type of substrate. In
new buildings, it is possible to insert anchor bushings (or
plates for attaching the anchors by welding) into the shell
construction. The anchors have cylindrical bolts, which
are drilled into the edges of the natural stone. For this
reason, panels that are to be fitted using anchors should
be at least 40 mm thick. This thickness of 40 mm is also
required in order to ensure that the material is frost-proof.
In existing buildings it is imperative to examine and test
the substrate in which the anchors are to be fixed. Should
the substrate be relatively soft, holes of a greater diameter should be bored in order to distribute the pressure
of the mortar-embedded anchors over a sufficiently large
area. Where the substrate is not capable of supporting
the imposed loads – or where areas of insufficient loadbearing capacity have to be bridged – substructure rails
can be used. These rails are also used around large openings. Special anchors are used to fix the panels at lintels
and reveals. Shell constructions with thin walls (<15 cm
thickness) are deemed to be special constructions and
result in higher costs because the usual anchoring depth
cannot be achieved. An important criterion when selecting natural stone is its resistance to water absorption
and its associated frost resistance. Only frost-resistant
stone is suitable for facades; this material can also be
used on nearly horizontal surfaces such as window sills
and the coping on parapet walls. This fact has a major impact on the design and the desired appearance of the
building, since it means that it is not necessary to use different materials in the facade.

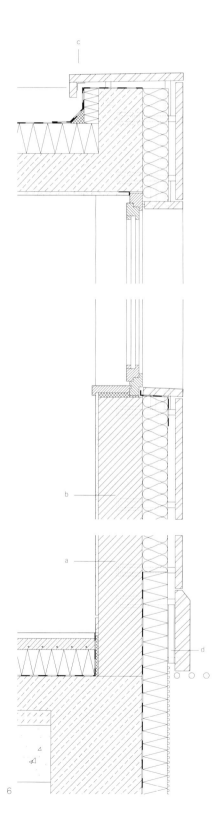

6

SUSPENDED FACADE – METAL

Metal facades come in a variety of designs and can provide a striking building envelope and an economic solution for a suspended facade with a long service life. Metal can easily be shaped, even into complex geometrical patterns, and provides long-lasting weather protection. To form the building envelope, only relatively thin material is required for the cladding elements in a back-ventilated facade. The back-ventilation is necessary to allow rainwater – which may penetrate through open joints and structures – to drain off or evaporate, and for the dissipation of any heat which may be generated owing to solar irradiation on the material. Porous insulation material is protected by a diffusive breather paper. A strong primary structure is required, one that is capable of carrying the considerable weight and is able to resist any deformation of the substructure due to thermal expansion and the resulting stresses.

MATERIALS AND TYPES OF CLADDING

Different types of alloy and pure metal can be used for metal facades, the choice depending on the type and format of the cladding, as well as the required strength and resistance to corrosion. Depending on the composition and design aesthetic, one can choose between claddings made of steel, aluminium, copper, zinc, or bronze, which produce a different effect in terms of colour, reflection and weathering.

STEEL, STAINLESS STEEL, CORTEN STEEL

Owing to its high density (7.8 g/cm³), its high modulus of elasticity and low thermal expansion, construction steel – which consists of white pig iron and alloy components – is well suited for use as a facade cladding material in the form of thin metal sheeting (0.35 to 3 mm thick), bands and panels. In order to protect the steel against corrosion and contact corrosion, it is possible to apply a metal coating – hot-galvanising or alloy galvanising – and, in addition, a plastic coating as protection against atmospheric and chemical influences. Stainless steel (a non-rusting, high-alloy steel) can be used without any additional coating. The colour of the material can be influenced by adding chemical solutions, while the texture can be modified using processes such as grinding, etching, enamelling and sandblasting. ⟶ p. 90

A facade material with a special look is Corten steel, the colour of which ranges between red and brown-black. Corten steel – the name of which is derived from 'corrosion-resistant' and 'tensile strength' – is a weatherproof construction steel. Owing to the addition of iron sulphate and phosphorous oxide with alloy additives, the material forms an impervious layer on the surface that resembles natural rust. Depending on environmental conditions and

the weather, this process can last between one and three years and then stops. In contrast to un-alloyed steel, Corten steel has greater resistance to corrosion but is more sensitive to the effect of pollutants in the air and to climatic conditions. The material comes in thicknesses of between 1.0 and 12.5 mm for panels or cassettes. When planning the thickness of the building components, it is important to take into account that the rusting process will reduce the thickness of the material. Another important factor is that of contact with other metals, for example in the substructure or fastening elements. In order to prevent contact corrosion, these should consist of stainless steel or powder-coated aluminium; otherwise they must be separated by must be separated by other means. ⟶ 2

ALUMINIUM

The raw material from which aluminium is produced is bauxite. Its good corrosion-resistance and the ease with which it can be shaped in different thicknesses, from metal sheeting to foils (0.02 mm thickness), make aluminium a popular material for many applications. In construction, aluminium is often alloyed with manganese, magnesium, silicium and zinc, so that high strength can be achieved in spite of its low density (2.7 g/cm³). The alloying of panels and bands is done in a hot- and cold-forming process or by finished casting. By anodising or applying an organic coating using foils and paint finishes, the natural oxide layer is strengthened. In view of the fact that the thermal expansion of aluminium is greater than that of steel, care should be taken to design a construction that is free of displacement constraint when using aluminium profiles.

COPPER AND ZINC

Owing to their good weathering properties and workability, copper (in an oxygen-free form, deoxidised by the addition of phosphorous) and titanium zinc (zinc alloy with added titanium and copper) are popular materials for facade design. While titanium zinc retains its shiny grey surface over time, the surface of copper changes from a shiny reddish hue and develops a patina with a dull green/anthracite colour shade due to the influence of the atmosphere. These materials are available in many forms – sheets, strips (pre-profiled roofing sheets), interlocking panels, cassette panels, shingles and sometimes perforated sheets – which permit a great variety of designs and geometrical arrangements.

DESIGN AND CONSTRUCTION

The external effect (form and joint pattern) is affected by the different types of construction available, some of which come as complete systems with the necessary

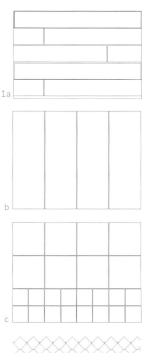
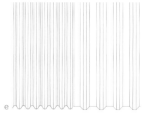
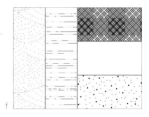

1   Profiles
a   Sheets/strips
b   Interlocking panels
c   Cassette panels
d   Shingles
e   Corrugated/trapezoid profile
f   Perforated metal sheeting/ metal fabric

2 In some cases, the substructure of a metal facade consists of timber battens, but the application of a support grid consisting of L- or T-shaped aluminium profiles 3–6 m in length is more common. The profiles are point-fixed with galvanised steel, aluminium, or stainless steel angles, which partly penetrate the thermal insulation and compensate for tolerances. Stainless steel is the preferred material, as it is corrosion-resistant and has comparatively low thermal conductivity. The angles allow lateral adjustment of the panels, and are fitted to the panel with one fixed point and several sliding points as required (depending on the weight of the facade and the wind load).

substructure. All types use rolled metal sheeting as base material (plate > 3 mm thickness, sheet < 3 mm thickness). A wide range of shapes and surfaces can be produced using various forming processes. One main purpose of these processes is to increase the sheeting's rigidity and thus the stability of the facade.

SHEETS / STRIPS

Sheets or strips have a maximum thickness of 3 mm and can be up to 2.5 m wide and 12 m long. They are usually produced by cold-rolling metal plate and are then rolled into coils, which are the base product for further processing. Prefabricated sheets (with edge profiling) made of stainless steel, enamelled or plastic-coated steel, copper, or aluminium fit together along the long side with a push-fit detail and are attached to supporting elements that are part of the system. Where these sheets are fitted vertically, additional screw fixing is applied. This system results in a facade with pronounced lines created by the longitudinal joints.

INTERLOCKING PANELS

Interlocking facade panels made of steel are between 4 and 20 mm thick depending on the size, which may be up to 2.2 × 3 m. On the back, the panels have welded L- or U-profiles, which are used to attach them to rigid holding pins. The panels are secured against negative wind load by their substantial own weight. Small elements are attached with visible screw fixings. The joints are open.

CASSETTE PANELS

Cassette panels are produced by single or multiple folding of the edges of metal sheeting to create rigid cassettes with a depth of approx. 4 cm. The elements are joined with a push-fit system or bolts. The substructure is a grid of rail sections made specifically for the system; the elements hook into it and are fixed with clamps or screws. Any secondary condensate must be drained off through holes. Depending on the width of the joint, cassette panels give the facade a flat or grid-shaped appearance. The thickness of the metal sheeting must be adequate (1.5 to 3 mm) to ensure that the surface does not buckle when the edges are folded, during installation, or from daily wear and tear.

FOLDED SHEETS

Metal sheets of up to 1.2 m in width are connected via seams. The sheets are folded on site to form the seams; they must not be too thick for this and they require a flat substrate as substructure. A typical construction detail is to install folded sheet facades on rough-sawn timber with an intermediate layer consisting of a draining foil and draining fleece. The fleece ensures that any water that

has penetrated and any condensate on the inside of the metal sheeting is discharged. The rough-sawn timber is capable of temporarily absorbing large quantities of vapour and condensate, but it needs back-ventilation so that it can dry out again. The rough-sawn timber substrate is mounted on wooden battens. The appearance of folded sheet metal facades is determined by the spacing of the longitudinal seams (resulting from the width of the sheet) and the cross seams.

SHINGLES

These are square or rhomboid sheet metal elements, which have a single fold along the upper and lower edges, to the front and back respectively. These help the elements to fit snugly together at the joint. Shingles are fastened by nailing, screwing, riveting, or with clips on a flat substrate that may consist of timber boarding or profiled metal sheeting. They create a small-format, regular pattern, suitable for cladding curved or free-form facades.

CORRUGATED / TRAPEZOIDAL PROFILE

Corrugated and trapezoidal metal sheets can be produced by cold rolling into a wide range of profile shapes and amplitudes; the profiling provides better longitudinal rigidity. Deep drawing forms metal sheets with greater amplitudes both upwards and downwards, further increasing their stiffness. Metal sheets formed in this way require a substructure designed for the respective application.

The appearance of profiled metal sheet facades can vary from a linear impression to an almost homogeneous texture. The determining factors are the shape and depth of the profile. When the cladding profiles run horizontally, it is important to bear in mind the likely soiling of the facade due to the accumulation of dust and rainwater. The sheets can be bent either along the longitudinal or the lateral axes. Common materials used are aluminium, powder-coated galvanised steel and stainless steel.

PERFORATED METAL SHEETING / METAL FABRIC

Perforated metal sheeting is made by punching holes – in a variety of patterns. This reduces its rigidity, so perforated sheeting subject to mechanical loads has either to be folded (profiles, cassette panels) or put in a frame. Expanded metal mesh is produced by making offset cuts in metal sheeting and then stretching it. It comes in many forms. Its strength is increased by using frames or by pretensioning. Metal fabric (mesh) is produced in an industrial weaving process using high-grade bar and wire. Perforated metal sheet is often used to create a uniform facade in front of opaque and transparent areas, also providing solar screening. The materials used are aluminium, stainless steel, coated steel, Corten steel and copper.

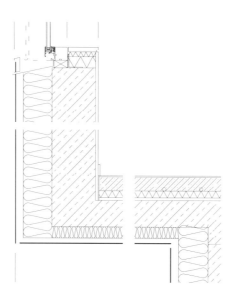

1   New headquarters building, Bad Laasphe , 2010, msah : m. schneider a. hillebrandt Architects: The client company works primarily with metal materials, which is why weatherproof, naturally aging construction steel was chosen for the facade. The fixing of the facade panels (4 mm thick) is concealed, suspended from the steel substructure; the depth of the construction allows the invisible integration of the roof connection detail, the installation of the water drainage system and solar screening in the construction plane.

2   New building for the De Young Museum, San Francisco, 2005, Herzog & de Meuron: For the facade, 7,200 copper cassettes were perforated and embossed with individual patterns as an analogy to the Golden Gate Park, where the museum is located. The material changes over time and gives the building its patina.

3   Extension to the Lenbachhaus, Munich, 2013, Foster & Partners: The gold-coloured facade of the new building is a contrasting element, and yet links it to the sand-coloured existing building which is listed as an historic monument. Tubes consisting of a copper-aluminium alloy, with a diameter of 10 cm and a height of approximately 4 m, have been installed in front of the two upper storeys. The round tubes are backed by yellow metal sheeting with concave profiling.

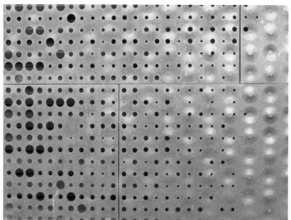

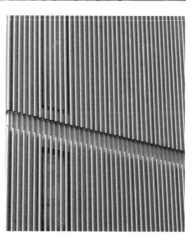

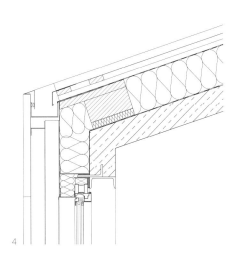

4   Upgrade of Bochum pump house, 2012, Heinrich Böll Architect: An almost archetypal example of a house with a double pitch roof was created by using a thin metal skin as cladding for a brick building typical of the mining industry in the Ruhr area. The external facade plane consists of anthracite-coloured trapezoidal metal sheeting, which covers both the walls and the roof areas. The metal is perforated in front of the windows, only a few of which can be opened. In keeping with the homogeneous style, the roof drainage is also concealed in order to avoid any visible elements on the facade surface.

5   New building for the Riverside Museum, Glasgow, 2011, Zaha Hadid: The intention was to emphasise the soft flowing forms of the architecture with the uniform material and appearance of the building envelope. For this reason, both facade and roof cladding were identically detailed. The substructure consists of trapezoidal steel sheets with a bitumen waterproofing membrane, mineral wool, wood-based panels and a roofing membrane attached to the steel structure. The cladding consists of titanium zinc with a thickness of 0.8 mm – installed on the facade using a single standing seam and, on the roof, with a double standing seam. The complex building geometry presented an enormous challenge to both manufacturers and installers with respect to design and execution. A total of about 200 t of titanium zinc was installed, primarily in band widths of 675 mm and 575 mm.

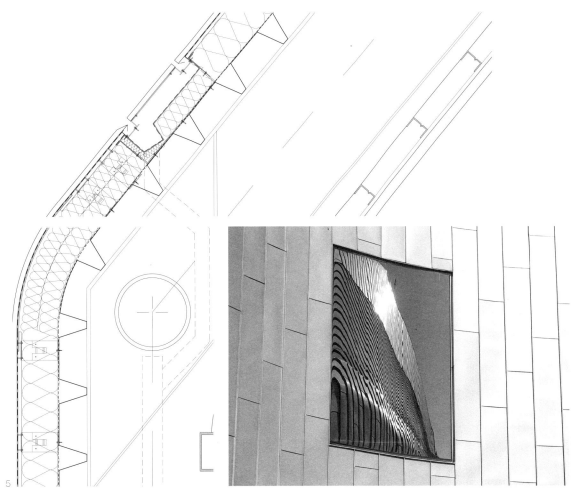

SUSPENDED FACADE – FIBRE-CEMENT BOARD

Owing to their different sizes and geometries, fibre-cement boards can be used in many different applications – in facades and roofs, as homogeneous areas or small elements, monochrome or in different colours. Typical applications of fibre-cement board are as self-supporting cladding for back-ventilated suspended facades, or as rigid waterproof infill panels in timber construction. The main ingredients are cement, powdered limestone, recycled ground fibre-cement material and water, as well as fibres (of glass, carbon or cellulose pulp) that, similarly to steel in reinforced concrete, act as tensile reinforcement of the board. The mixture is applied to format rollers as a homogeneous mass and is output in various formats, according to requirements, followed by a hardening and surface-coating process. With a density of > 1.4 g/cm³, the material is very light, but nevertheless holds its shape and is therefore suitable as cladding in mechanically exposed areas, such as around the plinth of buildings. Fibre-cement is frost-resistant, the board is waterproof, UV-resistant, does not rot and is non-combustible (DIN construction material class A2). Its surface texture can be grainy or smooth. The basic board is grey in colour due to the cement content, but can be coated in a translucent or opaque paint finish. However, boards in natural colours or pigmented are also on the market. The surface treatment prevents the penetration of moisture, although it is important that any edges resulting from cutting on site are re-treated. Textured surfaces are also available. The boards are produced in various formats in thicknesses between 5 and 20 mm.

MATERIAL AND EFFECT
Fibre-cement boards are produced either in large formats to create large homogeneous facades, in corrugated sheets, or in shingles which, with their small format, create a more animated appearance. In the form of shingles, fibre-cement elements are used both for wall and roof cladding. They can also be used as window sills and to line reveals, thus creating a uniform look in the same material. ⌐ 1
The effect of fibre-cement boards is determined by three important characteristics: the colour, the method of installation and the joint pattern. The choice of colour has an important impact on the appearance of the surface. The reflective effect of dark colours gives the impression of metal or natural stone materials. Natural grey colours look similar to concrete, while pigmenting the boards or applying a translucent paint finish leaves their fibres visible, which emphasises the material's own characteristics. Differently coloured boards can be used in a collage, in which their pigmentation or surface coating makes it possible to create vivid colour schemes. ⌐ 5

The method of installation and the associated joint pattern, as well as special fastening patterns, make a formal statement that contributes to the effect of the building. With the angular edges of the boards and their rigidity, fibre-cement boards emphasise the rectangular aspect of a building. The spacing of joints determines the facade structure, with the options including appropriately scaled rigid or free-flowing grids. The surface texture of facades with shingle cladding is determined by the shape of the shingle and the method of installation. One of the advantages of shingles is that they are suitable for curved surfaces. ⌐ 3

CONSTRUCTION
The substructure can be constructed using aluminium sections or timber battens. Where fibre-board is used – in particular in the context of energy upgrade refurbishments – it is backed with thermal insulation, which must be hydrophobic, fire-resistant, and have the benefit of back-ventilation, because it is possible that condensate forms on the back of the facade cladding or, in the case of open joints, that water penetrates them to behind the boarding. The boards are fastened with screws or rivets exposed to view. Rivets are faster and more economical, whereas screws make it possible to dismantle panels without damage. Concealed fixing can be achieved with undercut anchors or bonded surfaces, thus creating the impression of a monolithic envelope. In the case of visible fastening, the pattern of the fasteners is just as important as the joint pattern. Joints can either be left open, or can be closed using joint profiles. ⌐ 2
Since the substructure is independent, there is considerable design freedom with respect to the position and size of openings. It is possible to create a very homogeneous overall appearance when the joints are arranged to coincide with the openings and the same facade material is used to master element connections. It is important that adequate back-ventilation is provided at all reveals and openings. This is particularly critical where fenestration bands are flush with the outer face of the facade. However, it is more usual to place opening elements in the plane of the thermal insulation.

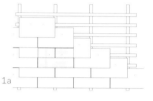
1a

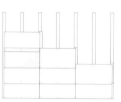
b

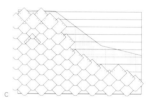
c

1 The following installation methods are available for shingle cladding, amongst others:

a Square, with staggered perpendicular joints
b Square, with perpendicular joints aligned
c Diamond-shaped

Each installation method requires a suitable substructure:
– Battens and counter-battens
– Counter-battens with back-ventilation
– Close-boarding/close sheathing with underlay membrane

Common formats are:
Long panels – 300 · 1194 mm
Rectangular shingles for staggered installation – 150/300 · 600 mm
Rectangular shingles for aligned installation – 300 · 600 mm
Square shingles – 300 · 300 mm
Shingles for diamond installation – 300 · 600 mm

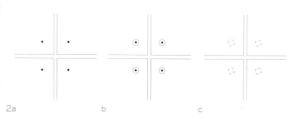

2a   b   c

2 Fastening methods
a Fastening with screws on timber substructure
b Fastening with rivets on aluminium substructure
c Concealed fastening with undercut dowels or staples

3 New building for the Grüne Schule, Mainz, 2010, eckertharms Architects / Interior Designers: The pavilion-type building is located deep in the botanic garden; the building geometry is reminiscent of a seedling. The exterior skin of white fibre-cement panels provides a canvas for the dappled effect of light through the surrounding foliage.

4 Patio houses, Rheinfelden, 2014, Raum.werk.plus: The high-density housing complex comprises four building volumes that form a unified ensemble due to the homogeneous material of the facade. At the maisonette apartments a perforated fibre-cement board 'filter' has been suspended in front of back-ventilated outer thermal insulation, resulting in a play of light and shadow in the interior and exterior spaces.

5 IBA Dock, Hamburg, 2010, Prof. Han Slawik: The floating headquarters of IBA Hamburg GmbH has been designed as a temporary exhibition and office building. The facade of the three-storey building consists of large-format fibre-cement panels in the IBA colours, arranged to look like freight containers stacked in the docks.

6 Schematic facade section, scale 1:20
a Fibre-cement panel, 15 mm
b Air gap, 40 mm
c Thermal insulation, 140 mm with hydrophobic treatment
d Metal substructure, thermally separated
e Metal sheet reveal lining, 15 mm
f Aluminium window, flush with the facade
g Metal sheet as parapet coping

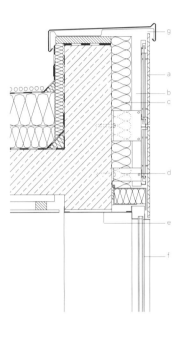

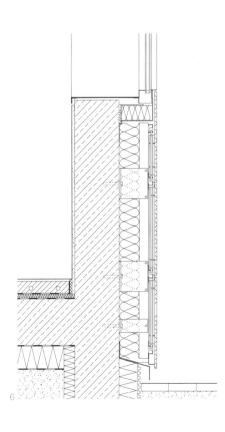

TIMBER FACADE

Facade cladding in timber can be found in all cultures. The regional availability of this natural and renewable material, its good workability and its low weight make it easy to use; in addition, its primary energy content is very low. When properly designed and well constructed, timber facades have a long service life and owe much of their characteristic appearance to the lively surface patina. Timber surfaces tend to go grey over time, and the intensity of this change in colour depends on the weather as well as the geographic and topographic situation. When choosing timber as a facade material, it is therefore important to choose construction details that provide appropriate weather protection. ⭢ 1 In the past, external timber cladding was typical of forested regions where timber was readily available, but nowadays various wood-based cladding materials for facades are offered with national distribution.

MATERIAL AND CLADDING METHOD
Suitable timber cladding materials are indigenous coniferous species such as fir, spruce, pine, larch and Douglas fir as well as deciduous species such as oak, robinia and chestnut. Fast-growing coniferous trees such as fir and spruce are not only available in sufficient quantity, they also have a greater resin content that improves the moisture resistance of the material – and hence its durability. On the other hand, facade elements made of larch, pine, Douglas fir and oak have a longer service life owing to the greater density of the material, even without surface treatment. The material comes in a range of different formats, with the main distinction being between solid wood (planks and battens) and large-format panels. The choice of cladding system depends on the desired appearance of the facade. Common cladding or siding systems are made of boards or slats, which are offered either rough sawn, planed or sanded. Boarded facades can be installed in vertical or horizontal layouts, using standard trade construction details to protect the wood. Vertical cladding – e.g. board-on-board arrangement – requires a substructure with vertical counter-battens to facilitate back-ventilation (with spacing between 40 and 60 cm), to which horizontal bearing battens are fixed to hold the board-on-board cladding. For a horizontal appearance, it is possible to choose lap siding or tongue-and-groove boards, amongst other systems. With the tongue-and-groove method it is important – for reasons of timber protection – to place the boards such that the groove faces downwards and the tongue upwards. The risk of deformation of the boards is reduced if narrower boards are used (minimum width 12 cm). ⭢ 2, 3
Traditional cladding such as shingles has also proven to be very durable. These are cut from solid wood using a

manual or machine process, and produced in different formats and shapes. They have the advantages of a long service life and even weathering, as well as being suitable for use both as a roof covering and as facade siding. ⭢ 6 Slats or vertical battens are used as open facade cladding. The construction layer behind the battens must be waterproof and UV-resistant. ⭢ 5
Where it is intended to achieve large homogeneous areas in the elevations, large-format cladding panels made of solid timber are used. In order to achieve dimensional stability and resistance to the weather / differential stresses, these panels require a multi-layer construction (laminated solid timber, plywood, or laminated veneer timber). Formats up to 5 m long should be fastened (visibly or concealed) to a substructure; it is important to ensure that joints and edges are neatly carried out. Windows and doors have to be integrated in terms of construction and design. It should always be possible to replace such components easily. ⭢ 4
There are a number of rules that govern the installation of timber cladding and siding, which allow swelling and shrinkage to occur in the structure to an extent that depends on the type of cladding chosen. The necessity of counter-battens depends on the evenness of the substrate and also on whether thermal insulation is to be placed in the structure. Counter-battens are also needed where a construction with back-ventilation is chosen, at least in the case of vertical siding boards.

TIMBER PROTECTION
In view of the fact that when exposed to driving rain or moisture, timber weathers relatively quickly, it is important to consider the available options for treating it. A basic distinction is made between protection by chemical means and protection based on construction detailing. In the latter, the timber is installed in such a way that any components that become wet or saturated can dry out again. Important details in this respect are: sufficient distance of the cladding from the ground or from projecting ledges; detailing around doors and windows that allows water to drain off; protection by roof overhangs or projecting upper floors, and detailing of fastenings and junctions to suit maintenance as well as replacement. Construction components that are severely exposed to the weather, in particular, should be easy to replace. ⭢ 1 Chemical timber protection is applied in the form of coatings or impregnations so that components under continual exposure to moisture receive lasting protection from damage by fungi and insect attack; this also provides the opportunity to apply colour in accordance with the design. With all types of cladding it is important to ensure that the fastenings are rust-proof (stainless steel screws are a good example).

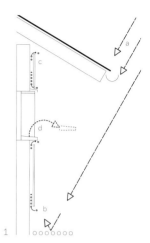

1 Schematic of timber protection with construction details:
a Rain protection
b Splash protection
c Ventilation
d Ease of replacement

4 Residence, Fislisbach, 2008, Renggli AG: Large-format timber panels emphasise the single plane of the envelope while displaying the rich colour variation of the wood.

5 House 11x11, Oberbayern, 2011, Titus Bernhard Architects: The continuous timber battens appear like a graphic structure in front of a black-coated, water-repellent substrate.

6 Conversion of the Fetz House, Egg, 2012, Hermann Kaufmann: The envelope of small-format shingles combines the scale of old and new while also reflecting the sophisticated styling of traditional forms.

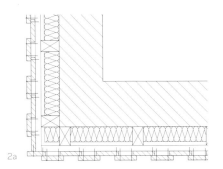

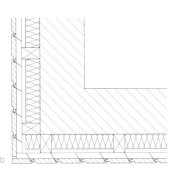

2a   b

2 Vertical siding
a Board-on-board siding
Base board only attached on one
side, air gap min. 20 mm
Minimum width of board 120 mm
b Tongue-and-groove siding
Concealed fixing in the groove

3 Horizontal siding
a Lap siding
Fasteners made of non-rusting
material, such as stainless steel
Insect screen, splash protection
at the base
b Tongue-and-groove siding
Concealed fixing in the groove
(tongue at the top, groove at the
bottom)
Insect screen, splash protection
with sacrificial boards which are
replaced when necessary

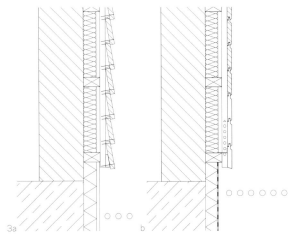

3a   b

To improve the durability of timber it used to be common practice to put it through a smoking process; this has now been developed into a controlled thermal treatment process. In this procedure, the timber is exposed to hot steam at temperatures between 160 °C and 220 °C for fifty to ninety hours, while reducing the amount of oxygen. The shrinkage, swelling and cracking of this thermally modified timber is reduced; furthermore it is more resistant to mould, fungus and insect attack. A visual side-effect of this thermal treatment is that the colour of the timber grows darker. The improved durability makes it an excellent choice for facade cladding.

SURFACE

As part of a natural weathering process, the surface of timber goes grey and forms a protective layer. However, additional surface treatment is necessary where the thickness of the material is not adequate. Open-pored translucent coating systems have been tried and tested for this purpose. They maintain the natural structure of the timber and are maintenance-friendly because they 'wash out' over time, rather than becoming detached as other coatings do. Paint is also frequently used although it obscures the grain of the wood as a result of its high pigment content, and has to be regularly renewed. Although dark colour shades provide more permanent coverage than light-coloured stain finishes, they promote the visible 'bleeding' of resin. The surface treatment of timber also acts as UV-protection.

4   5   6

PROFILED STRUCTURAL GLASS AND POLYCARBONATE PANELS

1 The Nelson Atkins Museum, Kansas City, 2007, Steven Holl: The external envelope of the museum consists of double-skin profiled construction glazing with a capillary insert of polymethylmethacrylate to disperse the daylight and hence protect the art exhibits. The inner layer consists of white laminated safety glass, one pane of which has been sandblasted, which tempers the shade of green inherent in the profiled glazing.

2 Workshop building, vocational training unit, Kirchseeon, 2004, Landau + Kindelbacher Architects: The transparent facades of the halls consist of vertically arranged profiled glazing, with an expanded metal insert as solar screening orientated to the cardinal directions.

PROFILED STRUCTURAL GLASS

Profiled construction glass (also referred to as industrial glass) is a type of cast glass in which the molten glass is formed into a wide profile (U or C-profile) using a rolling process while it is still hot.

A building envelope made of profiled structural glass can be used as a single-skin construction or as a double-skin in combination with internal transparent thermal insulation, which is used to increase the thermal transmittance coefficient. ⟶ 3

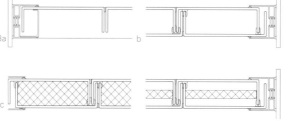

3 Schematic section of profiled glazing element in a thermally separated profile frame system, scale 1:10

a   Single-skin
b   Double-skin
c   With transparent thermal insulation integrated in the interpane gap.

Owing to their translucent properties, these elements transmit a large percentage of daylight without allowing views to the inside. The facade is perceived as a continuous glazed area which can be differentiated by colouring or by the insertion of structured elements. At night, the facade appears to dissolve and the light coming from the inside creates a luminous appearance. The frame structure, glass ribs and freestanding furniture in the interior become visible. The effect has to be taken into consideration at the design stage. Profiled structural glass was initially much used for industrial buildings, but nowadays it is also used in other functions and building types owing to the improved energy balance. ⟶ 1

MATERIAL AND CONSTRUCTION

Owing to the rolling process, profiled structural glass in its raw form diffuses light, has a rough surface and a somewhat greenish appearance. With the help of metal coatings it is possible to create shades of blue; other colour shades can be achieved with sandblasting and subsequent coloured enamelling. Glass that is low in iron content achieves greater translucence and is neutral in colour. Smooth and transparent profiles are also available, in addition to glass with infra-red-reflecting (low-e) coating and light-reflecting solar screening glass, as well as security glass. Longitudinal reinforcement in the form of stainless steel wires in the glass increases the strength of profiled construction glass, which may be required in the case of fire or as intrusion protection.

Owing to the shape of the profile, this type of glass is structurally very strong and lengths of up to 7 m can be produced. The width varies between 230 and 500 mm depending on the manufacturer and standard or non-standard production, with the profile depth varying between 40 and 60 mm. Owing to their structural strength in the longitudinal direction, the profiles do not require lateral framing, but are connected with each other via a slotting system (approx. 50 to 90 mm wide U-profiles made of aluminium or steel). The joints between the glass profiles are sealed with a permanently elastic compound; the joint with the frame profiles is sealed with sealing tape and additional permanently elastic compound.

Profiled structural glass only has to support its own weight while the horizontal loads are transferred to the primary system via the frames. Depending on the exposure to wind load, the span can be up to approx. 3.6 m for deep single-skin profiles and up to approx. 5 m for double-skin profiles. Double-storey elements are made possible by inserting an intermediate bearing on the

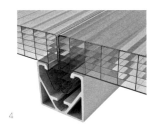

4

5

4 Polycarbonate multi-chamber element on a reinforced aluminium profile

5 Wall connection detail

6 Schematic section, scale 1:10 Polycarbonate panels can be used as facade cladding and as roof elements. In mullion/transom construction they can be installed with a pressure plate or, like profiled glazing, in a frame with thermally separated profiles. Multi-chamber systems are fastened with system-specific negative wind force anchors in mid-panel and in profiles at the edge.

a Polycarbonate multi-chamber element
b Substructure
c Wind suction anchor rail

intermediate floor slab. The high mass and air-tightness ensure good airborne sound insulation.

Uncoated, single-skin profiles achieve a U-value of approx. 5.7 W/m²K, while double-skin installations achieve approx. 2.8 W/m²K. Low-e coating on the inner skin can improve this to approx. 1.7 W/m²K. Thermally separated frame profiles improve insulation. Depending on the coating, glass composition and surface structure, the g-values vary between 0.65 and 0.8 and the light transmission values are between 40 % and 87 %.

POLYCARBONATE PANELS

An alternative to industrial glass is the polycarbonate panel, which transmits a high percentage of light and is therefore suitable for translucent building envelopes. These lightweight but strong elements are available in various degrees of transparency, different textures and colours.

The base material consists either of polyvinylchloride (hard PVC), glass fibre-reinforced polyester (GRP) or polycarbonate (PC). Owing to their greater strength, low weight, high impact resistance and good light transmission values, as well as the possibility of producing different cross-sections in the extrusion process, polycarbonate panels are primarily used in multi-chamber systems for element facades. PVC and GRP elements are used more for back-ventilated facades. The fast manufacturing process and the low cost of recycling make polycarbonate panels an economical alternative to glass.

MATERIAL AND CONSTRUCTION

Polycarbonate is a thermoplastic material which is extruded as an endless panel of up to twelve layers. The layers are connected by webs (multi-wall sheets) and can be profiled to improve longitudinal stiffness. Panels can be made of coloured material or finished with a coloured or solar screen coating, or with a coating to improve abrasion resistance, fire resistance (hardly flammable, no burning droplets) and/or UV resistance. Common sizes are 60–200 cm wide and up to 7 m long.

Depending on the thickness and stiffness of the element, as well as the prevailing wind forces, spans may be up to 2 m (40 mm thick) and up to 3.5 m (60 mm thick). The material is easy to cut, mill and drill; it can be folded or curved in a hot process, and can also be installed curved, provided it is held in place by the substructure. Owing to the considerable thermal expansion of PC panels, joints should not be sealed with permanently elastic compound but with rubber seals.

Polycarbonate multi-chamber elements have a rebate with pressure-equalising chambers along the edges. Air-tightness is achieved by an outer covering lip. Any penetrating driving rain drains off through a pressure-equalising chamber. There is an internal groove for attaching anchor profiles to counter deformation from wind suction, and to secure air- and water-tightness while allowing thermal expansion. The U-value varies with the configuration of panels, profiles and multi-layer constructions (panel thicknesses of approx. 50 mm and thermally separated frames can achieve up to 1.0 W/m²K).

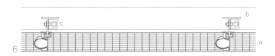

6

7 Joinery workshop, Pulling, 2010, Deppisch Architects. The 'shed' form and its simple treatment reflect the building's function. The joinery workshop is clad on three sides with a timber facade, while on the north side diffused daylight enters the workshop without glare through the polycarbonate multi-wall sheets, like in an art studio.

7

MEMBRANE FACADE

Buildings with membrane facades have a long tradition too. Early tent structures, which consisted of thin membranes enclosing the space in connection with a system of poles to take up the stress, are the precursors of today's membrane envelopes. Following the development of new high-strength materials, numerous construction methods and applications were created, both for facade envelopes and for roof areas. These materials have a very low weight and can be used as transparent constructions with large spans, representing an economic method for constructing the roof of buildings such as stadia. In view of the fact that membrane facades are often used in unusual designs, they must be considered as special cases requiring individual approval.

MATERIAL AND CONSTRUCTION

In membrane construction, a distinction is made between fabrics and films. ⌐ 1 The group of fabrics includes polyester fabric with PVC coating, PTFE-coated glass-fibre fabric (short: glass-fibre Teflon) and silicone-coated glass fabric. All fabrics have a long service life, translucency (including UV wavelengths), UV- and fire-resistance class B1 (hardly flammable), among other things. The surfaces are stabilised by pre-tensioning with tensile structural members. The pre-tensioning helps to create a surface free from creases and provides rigidity to the membrane skin. Since thermal expansion is considerable, this has to be taken into account in the pre-tensioning process and during installation. Where fabrics are applied in several layers, a moiré effect is created which can be controlled via the distance between layers and the weaving pattern of the fabric; this effect can be exploited to provide solar screening where the layers can be moved sideways. Some fabrics are also suitable for movable systems, since the material is not sensitive to buckling. After being cut to size and shape, parts are assembled in a thermal welding process or vulcanisation/bonding. Owing to their low mass, films do not provide much sound insulation.

In addition, the material must be strong enough to resist mechanical impact, for example from birds. The material used for films is ethylene tetrafluoroethylene (ETFE). In architecture, ETFE films are used in thicknesses from 100 to 300 μm, be it as multi-layer, pneumatically pre-stressed constructions, or single-layer mechanically pre-stressed systems. ETFE films are produced in colours or highly transparent, and can also be printed on. They have a very low weight and are highly permeable to visible and UV light.
ETFE film cushions consist of multi-layer, prestressed ETFE films. Pneumatically supported membranes have a synclastic geometry and require a constant internal air pressure to achieve the pre-tensioning required for supporting the structural loads. Several insulating layers of air can be produced by installing additional internal ETFE film layers. ⌐ Examples, p. 146
Back-ventilated construction systems are primarily created using tensile systems. The simplest construction consists of mesh or fabric clamped to steel or aluminium frames. Flat membranes are tensioned in one direction. They are then suspended in a secondary structure using specially profiled bars with springs and tensioning clamps. The secondary structure must be able to withstand the pre-tension loads and wind loads, which it transfers to the primary system. Pre-tension and wind loads depend on the fabric's flow resistance, the element's size, and the membrane's strength. Three-dimensionally shaped membranes require pre-tensioning and shaping. Depending on the shape, pre-tensioning may be required in several directions. Membranes can be held in a certain shape by compressive yokes or frames: either at points, along lines or along three dimensional curves. In the case of three-dimensionally shaped facades, the multi-axial loading results in a complex force distribution and superimposed stresses, and requires complex tailored elements that also take into account the expansion of the membrane from stretching during installation.

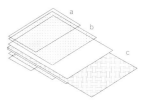

1 Structure of a fabric membrane (PVC-coated polyester membrane) compared to a simple film

a Coating (primer and top coat)
b Fabric
c Surface sealing
d Film

2 Unilever headquarters, Hamburg, 2010, Behnisch Architects: At an exposed location in the port area that experiences strong wind loads, the ETFE film facade serves as wind protection in front of the insulating glazing facade. In order to retain transparency, a single layer of film was used in construction with individual frames rather than the usual air cushion system. Maximum transparency was retained while achieving the necessary tension by using a cable construction in the frame fields.

3 In order to achieve stability of the intended forms, the tensile fixings at the edge must allow continuous transfer of the pre-tensile forces. Schematic illustration of the connections:

a HF weld seam, PVC polyester fabric – irreversible connection of components
b Cable in membrane pocket
c Cable and sewn strap in membrane pocket
d Extruded profile with grooves for cord edges

2

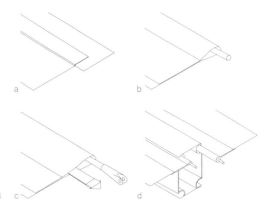

3

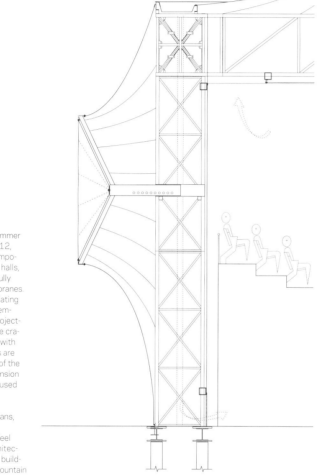

4   Shooting sport venue, Summer Olympic Games, London 2012, magma architecture: The temporary facility comprises three halls, the structure of which was fully wrapped in white PVC membranes. The facade is given its undulating surface by stretching the membrane from the framing to projecting inverted cones, rather like craters, which are accentuated with colour. The projecting fixings are necessary for the structure of the building envelope, as they tension the membrane, and are also used for natural ventilation.

5   Stanserhorn cable car, Stans, 2012, WaserAchermann Architects: The lightweight feel and transparency of the architectural envelope of the station building, set in the midst of the mountain landscape, has been achieved by installing single-layer, printed ETFE elements that are supported by cables. In spite of the extreme climatic conditions at 1,900 m above sea level, it is possible to use the ETFE material owing to sophisticated detailing and finishing.

6   The Allianz Arena, Munich, 2006, Herzog & de Meuron: The facade of the Allianz Arena consists of self-cleaning, ETFE film cushions, which can be illuminated on the inside. A total of 2,760 rhomboid cushions made of transparent ETFE film were needed to clad the 66,500 m2 of facade and roof. Fans are used to maintain the air pressure in the cushions at 350 Pascal. Each of these special hydraulic cushions supports a maximum load of 8 t and can withstand wind suction of 22 t.

COMPOSITE THERMAL INSULATION SYSTEM

Nowadays, building physics requirements stipulate that, to be fit for their purpose, walls must be constructed so that they remain dry and provide adequate thermal insulation. To achieve this, it is now common practice to install composite thermal insulation systems, which are not categorised as self-supporting envelopes in this book because they cannot be erected in front of the facade, independently of the loadbearing structure. In many cases, these systems can be confused with self-supporting materials, particularly when they are firmly attached to masonry. Composite thermal insulation systems consist of several layers of materials, including a layer of insulation. Different systems are distinguished by their type of insulation and weathering layer. Insulation materials can have a mineral or organic basis and they can be combustible or non-combustible; examples are rock wool, mineral fibre, wood fibre, silicate rock, hemp and polystyrene. Depending on the thermal resistance of the material concerned, the typical thickness of the insulation is between 80 and 300 mm.

The insulation can be fastened in various ways using an adhesive applied to the back (either in dabs or over the entire surface) and, depending on the height of the building and type of substrate, dowels or a rail system. Any protrusions must be ground flat, and open joints must be fully filled in order to create a homogenous surface without defects that could lead to damage. The insulation is reinforced with a fabric (glass fabric available in a range of mesh widths) and finished with a skim coat. This is followed by a render coat (either mineral-based or with an organic binder such as silicon-resin or silicate render), other coatings, or external face layers such as brick slips

and ceramic tiles. Back-ventilation of the insulation must be avoided as this would reduce the insulating effect and cause problems in terms of building physics. ⌐ 1 Composite thermal insulation systems are frequently used as part of energy upgrades of existing buildings, as they are also suitable for application on uneven substrates that are not homogenous. ⌐ 5 In that situation it is necessary, however, for the architects to consider the existing facade's architectural merits carefully, for example when dealing with historic facades that may warrant preservation. Where a composite thermal insulation system is applied as part of an upgrade operation, the detailing of connections to other building components must be carefully designed. Owing to the thickness of the thermal insulation, the reveals of windows become deeper and may restrict the amount of daylight entering the rooms. Likewise, window sills need to be deeper and the roof overhangs must be sufficient to cover both the insulation and the render coat, so that these are protected against the ingress of driving rain. Consideration must be given to the design of corners and the correct layout of expansion joints. The product approval is granted subject to the same system components being used throughout, including the adhesive, the insulation material, the fabric, skim coat and dowels through to the render and paint coat. The main relevant standards are DIN EN 13499 and 13500, as well as DIN 55699. ⌐ **Appendix**

As a rule of thumb, the substrate of all composite thermal insulation systems must be structurally sound and level enough to achieve an adequate bond between the panels and the substrate. Facades with insulation of

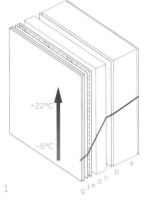

1 Composition of thermal sandwich insulating panels
a   Loadbearing structure
b   Fixing on the loadbearing wall (with adhesive or a combination of adhesive and dowels) and plinth rails
c   Thermal insulation
d   Reinforcement layer
e   Reinforcement fabric
f   External render
g   Facade paint

2 Welfenhöfe office and retail building, Munich, 2012, Hild & K Architects: The eye-catching render relief of the silvery, shining facade takes its cue from the surrounding Wilhelminian buildings. The raised areas around the windows overlay each other like scales, thus avoiding horizontal ledges where water could collect and damage the material. The shape of the render relief results directly from the properties of the thermal insulation sandwich system used.

3 Chemical laboratory of RWTH Aachen, 2014, kister scheithauer gross Architects. Rendered facade on a composite thermal insulation system; the different sides of the building have received different surface treatments of the render. Some areas of this mineral top coat render have been manually textured to create an irregular pattern, while other areas have been finished as a classic, smooth render.

more than 80 mm thickness tend to have low surface temperatures and therefore support the growth of algae. Using silicate renders and chemical additives in coating systems can reduce this risk but not fully eliminate it. The thermal expansion of coatings must be accommodated by placing enough expansion joints in the construction to avoid stresses. In contrast to mineral-based renders, these organic coatings cannot be modelled in much depth, as in the case of grooved or scratched render. Combustible insulation materials make it necessary to provide additional measures in the facade envelope, such as the insertion of fire barriers of non-combustible mineral wool between the floor levels. Like all systems, this construction requires building control approval. Installation mistakes, particularly defective fastening, lead to cracking at the junctions of boards, at building corners and at the corners of openings. Inappropriate storage of the thermal insulation boards can reduce their performance. It is therefore important to comply with the manufacturers' instructions and the applicable regulations. ↘ Appendix, p. 164

When deciding whether to install a composite thermal insulation system, any potential mechanical impact needs to be taken into consideration, particularly on the ground floor. In spite of the additional fabric reinforcement, the surfaces of the system are not as impact-resistant and easy to repair as directly rendered masonry. Assuming good technical installation, the service life of such systems is estimated to be thirty to forty years. Depending on the type of insulation material, a high proportion of primary energy is used in the manufacturing process, which also releases environmentally hazardous substances. In addition, the insulation material may be difficult to return to a material cycle because of the materials it is bonded to, such as the render, fabric and adhesive. These aspects must be weighed up against those of the cost of production/installation and the benefits of the energy upgrade of the building and should be reassessed for each building project in the context of current legislation and standards.

4 Installation of thermal insulation sandwich system
a Conventional solution
Mineral insulation board, between 80 and 200 mm thick
b Solution for refurbishment projects
High-tech thermal insulation sandwich system based on aerogel, thickness 40 mm

5 Schematic section through wall construction with thermal insulation sandwich system, scale 1:20
a Internal plaster
b Vertically perforated bricks
c Mineral insulation
d Skim coat with fabric and render
e Plinth render
f Perimeter insulation

4a

b

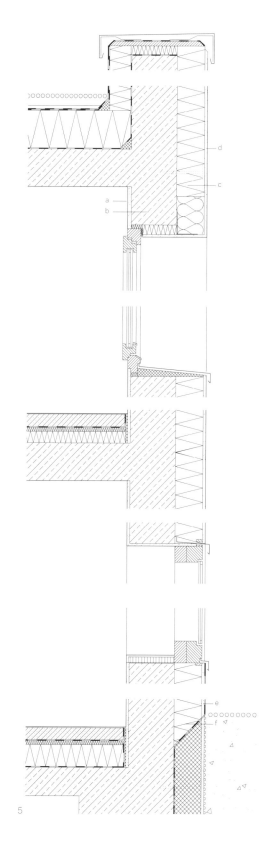

5

ENCLOSE | BUILD
ROOFS

FROM LEAF THATCH TO ROOF ENVELOPE

The roof is mankind's earliest form of creating a protected space, and is the element from which today's building envelope has developed. When people settled, they created habitable spaces by using the materials they found in the vicinity; thus roofs and walls were constructed. The roof is not just the upper part of the building envelope, but also part of the structure, always depending on – and supported by – the construction chosen. As roofs became more sophisticated and differentiated, they not only had a protective function, but were also used – in combination with the other parts of the building envelope – to give buildings a specific expression, in both secular and sacral architecture.

In view of the fact that the building envelope comprises not only the vertical facade, but also the roof, this chapter is dedicated to roof construction, of which it presents the most important standard forms. Developments in recent years have shown that the classic separation of plinth, main elevation and roof is being adhered to less and less, and that the shape of buildings is increasingly being determined by independent envelopes which subsume the roof. These envelopes rely on the basic principles of traditional roofs, but also involve specific solutions and details. For this reason, the chapter on roofs has been included here with the building envelope, complementing Volume 3 of the Scale series, Support | Materialise.

The shape and construction of roofs, as well as their use, appearance and architectural significance, are closely interrelated. Specific regional climates, in combination with the respective functions of the building and the attic space have, over time, led to the development of typical construction methods and building styles. Different climatic conditions, in particular, have led to the most striking difference in roof type, the sloping and the flat roof. In the temperate zones of Central Europe, with their changeable weather, a roof has to be designed for a wide range of conditions. In the northern part of Central Europe, pitched roofs with a range of different covering materials are therefore common, as they allow precipitation water to run off quickly. Some roofs reach down close to the ground in order to protect the external walls from driving rain and splashing water. By contrast, houses in Southern Europe tend to have roofs of a shallow pitch, with large overhangs that protect the timber beneath from rain and solar radiation. Owing to the shallow pitch of the roof, any snow that falls in winter accumulates and acts as a seasonal insulation material. Roof shapes vary widely. They range from the steep roof assembled from branches in the 'primal hut' described by Vitruvius and drawn by Alberti, ⌐1 to landscaped roofs that allow buildings to merge seamlessly with their natural surroundings. ⌐5 The history of their development starts with the technical improvement of roofing materials. Bit by bit, the space beneath the roof acquired ever more sophisticated purposes. At first, it was used to store and dry goods and provisions, then as simple living accommodation for servants; today, stepped-back top storeys are constructed specifically for luxurious penthouse apartments, in allusion to a pattern of use that, owing to the warmer climate, is common in Mediterranean countries.

There, the roof terraces behind the decorative parapets of Medieval and Renaissance townhouses were used as dining rooms in summer. The history of development of roofing materials has also spawned different urban forms. While slate was often used as a roofing material in the towns of Central Europe, resulting in dark roofscapes, the predominant feature of the roofscape of towns in Southern Europe is the terracotta colour of fired clay roof tiles. ⌐3

Similar to the plinth of a building, the roof plays an important role in the overall composition of the building envelope. The shape of the roof can have a major impact on

1 Primeval hut by Alberti/Vitruvius from Marc-Antoine Laugier, Essai sur l'architecture, Paris 1755.

2 Traditional adobe buildings with flat roofs in Morocco.

3 Historic roofscape with tile-covered pitched roofs in Siena.

the proportions and silhouette of a building. The historical canon ranges from the classic proportions of temples in ancient times, and the strict order of a Medieval townhouse to the complete dissolution of the balanced composition in modern times, in which the roof can only be seen as a thin line that confines the building at the top. Of course, the flat roof is by no means a modern development. Different forms have been created throughout history, just as with sloping roofs. Notable examples are the adobe buildings of the Pueblo Indians, and traditional Moroccan houses, ⤳2 the flat roofs of which were used for drying foodstuffs. The nomadic peoples of Siberia constructed log cabins with flat roofs covered with earth and turf. By contrast to the sloping roof, which creates usable space beneath the envelope, the upper surface of the flat roof can be used for various purposes, for example as a summer living space, or as a roof garden. While in arid zones it was possible to keep roofs leak-proof through regular maintenance with natural materials such as adobe, flat roofs did not become practicable in climate zones with more precipitation until roofing membranes, such as bitumen or tar-saturated roofing felt, were developed. This development led to longer-lasting solutions that were more leak-proof. As a result, the flat roof began to displace the sloping roof, particularly in densely developed urban locations. Better utilisation of the built volume and the omission of complex roof structures facilitated the creation of large building projects. During the 1920s, under the influence of Modernist thinking, sports and leisure facilities started to appear on the roofs of buildings, such as the test circuit on the buildings of the Fiat factory in Turin, Il Lingotto, designed by Giacomo Matte-Trucco in 1923, and later the swimming pools and kindergartens on the roofs of the Unité d'Habitation in Marseille by Le Corbusier, from 1952. The flat roof increasingly became a means of extending functionality at little extra cost. This trend has continued and today, flat roofs are ubiquitous in dense, urban locations, where their value for 'urban gardening', including 'urban food', is appreciated in addition to their use for leisure purposes. The possibility of planting on roofs and creating gardens, even parks, is leading to more and more intensive use of these spaces, which are integrated into the existing landscape, thereby compensating – in terms of planted area – for the loss of natural land under the building. For example, the new Learning Centre of the ETH Lausanne is a built landscape on the shore of Lake Geneva; similarly, the underground extension of the Städel art museum in Frankfurt has been built so as to retain the existing inner courtyard with its qualities as a green space. Whether we are contemplating a sloping roof, a flat roof, a dome or a landscaped roof, and whether it is covered in roofing material, planted, or covered with gravel, the choice of the 'right roof' is always a question of the appropriate shape for the building, for its envelope as a whole. The roof can make a significant contribution to how we understand a building – its spatial structure, its function, and not least its quality – if we consider it not only as a necessary adjunct to the building, but as a space-forming element in its own right, impacting on the design. Today, the seemingly ubiquitous availability of materials and construction know-how opens the door to the largely free design of buildings and their roofs, and hence of the entire building envelope.

4 Roof House, Hatano-shi, 2001, Tezuka Architects: The roof of a house on a restricted site in Hatano-shi is not just used for protection from the weather, but also serves to extend the usable area.

5 New building for the MRT laboratory of the Physikalisch-Technische Bundesanstalt (PTB) in Berlin, 2013, huber staudt architects: With the planted roof construction, the extension of the research building becomes part of the context and also a landscape sculpture, which interacts confidently and yet in a restrained manner with the surrounding historic buildings.

STRUCTURE AND LOADS

The shape of the roof is affected by – and determined by – its structure. The roof structure should be integrated into the design and construction at an early stage of the design process. The following aspects must be taken into account when designing a roof structure:
- size of the roof area and construction spans
- imposed and dead loads
- loads from local climatic conditions, such as wind or snow
- restrictions imposed by the available bearing options where a building is placed on an existing, older structure
- structural potential of the material.

Usually, roof structures are constructed using timber, metal, or concrete. More rarely, natural stone is used for historic buildings and, more recently, structures made of plastic. The choice of material and construction is primarily determined by the existing resources, the required loadbearing capacity and spatial and design requirements. In timber structures there is the additional distinction between traditional, carpenter-built constructions and engineered roof structures with calculated proof of structural integrity; as a rule, the latter are only commercially viable when covering spans in excess of five metres. While in carpenter-built constructions, the dimensions of solid construction timber from the grown timber logs have a determining influence, engineered timber constructions involving glulam girders and lattice girders are also viable for larger roof constructions. Today, solid construction is used commercially for both sloping and flat roofs. As with engineered timber constructions, steel is used for roof structures with larger spans and more complex designs ⟶ SCALE, vol. 3, Support | Materialise. For example, structures using timber framing, dome or shell construction have been used to create impressive buildings such as the Roman Pantheon in ancient times, modern glass constructions in many contemporary airports and railway stations, and even the solid shells of the Sydney Opera House.

DEAD LOADS AND IMPOSED LOADS
One of the functions of the roof structure is to brace the building against horizontal loads (wind, earthquake, bearing loads), and the roof itself also absorbs horizontal loads. This means that the roof plane must be sufficiently stiff for the forces to be transferred to the structural system at the bearing points. The loads on a roof structure are categorised as either dead loads or imposed loads. The dead load comprises the weight of the structure itself and the layers carried by the structure, such as the substructure, roofing, thermal insulation and any installations such as solar collectors or technical equipment;

for example, thin metal sheet roofing or metal trays with formwork weigh approx. 3 to 25 kg/m², roof covering consisting of stone or tiles weighs approx. 50 to 100 kg/m², and intensively planted roofs up to 1,000 kg/m²). The imposed load may, at one end of the scale, be that of persons entering the roof for the purpose of maintenance (up to approx. 100 kg/m²) or that of persons and furniture etc. in habitable roofs (accommodation, restaurants, up to 400 kg/m²) or, at the other end, heavy imposed loads such as those of a parking deck (up to approx. 500 kg/m²) or helicopter landing pads. Pitched roofs are usually only walked on for the purpose of maintenance. In addition, there are loads from wind, snow, or ice and, in the case of green roofs, ponding water, layers of earth and plants. In special types of building (multi-storey car parks, warehouses etc.) exceptional loads are taken into account, such as those resulting from the impact of vehicles or heavy goods.

RAIN, SNOW AND ICE LOADS
The main purpose of a roof is to keep out rainwater. Any water penetrating the covering layer must be allowed to drain off, usually via the layer beneath. The ability of the roof to protect against driving rain depends on the selected roofing system (size of elements, length and design of joints) and the pitch of the roof. The roofing elements must be water-repellent and frost-proof, and any path the water might find through the joints should be as long as possible. The possibility of water penetrating joints or ponding also necessitates a means of discharging such water beneath the roof covering, usually in the form of a sealing membrane or a tear-resistant, reinforced roof underlay membrane, which can be additionally supported by a substructure layer such as closeboarding or wood-based boards. For this reason, the German standard, for example, specifies a rain zone map ⟶ Appendix, p. 159 which contains a load classification. Similarly, the snow load depends on the geographic location and increases with the altitude of the terrain. The shape of the roof also has to be taken into consideration. Although steep and only slightly insulated roofs do not retain much snow, any snow melting due to transmission heat may freeze and thereby add to the load to be supported. Likewise, fine drift snow may penetrate through openings in the construction, icicles and ice sheets may present a hazard to building components and users, parts of a building may be forced apart by the formation of ice, while melt water must be reliably discharged. For this reason, the snow zone map ⟶ Appendix, p. 159 divides Germany into three zones, with the values for locations above 1500 m above sea level being determined by the local authorities.

1 The image shows the loads impacting on a roof structure described in DIN 1055 Actions on structures. Actions include dead and imposed loads, as well as the loads from wind, snow and ice.

The wind pressure is calculated by multiplying the aerodynamic factor c, which can be found in a table in the DIN standard, by the velocity pressure q, which depends on the wind speed and the air density.

$$w = c * q$$

The resulting wind force F acting on a building or part of a building is

$$F = c * q * A$$

whereby A is the reference surface of the building affected by the force, c is the sum of the aerodynamic factors and q the velocity pressure.

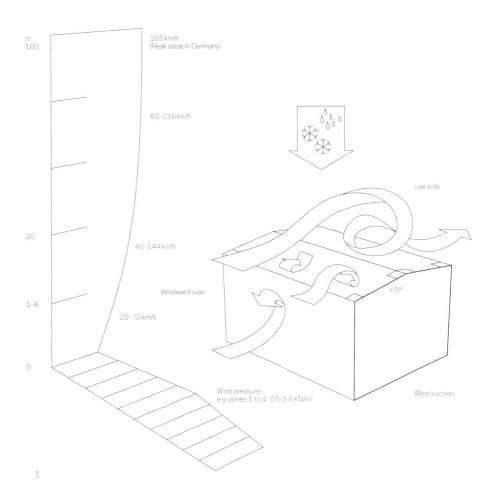

2 Classification of some wind forces according to Beaufort

	km/h	
0	0–1	Calm
1	1–5	Light air
4	20–28	Moderate breeze
6	39–49	Strong breeze
7	50–61	High wind, moderate gale, near gale
8	62–74	Gale, fresh gale
9	75–88	Strong gale
12	>117	Hurricane force
	Up to 194	Hurricane

WIND LOADS

Strong wind, as well as rain and snow, not only impacts a building horizontally but, owing to suction or negative pressure, may also act on it in an upward direction and result in specific loads on the construction. For this reason, the method of attaching the roof to the building, as well as the weight of the roof covering material, are important considerations in very exposed areas.

Depending on the height of the building and the altitude of the geographic location, the wind forces acting on buildings and their roofs can be extreme. Wind load increases with wind speed. On the other hand, obstacles on the ground (buildings, trees, topography) reduce the wind speed. Free-standing buildings, domes and higher parts of a building are more exposed. In coastal areas, wind speeds are significantly higher than inland, which means that the wind pressure on the building surfaces is increased. In extreme cases, the wind impacts purely horizontally on a building. In those cases, the windward side of a roof with a pitch of approx. 30 to 35° or greater is subject to wind pressure; below this pitch it will be subject to wind suction. As a rule, the lee side of the roof is subject to wind suction, which will apply a pulling force on the roofing material. For this reason the weight of the roof covering material and the fixing method (e.g. nails, wind brackets) must be designed to counteract the suction force. In pressurised areas (e.g. under cantilevers) and in buildings with an open envelope, it is possible for roofs to be subject to an upward force or, conversely, to a downward force where wind passes beneath them. Where wind is periodically interrupted at the edge of a building, there is likely to be negative pressure with eddies. Wind will also impact on the coping of parapets, sealing devices and components at the edge of buildings (eaves, flashing), which means that these parts have to be designed for the location and the prevailing wind speeds. For this reason, the standard specifies calculatory loads for various building and roof shapes, again highlighting the interaction between form and structure.

VENTILATED, UNVENTILATED, SLOPING, FLAT

When selecting a roof, it is possible to apply various basic principles that derive from the protective function and the arrangement of layers. A distinction is made between ventilated and un-ventilated roofs (the former terminology was 'cold roof' and 'warm roof', which simplifies the issue but could also lead to misunderstanding). This terminology relates to the different construction layers of a roof. It is rare for the many different requirements that apply to a roof – such as insulation, weathering and wind-proofing – to be fulfilled by a single-skin construction (as in the case of an igloo). Usually the various functions are fulfilled by different layers. The top layer, which protects against rain and snow, consists of either scale-like elements such as tiles or shingles, or of roofing membranes. The structure can be built in solid construction or with framing, the roof can be sloping or flat, and the insulation layers (and hence the overall construction) can be ventilated or un-ventilated.

VENTILATED ROOF

Owing to the temperature gradient from inside to outside and the resulting effect on the moisture suspended in the air, it is possible for condensate to form on the inside surface of the outer roof layer. In addition it is possible, in the case of scale-like roofing material, that some water from heavy rain is driven into the roof. In order to protect the space and layers underneath, an air gap is formed between the covering layer and the layer beneath, in order to discharge any water with the help of air ventilation – similar to a curtain wall facade. Since lofts were traditionally ventilated and unheated (only the storeys below were heated), the term 'cold roof' was applied to such roofs. Owing to improved building materials and the resulting possibility of using lofts for the purpose of (heated) accommodation, this term has now become misleading. Now the term 'cold roof' only refers to a roof with a ventilation gap between the outer skin of the roof and the thermal insulation. In ventilated roofs, humid air diffusing through the structure and forming condensate

underneath the outside roof layer in winter, and humid air penetrating the roof in summer, is discharged to the outside. The ventilation cross-sections have to be calculated for each roof in order to ensure that any condensate is discharged in accordance with the applicable standard (e.g. DIN 4108-3). Assuming that the building components have good thermal storage capacity, a roof with ventilation will provide better thermal protection than one without.

Sloping roofs in particular lend themselves to the ventilated roof construction, since the air entering at eaves level will rise and can easily be discharged at the ridge. In the case of flat roofs, which are often constructed as ventilated 'cold' roofs, particularly in existing buildings, it is important that both the size of the air gap and the flow of cross-ventilation are sufficient, since otherwise moisture damage can result. For this reason and in order to reduce the volume of the building, flat roofs today are usually constructed without ventilation.

UN-VENTILATED ROOF

By contrast to the ventilated roof, it is important that no moisture penetrates the various layers of the un-ventilated roof. This means that a vapour barrier has to be installed (usually supported on the loadbearing structure) to prevent any moisture/humidity from the room below penetrating the thermal insulation. The weathering, water-repellent covering layer is then applied directly on top of the thermal insulation (without an air gap). This means that both the thermal insulation and the roof remain dry. Although this requires precise detailing and accurate execution, it is now the standard construction for all flat roofs. Special care must be applied to penetration and corner details. Currently, the 'inverted roof' is still considered to be a special form of the un-ventilated flat roof. In 'inverted' roofs, the weathering layer is placed directly on the loadbearing structure and the thermal insulation is placed on top, acting as protection for the sealing layer. In this case, the insulation must be waterproof and rot-proof.

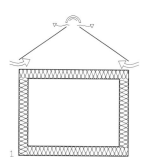

1 Traditional house with an unused, ventilated 'cold' loft space; air enters at the eaves and is discharged at the ridge.

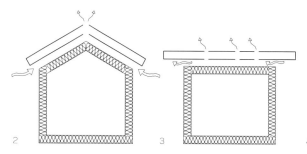
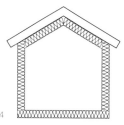
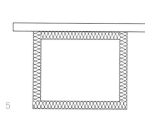

Principal roof constructions:

2 Sloping roof, ventilated
3 Flat roof, ventilated
4 Sloping roof, un-ventilated
5 Flat roof, un-ventilated

6 The diagram shows an overview of the relationship between roofing materials and their respective suitability for different roof pitches. When selecting a roofing material for a certain shape of roof, the designer must check whether the chosen material will provide adequate impermeability. The diagram clearly shows that historic roofing materials such as straw and reed, or plain tiles, require the steep roof pitches that are so characteristic of northern European Medieval townscapes, while the introduction of roofing membranes and metal roof coverings made flat roof construction possible in this climate.

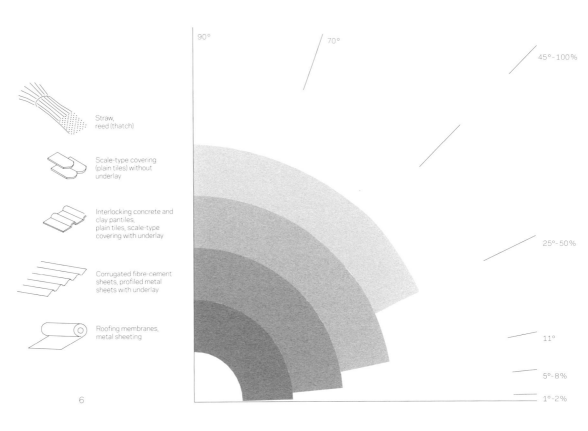

Straw,
reed (thatch)

Scale-type covering
(plain tiles) without
underlay

Interlocking concrete and
clay pantiles,
plain tiles, scale-type
covering with underlay

Corrugated fibre-cement
sheets, profiled metal
sheets with underlay

Roofing membranes,
metal sheeting

90°   70°   45°–100%

25°–50%

11°

5°–8%

1°–2%

6

SLOPING ROOF

In addition to the distinction between ventilated and unventilated roofs, the different roof shapes can be categorised as either sloping or flat. The choice is not just a formal decision, but one that has to take the construction into account, since different materials are only suitable for certain inclinations. To provide an overview, different material groups are shown in ↘6 with the matching roof inclination. In any case, information on the respective materials should be obtained from their manufacturers. While roofing materials such as thatch, shingles, and clay or concrete tiles can only be laid on sloping roofs, covering layers such as roofing membranes and metal roofing materials can also be laid on flat roofs. The term 'covering layer' refers to a waterproof skin, while the elements broadly classed as scales, boards or sheets that are used on sloping roofs are laid such that precipitation water can drain off. Impermeability increases with the coverage density of the roofing materials. Roofing materials such as wooden shingles and plain tiles (sometimes referred to as single-layer covering) have a larger proportion of open joints compared to multi-layer cover-

ing and thus provide less protection. For this reason, any scale-type covering method on a roof with an inclination of less than 20° requires an additional underlay to provide sufficient protection against driving rain and water that may not be able to drain off the roof in winter. If such an underlay is provided, these materials can also be laid on roofs with inclines as low as approx. 11°. The shallower the pitch of the roof is, the higher the demands are regarding quality of the materials, the dimensional stability of the elements and the quality of execution. The thinner such roofing elements are, and the better they fit with their adjoining elements, the more suitable they are for shallower pitches. In the case of sheet and membrane layers, the quality of the joints is particularly important. However, even though flat roofs without any fall are feasible in theory, it is recommended that a slight fall of at least 2 %, preferably 5 %, be provided in order to prevent the formation of puddles and ponding and thereby avoid this additional potential cause of damage, particularly at the seams of sheets and membranes. It follows that the choice of roofing material also determines whether a sloping roof or a flat roof can be used.

MATERIAL, CONSTRUCTION, STYLE, ROOF SHAPE

The shapes of roofs are just as varied as the materials they are constructed from. The dome shape of the Inuit's igloo, the textile yurt of the Mongolian nomads, the ridge roof made of timber and tiles in Central Europe and the flat, adobe roof of the Pueblo Indians of North America all have this in common: they are built from the locally available materials and are suited to the climate of the region. In spite of all the differences, the constraints of geometry and construction have led to similar shapes over time. Scale-type roofing materials were placed on a sloping substructure so that any precipitation water could drain off as quickly as possible and in order to prevent the ingress of humidity and driven snow. While the Gothic style of northern Europe features steep roofs with an incline of over 60° owing to the severe climate, shallower roof pitches were sufficient in the Mediterranean area with its low rainfall. In regions with heavy snowfall, the hipped roof was developed to protect the gable ends of the buildings, such as the Black Forest farmhouses or the 'Haubarg' farmsteads near the North Sea. Other versions of pitched roof construction still in use today include the tent roof, single-pitch roof, mansard roof and valley roof. The French mansard roof and the Medieval valley roof in particular demonstrate how the shape of the roof is influenced by the use of the space below it, because both forms were created to provide more usable floor area within a certain volume.

These regional types of roof construction created characteristic town roofscapes, which are increasingly changing nowadays, owing to changes in construction technology. As a first consideration, the shape of the roof is determined by its pitch, which has to suit the chosen material. For example, materials such as straw and reed require a minimum pitch of about 45°, while roofing membranes provide adequate sealing at all pitches. While metal, as a very valuable material, was traditionally used for important buildings, such as churches, which required complex roof shapes, new pliable sheet materials today make it possible to create a nearly unlimited variety of roof shapes, since they can be used to seal many different shapes and geometric compositions. This apparent freedom requires careful design and execution, however, in particular in the case of complex configurations and with respect to the application of several roofing layers. In addition, the durability of the construction and the serviceability for the purpose of maintenance have to be taken into account.

The design freedom resulting from technical developments requires that special attention be paid to the design of the roof shape. The expression of a building is dominated by the shape of the roof. The original form of a dwelling is still considered by many to be the rectangular building with a pitched roof. This is supported by various cultural traditions in different regions. However, both with the sloping roof and the flat roof it is possible to identify similar, formal effects. While a roof with a large overhang ⟍ 4 protects the building fabric beneath it, and hence the roof becomes the primary expression of the overall composition rather than being just an added element, a roof without any overhang ⟍ 5 has the effect of highlighting the sculptural appearance of the building volume. This building will appear more compact and closed, even though – as shown in the picture – it has a fully transparent ground floor. The different appearances illustrated by these examples can be used deliberately to achieve different design effects, particularly since the technical possibilities are now available and restrictions regarding materials no longer apply. Historically, these two types of design have evolved in response to the respective weather conditions. The roof with a large overhang can be found in many areas with heavy rainfall – in the jungle as well as in the mountains; the purpose of the overhang is to provide some space close to the house that is protected from the rain.

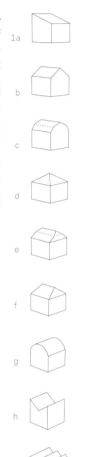

1 Principal roof shapes
a Monopitch roof
b Ridge roof
c Mansard roof
d Pyramid roof (tent roof)
e Half-hipped roof
f Hipped roof
g Barrel roof
h Valley roof (butterfly roof)
i Shed roof

2 New community centre, Ginsheim-Gustavsburg, 2010, Hille Architects: The envelope and roof of the building consist of one material and do away with the effect of separate building components.

3 Art Museum, Ahrenshoop, 2013, Staab Architects: The traditional form of the thatched roof is replicated with a new material, and there is no longer a distinction in the envelope between the roof and the wall material.

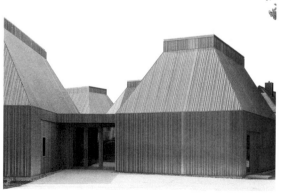

The compact gable roof, in which the roof is set between the two gable ends, can often be found in windy areas such as the coasts of Ireland and France, since this geometry helps to resist the strong wind forces and horizontal driving rain. On the other hand, the additive principle used by Mies van der Rohe in his exhibition pavilion ➔ 6 leads to an artistically emphasised form that creates appealing and differentiated rooms and assigns a protective and connecting effect to the flat roof too. The compact shape in ➔ 7 on the other hand reduces the spatial diversity, creating a precise geometrical figure. In addition to these geometric effects, the building in ➔ 3 illustrates how a historical roof shape, such as the thatched roofs found near the Baltic Sea, can lead to an independent design effect when used in combination with new materials. The fusion of roof and wall shown in ➔ 2 leads to a unique roof shape that nevertheless reflects the existing roofs in the neighbourhood. Material and construction as well as the form and use therefore determine the shape of the roof and imply a strong potential for visual expression.

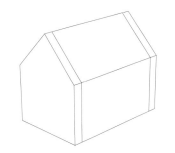

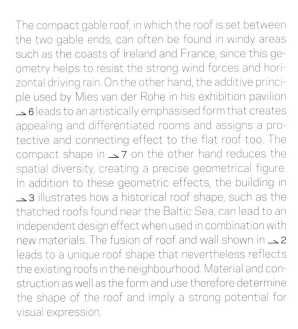

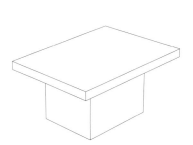

4 House in Balsthal, 2014, Pascal Flammer: The ridge roof with large overhangs and gable projections emphasises the protective and sheltering function of the house.

5 Summer house, Lagnö, 2012, Tham & Videgård Architects: The angular form of the roof generates an enclosed, severe image.

6 Barcelona Pavilion, 1929, Ludwig Mies van der Rohe: The building components are put together as open areas; the function is embedded in the sculpture, the building appears open, the spaces flow into each other.

7 Seepark building, Zülpich, 2014, Wollenweber Architects: The building is reduced to the basic shape of a cube. It creates an undifferentiated, enclosed shape.

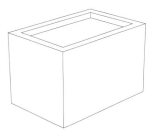

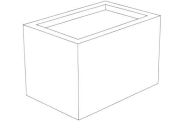

PITCHED ROOFS

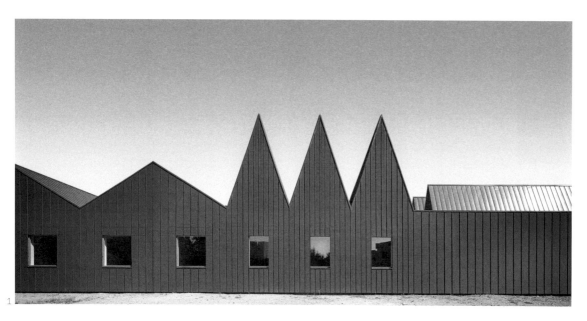

Roofs with different pitches come in many different design variations, but they nevertheless share some clear basic principles with respect to their structural system, such as with the rafter roof and the purlin roof. The sides of these roofs are dealt with as planar structures that transfer their loads in one direction, in the plane. More complex spatial designs in which the loads are transferred in several axes are referred to as shell structures. These structures are supported either linearly (walls, beams) or at points (columns).

The load to be transferred by the roof (covering material, snow, wind etc.) acts vertically on the respective support elements referred to as rafters. The rafters rest on the longitudinal walls of the building, usually placed in parallel to each other. Traditionally the rafter feet are attached to plates, horizontal timber sections that facilitate the fixing and connection of the rafters to the loadbearing structure. These plates may also be referred to as purlins. At the head of the rafters there may be a ridge purlin, and at the feet, an eaves purlin or plate. The required span of a roof is determined by the functions to be accommodated in the building; the possible span results from the construction height, the building material and the structural principle, as well as from the loads acting on the roof.

The external shape and the interior space of the pitched roof are usually directly determined by the structure. For example, external walls supporting a roof make unobstructed interior spaces possible. Roof constructions with wide cantilevers make independent facade constructions possible when the loads are transferred via additional loadbearing structures on the inside. Where the roof structure reaches down to the ground, the roof shape alone determines the building. All roofs require detailing of the edges, such as the ridge, eaves and verges to deal with the functional aspect of water drainage; however, these elements have also acquired a formal aesthetic aspect in many cases.

Sloping roofs do not require a specific material; they are frequently built in timber, but reinforced concrete and metal are also used. In simple timber structures – also referred to as 'carpenter-built constructions' as opposed to 'engineered timber constructions' – the span of the rafters usually does not exceed approx. 5 m and rafters are spaced at approx. 0.8 m centres. Construction timbers are joined by a variety of methods to form lattice trusses or girders as well as nailed roof trusses or solid web girders. Timber sections can be assembled with rigid joint connections to produce frames, which in turn can be connected via movable joints. Although frames largely resist deformation, they are subject to significant stresses in the rigid nodes. For this reason the corners of frames require larger cross-sections, for example for the insertion of metal connectors in glued laminated timber, for additional reinforcement in reinforced concrete, or for large gussets with screwed connections in metal construction. Frames also require greater strength of the concrete or metal material. Truss and frame constructions can be adapted to the respective load case. They have a linear loadbearing effect and geometry, and thereby subdivide the loft space into various sections, both formally and as part of the construction. The timber, reinforced concrete or metal profile sections, together with frames and trusses, form flat structures for larger loads or wider

1 Young Disabled Modules and Workshop Pavilions, Zaragoza, 2011, José Javier Gallardo: The expressive and significant shape of the building is determined by the roofs with their different pitches and widths.

2 Principal elements of a sloping
roof
a Rafter
b Tie member (doubled up)
c Ridge
d Ridge board as construction aid
e Eaves purlin or plate
f Battens, counter-battens
g Close-boarding
h Thermal insulation
i Covering layers
j Eaves
k Dormer window
l Valley
m Wind brace (for longitudinal
bracing)

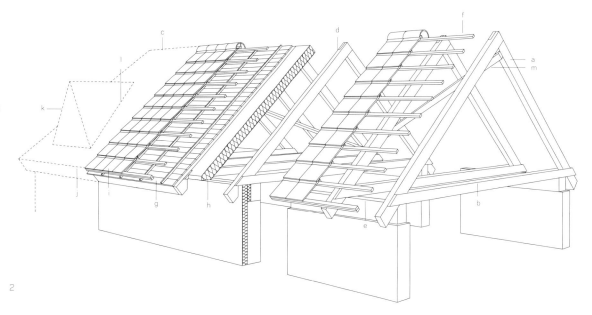

2

spans which, in the context of the completed roof, form a rigid structure. ➔ p. 118, Other Structures
In addition to the function of protection from precipitation and the weather generally, which is the original function of sloping roofs, it is also necessary to take sound insulation and fire safety into account. Roofing materials are classified either as soft materials (building material class B) made of combustible material such as reed, straw, wood shingles and some bitumen and polymer bitumen membranes, or as non-combustible building materials (building material class A) which are hard and are resistant to spread of flame, flying sparks and radiant heat. When developing the design of a roof, it is advisable to aim for simple jointing methods and forms. The simpler the shape of the roof, the less risk there is of defects occurring during execution. Since the roofing of complex dormer windows, valleys and ridges involves an increased risk of faulty execution with all types of roofing material, it is advisable to design with foresight and to apply great care.
The overall shape can also help to minimise risks in sloping roofs; the steeper the pitch, the faster the precipitation water can run off. Depending on the roof pitch, only certain roofing materials can be used. ➔ p. 109 However,

this rule of the roof pitch can be modified if an additional underlay is used, which must be appropriately waterproof. Such an underlay may consist of a layer of close-boarding attached directly to the rafters and lined with a waterproof roofing membrane. Likewise, in areas with heavy snowfall, it is common to construct an additional layer beneath as a safety measure in order to reduce the risk of ingress of drift snow. Depending on the region, it may also be sufficient to install an underslating membrane that is vapour-permeable and tear-resistant, and provides a run-off layer for the water. This membrane is usually attached directly to the rafters and fixed using counter-battens; during the shell construction stage, it is a useful way of providing weather protection. Above this layer is the ventilation plane and below, that of the thermal insulation.
Usually, the rigidity of sloping roofs across the building is achieved directly via the rafters. In the longitudinal direction, rafter roofs and suchlike are stiffened with wind braces in the form of diagonally fixed boards or steel straps. It is important that these braces are not attached in the area of roof skylights or dormer windows, as they would cause an obstruction. If necessary they have to be subdivided, and fixing is directly to the rafters.

RAFTER ROOF

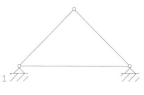

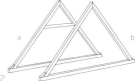

RAFTER ROOF

Simple sloping roof constructions consist of rafters leaning against each other in linear fashion (ridge roof) or rafters coming together at a point (tent roof). A rafter roof must be symmetrical and must have a clear, simple shape. A pair of rafters with a tie member form a stable triangle of forces, consisting of two compression members (rafters) and one horizontal tensile member (e.g. tie beam, ceiling joists, a ceiling slab with bearing upstand, or alternatively, walls as counter-bearing) that form a triangular frame. ⬎1 At the feet of the rafters, the loads are divided into vertical and horizontal forces. This type of roof requires a minimum pitch, otherwise the horizontal component of the rafters' loads will be too great. The roof incline should preferably be more than 30°. Rafter roofs are considered to be commercially viable for inclines of down to 20° and widths of approx. 8 m; beyond that, it is necessary to apply more complex detailing to absorb the compression forces.

The rafter roof is an early form of roof construction, which was superseded by the purlin roof owing to the latter's simpler construction. After the Second World War, rafter roofs again became the standard in Germany, initially as emergency roofing with layers of boarding, because they needed less material to build, and later in general housing construction, owing to improved connectors and cal-

culation methods. The advantages of the rafter roof are that it covers the loft without intermediate supports and that it uses less timber than a purlin roof. The geometry of the construction requires that timbers be cut and fixed very carefully, necessitating additional work. Also, trimming a rafter, for example in order to insert a dormer window, is more involved than with a purlin roof since it is always necessary to interrupt the force triangle and provide another means of counteracting the force exerted from the opposite rafter. Likewise, the transfer of tensile forces at the rafter feet requires more involved detailing. If the horizontal forces are absorbed by a timber joist ceiling, the rafters are usually attached to a purlin or plate that rests on the ceiling joists. ⬎3 In the case of a reinforced concrete ceiling, which is the common solution today, the tensile forces are absorbed by the reinforcement. Here too, the rafters are attached to a purlin or plate, or are attached directly to the concrete using special metal connectors and rafter feet anchors, together with an upstand formed in concrete.

In historical constructions, the foot of each rafter is attached to the tie member at a short distance from that member's end so as to help transfer the tensile forces, with an additional short rafter piece (firring) with a somewhat shallower pitch dowelled to it to cover the remaining length of the tie member. Today, however, the connection

1 Structural system
Rafter roof: triangular system with tie member (e.g. timber joist ceiling or reinforced concrete ceiling)

2 Isometric
a Collar tie roof with firring
b Rafter roof with firring

3 Rafter roof connection details
(from top to bottom)
Ridge, rafter collar tie (collar tie
roof), rafter feet

a Rafter
b Lap joint
c Collar tie
d Ridge board
e Plate (rigid collar tie roof)
f Tie beam
g Plate
h Firring

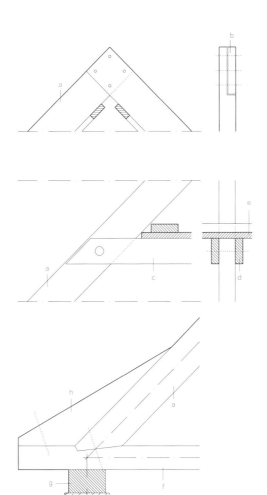

is made one-on-one using steel connectors. The traditional joints used for the ridge (scarf or lap joints) have
likewise been superseded by nailed boards, construction
plywood, or metal connectors. In order to make the construction process easier, it is common to use a ridge
board, which is similar to a ridge purlin, although it does
not have any structural function.

The commercially viable span of a rafter roof can be increased by using collar beams to support the continuous, symmetrical rafter pairs as compression members.
↘ 2 When they are fitted in the right place, the collar
beams can also function as ceiling joists for a habitable
space in the loft or, at least, for a cockloft. If the collar
beams are constructed as a ceiling, and hence as a rigid
plate, this additionally counteracts the effect of asymmetrical loading, e.g. when wind suction on one side
coincides with wind pressure on the other.

While a rafter roof is sufficiently braced by the triangular
arrangement of the construction members, additional
measures to give it sufficient stiffness in the plane of the
roof surfaces are required. A simple solution is to fix roofing battens diagonally to act as wind braces. Alternatives
to these are steel straps, or close-boarding over the
entire roof area. If it is intended to insert roof windows or
dormer windows, care must be taken to arrange the bracing elements such that they do not interfere with these
openings.

4 Community and Cultural Centre,
Altötting, 2012, Florian Nagler
Architects: The succinct ridge roof
shape is created by lattice trusses
that are combined to form a space
frame. This ↘ p. 118 spans the
space beneath without the need
for columns and accommodates
the services installations; it creates
a most impressive hall. In historical
buildings, one can also find roofs
with large spans, for example in
churches, which were frequently
mastered with complex hybrid constructions, because the roof structure was devised from experience
rather than from the purely structural principles that were developed
later in rafter and purlin roofs.

PURLIN ROOF

A sloping roof with rafters attached to – and supported by – horizontal beams called purlins is called a purlin roof; in this case, the loads acting on the rafters are transferred vertically to the purlins. Where the rafters are only supported by a purlin at either end, the foot purlin is supported by the external flank wall and the ridge purlin rests on the gable walls or on specific loadbearing structures. In view of the fact that the foot purlin in purlin roofs does not have to absorb any horizontal load, the detailing of the joint between the rafter feet and this purlin can be simpler. In addition, it is easier to make larger openings and insert dormer windows, since trimming the rafters only affects one side of the roof, and the load from the trimmed rafter can be transferred directly to the adjacent rafters via the trimmer beam. Furthermore, it is possible to create sizeable roof projections by cantilevering the purlins beyond the gable walls. Owing to the simple additive assembly of their components, purlin roof structures can be used to cover larger spans than rafter roofs. Over time, three main principles have developed, which in turn have developed further into different variants. In all systems, the rafters are usually spaced at approx. 0.8 m centres and a commercially viable span between the bearing points – both of purlins and uprights – is between approx. 4.5 m and 5.0 m in the case of carpentry-built timber constructions. In addition to the frequently used queen post truss, there is the king post truss and the modified queen post truss (in America also known by the German term as *liegender stuhl*).

QUEEN POST TRUSS
In a simple queen post truss roof, with ridge purlin and foot plate, the rafters are single span beams supported at the ridge and feet; in more complex versions (with foot plates and middle purlins) the rafters cantilever upwards beyond the middle purlin and, where there are three supports (foot plate, middle and ridge purlin) the rafters act as continuous beams. ↘ 2 a-c In contrast to the rafter roof, the rafters meeting at the ridge in the purlin roof do not impose any load on the opposite rafter. Purlins can be extended in the longitudinal direction (single-span beam, Gerber's beam). Longitudinal bracing is achieved using short diagonal members (braces, ties) beneath the purlins or by anchoring the structure in the masonry. Cross-bracing is provided by double ties between pairs of rafters (at right angles to and beneath the purlins). Both the roof plane and double tie plane are braced as in the rafter roof. With a queen post truss it is possible to construct roofs of any pitch, asymmetrically and in complex shapes. Owing to today's improved connecting fasteners, purlin roofs are now usually braced without timber struts. This system makes use of the rafters above the vertical supports (posts), together with which they form

a cohesive structural element. The connection can be made with nail plates or timber gussets, which then carry on to the next structural element, sometimes in the form of a double member, thus creating a stable and simple base structure for the roof. In this case, the loft can also be used as habitable space. The supports (posts) of the roof should preferably be placed above internal walls below, so that no additional load has to be transferred to the floor construction. However, small deviations from the vertical alignment can be accommodated. The supports (posts) transfer only vertical loads, since all horizontal loads are transferred via the rafter feet.

MODIFIED QUEEN POST TRUSS
In this modification of the queen post truss system, the vertical posts are modified into diagonal struts resting on the perimeter walls and thereby freeing up the space that before was obstructed by the queen posts. Cross-bracing is normally achieved via the struts and tie beams, similar to the tie members, which create a framing effect in the system. However, the diagonal struts transfer some horizontal forces at their bearing point, which can be counteracted by the joists of the ceiling construction or tie beams at the same level. The diagram in ↘ 2 e is a good illustration of the additional space created by this construction. In order to achieve sufficient bracing also in the case of one-sided wind load, the diagonal struts are connected to the rafters using metal plates or double timber plates. Today, the empirically developed modified queen post truss has been mostly replaced by timber frame constructions based on exact engineering calculations.

KING POST TRUSS
In order to achieve even larger spans, roof structures in historic buildings combined the collar tie roof system with that of a purlin roof. In this system, long tie beams have

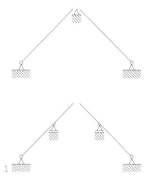

1   Structural system
Purlin roof

2   Schematic cross-section of different roof constructions
a   Basic queen post truss
b   Queen post truss (with double support)
c   Queen post truss (with triple support)
d   Basic modified queen post truss (purlin construction)
e   Modified queen post truss (with double support)
f   Basic king post truss (purlin construction)
g   King post truss (with double support)

3   Isometric of purlin roof
a   Basic queen post truss
b   Modified queen post truss (with double support)
c   King post truss (with double support)

4   Purlin roof; connection points
Ridge, rafter / purlin, foot point (from top to bottom)
a   Rafter
b   Ridge purlin
c   Rafter peg
d   Middle purlin
e   Post
f   Eaves purlin or plate
g   Rafter anchor
h   Fastening

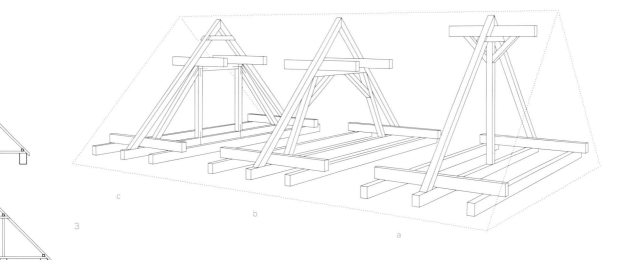

3

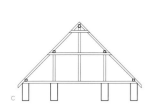

2a

b

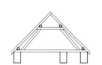

c

d

e

f

g

a central support not from below, but in the form of a tensile member 'hanging' from the ridge, with the load being transferred via the rafters or diagonal struts. In contrast to the queen post truss, where a support is needed beneath the two queen posts, no additional support is needed beneath the king post since this is suspended from the ridge. The horizontal tie beam with its central suspended support absorbs any horizontal or asymmetrical loads, which means that the latter must be designed not only for tensile, but also for compressive stresses.

MODIFIED KING POST TRUSS
The king post truss can be modified in that the diagonal struts (also called principal rafters) are connected to the upright post not with a tensile connection, but with a pivot pin, thus securing the position of the post and holding the tie beam. In the case of a symmetrical load resulting from snow and the construction's own weight, the pivot pin remains vertically above the tie beam and the forces are transferred via the rafters and bracing members. The pivot pin only transfers compressive forces and is only needed when asymmetrical loads occur, for example from wind; in that case the post makes a tight connection with the tie beam and the resulting load is transferred to the construction beneath through deflection of the strut.
This type of construction is no longer in use today, since the pivoting function of the pin cannot be reliably proven by calculation. Nevertheless, the existing examples of this construction have stood the test of time. In all roof constructions, it is possible to increase the loft space by moving any vertical structural members sideways to create what are known as jamb walls, and supporting the rafters with a purlin supported by these.

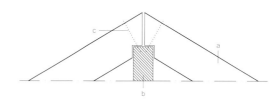

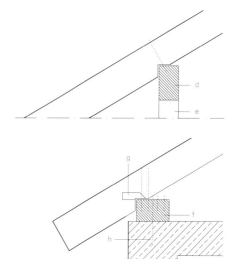

4

OTHER STRUCTURES

In addition to traditional standard roof construction systems, a range of structural systems has been developed to cover buildings with requirements for wide spans, such as theatres, stadiums, exhibition halls, industrial premises, as well as tunnels and airports; some of these systems are presented here. Each of these systems has its specific impact on the building envelope.

SPACE-FRAME STRUCTURES
Frames or lattices can be combined to create complex, planar or curved structures with wide spans. In such systems, the forces are not only transferred linearly via triangulation, but rather spatially in the form of pyramidal or cubic structural units.

SPATIAL SHELL STRUCTURES
Concrete or steel sheet shells, domes, or barrels are three-dimensional structural systems which transfer forces in the geometric form dictated by the respective system. At inclines greater than approx. 35°, in-situ concrete plates or shells require special formwork in order to achieve the required shape during the construction process. Folded-plate roofs consist of plates or shells joined linearly or prismatically to create a three-dimensional structure. This makes it possible to achieve larger spans owing to the increased edge stiffness and construction height. Plates and shells tend towards lateral deformation (spatial deformation, distortion). Only minor forces (primarily linear) can be transferred to the shell or plate. Openings can only be inserted where the geometry allows, otherwise they have to be small and follow the shape of the respective element (load diversion). The forces in simple, regular surfaces (rotation, hyperboloid and paraboloid surfaces) can be calculated and therefore allow the insertion of integrated elements (such as windows).

CABLE AND MEMBRANE STRUCTURES
Tensile cables or single/multiple-layer membranes can be used to produce very lightweight shell structures with wide spans, such as solar sails, building roofs or large tent structures. To make this type of construction stable, low and high points are required. The high points are achieved by the insertion of compressive struts. In order to reduce the risk of buckling, these may be in the form of framed or inverted bowstring supports, which have to be formally integrated into the overall design. Lightweight structures are at risk from vibration and wind suction, which means that the pre-tensile and bearing forces are considerable, and high-strength material is required. Cables and membranes are subject to stretching during installation. Many points of penetration (supports, cables) and the low points and valleys that are a necessary part of the con-

struction have to be taken into account. Regular surfaces are easier to calculate and predict than any free shapes or special constructions. The transfer of forces and geometry of openings are determined as for all shell structures. The shape is a direct result of the geometry of the structure.

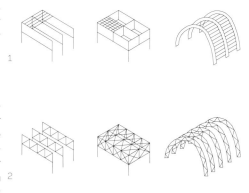

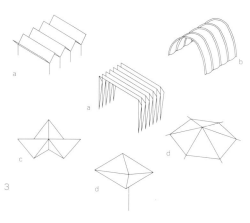

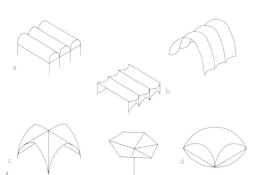

Structural systems:

1 Girder

2 Lattice girders

3 Folded plate structures
a Linear folded structures
b With curvatures
c Penetrations
d Prismatic folded structures

4 Shells
a One-directional curvatures
b Two-directional curvatures
c Penetrations
d Curvatures in the same and opposing direction

RIDGE, VERGE, EAVES

5 Roof edge details

All roofs – which could be considered a continuation of the walls – have a geometric high point referred to as the ridge. They also have eaves, which is the point of transition from the roof to the longitudinal wall, and verges. The latter is the name given to the junction of the roof with the gable wall. These three junction points contribute to the appearance of the roof. ➔ p. 110 For this reason, we are showing here standard details for a ridge, eaves and verges of a standard tiled roof. When producing detailed drawings for a building, appropriate details should be agreed with the manufacturers of the roofing materials and sealing membranes.

a Ridge
b Verge
c Eaves

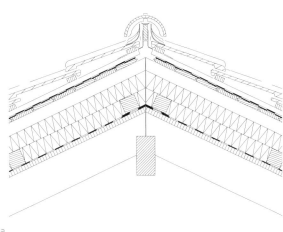

5a

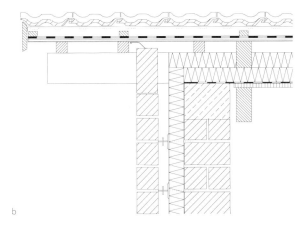

b

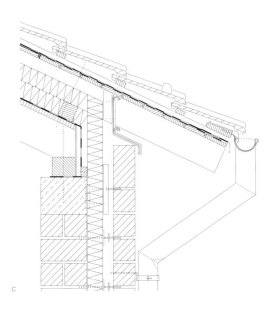

c

The upper horizontal part of a roof – the ridge – is particularly exposed to the weather and therefore has to be carefully designed and attached. It frequently ventilates the roof space and significantly impacts on the appearance of the building. Its free ventilation cross-section must be at least 2 cm high and the total ventilation area must be at least 0.5 % of the associated roof area and 200 cm² per linear metre of the roof length. This is only possible when using a dry-installed ridge, as is common practice today; in this system the ridge tile is fastened with special brackets, and the ventilation opening is made using special ventilation strips attached to a timber profile on top of the rafter ridge point. At the ends of the ridges, perforated end caps or special elements are fitted. Ridge tiles fitted in the traditional way – embedded in mortar –are only used nowadays for historic buildings, or in roofs where the roof space is not heated and is therefore not thermally insulated. In these cases, the roof space is ventilated via ventilation tiles.

The roof structure is frequently used to provide bracing to the gable wall, unless this is already sufficiently braced by interior walls. The gable wall can be connected to the rafters and the roof structure ➔ 5b via a ring beam or metal straps attached to the purlins. It is also possible for wind suction forces to act on roof tiles and dislodge them. For this reason, depending on the regional wind forces and the material used, the last courses of roof tiles have to be attached with brackets or nails, unless the gable wall extends above the roof level. At the end of the battens, a barge board is fitted to exclude wind suction and close off the space. Frequently, the overhanging part of the rafters is covered with close-boarding. Owing to their specific construction method, rafter roofs can only have a small roof overhang.

The eaves of the roof can be detailed with visible rafter heads or be boxed-in with boarding. In traditional constructions, the heads of rafters were frequently protected by embellished boards that protected the end grain. The air needed for ventilating the roof enters via the eaves. The ventilation openings must be protected against insects with a ventilation grille. Likewise, the space between the rafters must be closed off. This can be done by extending the wall beneath upwards, or as shown in the example, by forming a dummy joint with a folded metal sheet which is also used as a ventilation grille. The area is protected from the rain by the projection of the roof. The lower tile course requires a double-thickness batten or a gutter board so that it has the same pitch as the other tile courses. This gutter board is also used to hold the gutter and to attach the eaves flashing.

ROOFING METHODS

REED/STRAW Roofs thatched with reed or straw present a considerable fire hazard as they can catch fire from flying sparks. They are therefore subject to minimum distances between buildings under building regulations. The minimum pitch of thatched roofs is 45°. Depending on the covering material and the region, different thatching methods are used. The thatch can be attached using a variety of methods, one of them being with twisted hazel sticks called spars. The material has good thermal insulation properties and, provided it is well maintained, is long-lasting. The weak point of a thatched roof is the ridge area, as this is the point where the reed bundles (also called yelms) meet, and the risk of damage is considerable. Owing to the brittleness of the material, it is not possible to bend the thatch so that it crosses the ridge with part of the length being on either side of the roof. The ridge is often covered with a different material such as sedge or heather. This is then held down by crossed hazel twigs that reach across the ridge. Another fastening method uses twisted straw ropes.

TIMBER Timber has a long tradition as a roofing material and is used in the form of shingles. These are usually made of indigenous timber, for example spruce, pine, larch, or oak in the Alps and from cedar in North America. A distinction is made between sawn shingles and split shingles (also known as shakes). Whereas the surface of the wood is opened up during sawing, making the material more susceptible to water, the fibres of split shingles remain intact. A roof covered with shingles should be watertight from an angle of 22° thanks to the overlap of the shingles. There are different methods of laying shingles, which are available in many different forms. The thicker type of shingle has a thickness of 15 mm and is up to 350 mm wide and up to 1200 mm long. Thinner shingles may be as thin as 7 mm, up to 350 mm wide and up to 800 mm long and are laid either on battens or on close-boarding. The nail holes are pre-drilled. Shingles can be re-laid with the bottom end up so as to double the service life of the roof.

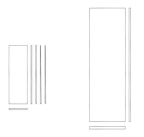

CLAY AND CONCRETE ROOFING TILES Clay is put through a firing process to manufacture tiles; these are impervious to water and are resistant to frost, chemicals and UV radiation. There is a wide range of different tiles, with regions having developed their specific shapes, formats and colouring. A distinction is made by the method of manufacture: extruded tiles (pantiles, flat tiles, plain tiles etc.) and pressed roof tiles (flap tiles, interlocking tiles and pantiles. The traditional method of laying plain tiles with a large overlap embedded in mortar has been largely replaced by interlocking tiles which provide better impermeability and allow a shallower roof pitch (as low as 10° with an appropriate construction and underlay). Further advantages of tiles are their fire-resistance and the small format, which is advantageous during installation. Roofing tiles made of concrete essentially function in the same way as those made of clay.

NATURAL STONE AND SLATE Natural stone is a traditional roofing material and is typical of certain regions. Depending on the available resources, slate, limestone, or sandstone is cut, split, or sawn to form flat rectangular elements. Natural stone is an expensive, but very durable roofing material. Slates are supplied in several shapes, including rectangular, scale-shaped, diamond and bow-shaped. Specifications for laying slate roofs can be found in EN 12326 and specialist trade instruction manuals. Different patterns result depending on the shape of the slate and the laying method, for example the Old German pattern or patterns using different sizes of rectangular slate. As a rule, slates are fastened with special rust-proof nails, pins, or hooks. The roof surfaces must have an adequate pitch, the minimum being 22°. Battens must be dimensioned according to the weight and thickness of slates and natural stone slabs.

METAL Metal roofing consists of plain or pre-profiled metal sheets installed perpendicular to the eaves. Materials in common use today include zinc, copper and aluminium. Because the material is completely impermeable, it is preferable to opt for a construction with back-ventilation. It is important to ensure that the metal layer is flexible enough to allow for expansion and contraction due to changes in temperature. The material has high thermal conductivity, is electrolytically conductive and is classified as non-combustible. The minimum pitch of metal roofs is 3°. The substructure needs to be close-boarded, either in the form of boards or wooden panels. Different forms of seams are used to connect the long side of the metal sheets, such as single or double standing seams, angle standing seams and batten seams. Batten seams have an advantage compared to standing seams because they allow the sheets to move independently, being separated by the battens.

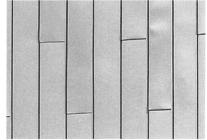

FLAT ROOF

The flatter a roof is, the more impermeable the roofing material must be. Membranes are typical of flat roofs, whereas various kinds of roofing material can be used on sloping roofs. The installation of roofing membranes is subject to complex regulations, which must be carefully observed for each of the different membrane types. Standard industry practice is incorporated in the directives on the installation of flat roofs, which must be applied in each individual case. Flat roof coverings must be impervious to water, including flashing, penetration and jointing details. In order to avoid ponding and the permanent exposure of seams to water, flat roofs are built with a slight fall. According to the flat roof directives, the minimum fall has to be 2 % or approx. 1.1°, although approx. 5 % is preferable. If the fall is generated by the structure of the roof, the need for additional sloping elements can be avoided. The fall is usually created either by designing the structure with a slope, by installing sloping insulation material, or by laying a sloping screed. The overall appearance is determined by the loadbearing structure, which must be suitable for the different loads as well as for maintenance purposes. Loadbearing and insulation layers must be even and resistant to compression; protective layers must be strong enough to withstand mechanical loads and safeguard the sealing function. Flat roofing layers with sufficient weight must be designed to resist wind suction and to provide fire protection (flying sparks), resistance to impact from the environment (ozone, UV radiation, mineral oil, solvents) and to reduce or prevent thermal impact on the roof structure and roof sealing. The top roofing skin is either bonded along linear seams or at certain points, or is mechanically fastened with rails or fixing plates, in order to counteract wind suction and movement, as well as to limit thermal expansion (folding of the material). Chemically incompatible layers require separating membranes (films); shear stresses on roof sealing layers require sliding layers (fleece, several layers of film, layers of gravel).

In order to be able to form a waterproof flat roof with upstands all round, the sealing membranes are installed at least 15 cm high at the surrounding walls, so as to reach above the level of splash water, snow and water ponding, with the top detail finished mechanically with a sealing strip. The water ponding level must be considered when inserting a door opening to the flat roof; however, the height of the threshold may be reduced in order to make access to the roof easier, as long as a roof overhang and a covered gutter (grating) can be provided. A flat roof with a surrounding upstand must have a drainage point at the lowest point of the fall (in the form of an outlet or a gully) and an emergency outlet. Melt water must be able to run off without re-freezing; for this reason, the gully must be exposed to sufficient solar radiation or be fitted with an adequate pipe heating system. As a rule, flat roofs are constructed nowadays as non-ventilated, insulated roofs ⌐2, the layers of which must take the planned future use into account. In contrast to flat roofs that are only walked on for maintenance purposes, flat roofs subject to regular use must have a layer of insulation that resists compression and, in the case of parking decks, also a wear-resistant top layer above the sealing layer, which altogether results in complex, special constructions. Green roofs ⌐ p. 126 are designed to suit each particular situation. In addition to the standard construction for a ventilated roof ⌐1 – which is normally not regularly walked over – an additional solution has been developed in the form of the inverted roof. In this system, the sealing layer is applied directly to the structural layer, separated by a vapour pressure equalising layer, and the thermal insulation is installed as protection on top of the waterproof layer. This protective layer serves not only as insulation, but also has to be waterproof, rot-proof and UV-proof. Today, a wide variety of robust roof construction layers and roofing membranes is available. In addition to the tried-and-tested bituminous sealing layers, there are now plastic films and liquid plastic coatings for covering flat roofs reliably.

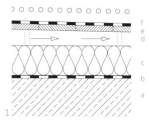

1

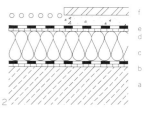

2

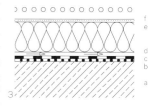

3

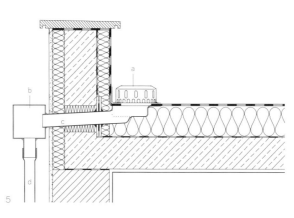

4

5

4 Two-part roof outlet for flat roof with vertical gully, inserted in a larger hole in order to allow for tolerances of the piping. Following installation the hole must be closed to provide adequate fire protection.
a Grid (for leaves)
b Connecting sleeve and sealing profile
c Gully insert
d Connecting sleeve and sealing profile
e Gully pot

5 Parapet drainage outlet with bonded flange to connect to the bitumen sealing membrane
a Parapet drainage outlet
b Collection pot
c Sliding flange
d Rainwater downpipe

1 Solid flat roof, ventilated
a Loadbearing layer
b Vapour pressure equalising layer
c Thermal insulation
d Air gap
e Timber boarding on substructure
f Sealing membrane

2 Solid flat roof, non-ventilated
a Loadbearing layer
b Priming coat, vapour pressure
equalising layer/emergency sealing
layer
c Thermal insulation laid to a fall
d Separating layer
e Double sealing membrane
f Imposed load

3 Inverted roof
a Loadbearing layer
b Vapour pressure equalising layer
c Sealing membrane
d Drainage layer
e Thermal insulation, resistant to
pressure and water
e Separating layer
f Imposed load

6 Illustration of roofing membrane
solutions as specified in the flat
roof directive
a Parapet sealing detail
b Sealing of vertical masonry, at
least 15 cm above the waterproof
layer
c Sealing of penetrations, up to
at least 15 cm height above the
waterproof layer
d Special construction, for example with gulley grating for barrier-
free roof access

7 Two contrasting design versions
of the detailing of the edge of a
ventilated flat roof

a Projecting roof with a narrow
folded metal edge profile
b Projecting roof with a large
upstand covered in boarding

For the following heights of building
(h), the external downstand of the
metal parapet coping sheet must
overlap the upper edge of the
render or any cladding as follows
h up to 8 m > 5 cm
h up to 20 m > 8 cm
h over 20 m > 10 cm

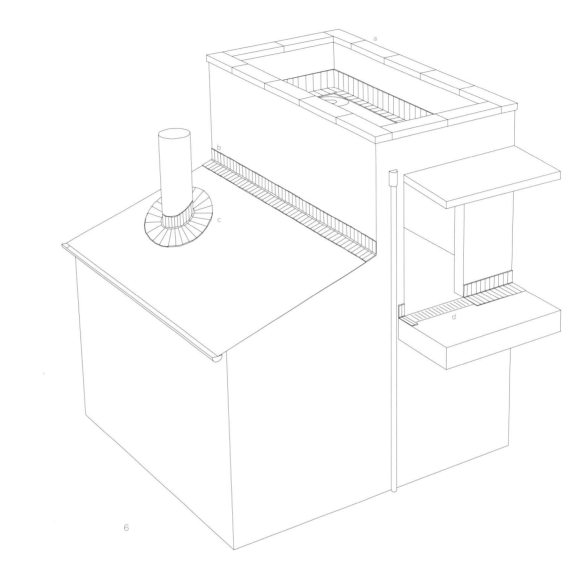

6

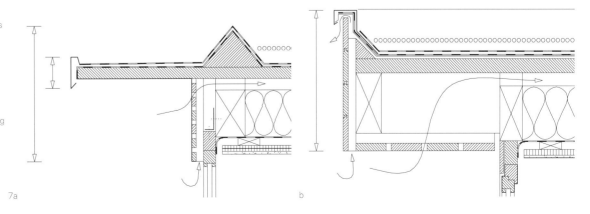

7a   b

ROOFING MEMBRANES

BITUMEN

Bitumen is a crude oil product and has a special characteristic: at approx. 130°C it becomes viscous, but returns to a solid state at lower temperatures. Owing to this special property it is possible to weld bitumen sheets together into a continuous layer using a heating process that leaves the junctions waterproof once the material has cooled down. Bitumen membranes are manufactured with a backing fleece consisting of plastic or glassfibre, the quality of which determines the sheet's resistance to expansion and tearing;

furthermore, it is possible to insert metal fabric into the backing material to suit certain functions, such as that of a vapour barrier or root protection membrane. By contrast, roof sealing membranes – also colloquially and misleadingly referred to as 'roofing felt' – are laid loose, then nail-fixed or bonded with hot bitumen. Nowadays these membranes consist of a bitumen-saturated base material and are frequently used as a separating layer or underlay. The membranes are supplied with various top finishes, such as sand, chippings etc.

VitraHaus, Weil am Rhein, 2010, Herzog & de Meuron

PLASTIC ROOFING MEMBRANES

Thermoplastic sealing membranes made of plastic are laid in a single layer and provide a waterproof roofing finish. The available materials include polyvinylchloride (PVC), ethylene copolymer bitumen (ECB), polyisobutylene (PIB), polyolefin alloys (TPO/FPO), ethylene vinyl acetate copolymer (VAE/EVA), chlorinated polyethylene (CPE). The minimum thickness of these plastic-based roofing membranes is 1.2 to 1.5 mm. Where the roof is used as a terrace or for a similar purpose,

the minimum thickness is generally 1.5 mm, preferably 2 mm. The thicker the membrane, the longer it will last. To achieve a waterproof finish it is essential to install the membranes correctly and to ensure a continuous join at the seam, which in the case of thermoplastics is made by welding with hot air. Several different materials are used as backing, the most common being glass-fibre or plastic fleeces, or mesh fabric. The edges and connections should be firmly attached.

Refurbishment of glass blowing workshop, Völklinger Hütte, Völklingen, 2009

ELASTOMER ROOFING MEMBRANES

Elastomer sheeting is a distinct type of sealing material that is also often referred to as caoutchouc sheeting, owing to the synthetically produced base material. Today, it is most common to use membranes consisting of ethylene propylene diene monomer (EPDM). In addition, there are membranes consisting of chlorosulfonated polyethylene (CSM), nitrile rubber (NBR) and butyl rubber (IIR). The sealing membranes are produced either with or without a carrier insert, and optionally with

a glass or polyester fleece lining on the underside. EPDM sealing membranes are not resistant to mineral oil, aliphatic and aromatic solvents and nitric acid. The membranes are installed either in a single layer or in multiple layers, using either a welded edge fixing or a melt layer. The membranes are subject to considerable thermal expansion and contraction and should therefore always be cut to allow an additional 1 % in length. The edges and connections should be firmly attached.

Stonehenge Visitor Center, 2014, Denton Corker Marshall

LIQUID SEALING

Liquid sealing compounds may be single or multiple-component materials and are applied on site in liquid form without seams; the finished sealing layer is the result of chemical reaction or of physical drying. It is also possible to insert reinforcement in the form of a fleece. The basis of this material is usually polyurethane or epoxy resin. Owing to the chemical reaction, the material cures to form a permanently elastic sealing layer without joints, which can adapt to complex

roof geometries. The sealing layer is attached to the substrate continuously over the entire surface, which means that water cannot run underneath the layer. Surfaces exposed to pedestrian or vehicular traffic must be covered with a protective layer. It is possible to apply pigment to the sealing layer, as well as a range of different surface finishes such as an anti-slip finish. The material is compatible with many other sealing materials and is therefore suitable for refurbishment work.

Extension of Städel Museum, Frankfurt am Main, 2012, Schneider + Schumacher

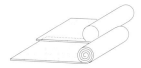

Bitumen membranes are installed in several layers with the seams overlapped. The membranes are fully bonded over the entire surface by heating the underside of the membrane. In addition, there is a cold-bonding, self-adhesive process. Where it is important not to damage insulation material that is sensitive to heat, both methods can be combined. This method of installation is not sensitive to heat but does require measures to safeguard against fire.

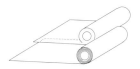

Plastic roofing membranes are laid out from rolls on top of a plastic fleece separating layer. They are then welded together and bonded to the substrate in strips or at points. Mechanical attachment is also possible using flat metal strips or holding plates. The membrane sheets are connected to each other using a hot air welding process to form a sealed waterproof layer. The installed membrane is permanently held in place by heavy material placed on top, such as gravel or concrete slabs.

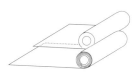

The membranes are fully bonded using a self-adhesive layer or specific system adhesives, such as polyurethane or hot bitumen (in the case of membranes compatible with bitumen). Mechanical fixing can be carried out using linear flat metal strips or holding plates. The membranes are secured against wind suction by placing heavy material on top, such as gravel, concrete slabs, or green roof systems.

Liquid sealing materials are applied in a three-stage process. The substrate must be appropriately prepared and the work has to be carried out during dry weather. The liquid polyester resin is applied using two thirds of the material; then, if required, the plastic fleece is inserted (without bubbles and creases) and then the remaining third of the material is rolled on until the fleece is saturated; if required, a final sealing coat may be applied.

GREEN ROOF

Planting greenery on roofs has become an established, ecological way of finishing a building envelope. While the rough climate in Northern Europe gave rise to effective roof planting – referred to as turf roofs – on simple traditional houses, today it is the high degree of urbanisation that drives the development of green roofs, as well as – increasingly so – of planted facades, which could be seen as a new interpretation of the original leaf thatch. The plants thus used measurably improve the micro-climate by increasing the relative humidity and cooling the environment, binding dust and noxious substances, emitting oxygen, providing an effective thermal insulation layer and storing rainwater. In addition, the planted areas can be used for a range of different activities, primarily on flat roofs in the inner city, such as sports and gardening. The special roof construction required and the resulting additional height must be taken into account during the design process. Distinctions are made between extensive and intensive planting, and between single-layer and multi-layer construction. The principles and technical details – whose execution requires careful professional supervision – are included in the roof planting directive

issued by the German Research Association for Landscaping and Gardening (FLL). The depth of construction required for extensive planting is less than that for intensive planting, which means that it can support only comparatively thin vegetation layers with a low water requirement. Typical plants are drought-resistant flowers, mosses, pre-cultivated types of plants, lichens and sedums, which are used on substrates that have been secured against wind suction by additional mesh inserts or by their own dry weight. Intensive roof planting may require different layers of humus soil, depending on the type of plant chosen. Turf, for example, normally requires about 20 to 30 cm, while shrubs need about 50 to 70 cm and trees 80 to 130 cm. The resulting high loads must be taken into account in the structural calculations for the building; in addition, the rather more involved maintenance has to be planned for, including the option of an automatic irrigation system. The sequence of layers follows the same basic principles in every case, be it an economical (but riskier) single-layer construction, or a complex multi-layer system.

1 Simple extensive roof planting as a single-layer
a Roof construction with sufficient loadbearing capacity, thermal insulation if required
b 0.5 to 1 cm roof sealing and root protection membrane to FLL guideline
c 0.5 to 1 cm separating layer, e.g. rubber granulate mats, also as storage layer
d 8 to 10 cm extensive layer substrate as vegetation support layer and to provide drainage
e Vegetation layer: planting with drought-resistant types of plant such as sedum seedlings, pre-cultivated herbaceous perennials and plant mats

2 Multi-layer extensive roof planting
a Roof construction, with thermal insulation if required
b 0.5 to 1 cm roof sealing and root protection membrane to FLL guideline
c 0.5 to 1 cm protection layer, e.g. fleece
d 2 to 6 cm drainage layer using bulk material, e.g. lava stone (bulk material drainage) or plastics (solid element drainage)
e 0.5 cm filter fleece
f 8 to 20 cm extensive layer substrate as vegetation support layer
g Vegetation layer consisting of drought-resistant types of plant, applied as seeds, sedum seedlings, pre-cultivated herbaceous perennials and plant mats

3 Multi-layer intensive roof planting
a Roof construction, with thermal insulation if required
b Roof sealing / root protection membrane
c 1 cm fleece or rubber granulate mat protection layer
d 6 to 12 cm drainage
e 0.5 cm filter fleece
f 20 to 120 cm intensive layer substrate as vegetation support layer
g Vegetation layer
Planting can be like that of a ground level garden using turf, herbaceous perennials, shrubs and trees.

The roof structures described here show examples of the different layers and construction heights used in extensive and intensive roof planting. All systems contain the following basic layers which, depending on the construction method, consist of different materials. Above the loadbearing structure / thermal insulation layer, a sealing and protection layer is provided to prevent root damage. This is topped by a separating and sliding layer to protect against mechanical damage, and a drainage layer for temporary water storage and the drainage of excess water to the drainage points. A filter layer prevents any fine particles from penetrating the drainage layer from the upper layers: the vegetation support layer and the vegetation layer. The planting chosen determines the thickness of the support layer.

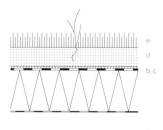

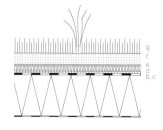

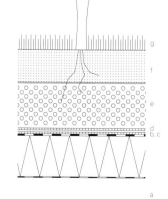

1

2

3

4   California Academy of Sciences, San Francisco, 2008, Renzo Piano Building Workshop: The museum roof becomes an additional open space in the inner city context

5   Edgeland House, Austin, 2012, Bercy Chen Studio: The building merges with the landscape owing to the extensively planted roof.

6   Standard details of extensive roof planting on a ridge roof, including the ridge detail, and on a mono-pitch roof, including ridge and eaves details

a   Vegetation layer
b   Vegetation support layer
c   Filter layer
d   Drainage layer
e   Separating layer
f   Root protection layer
g   Sealing layer
h   Thermal insulation layer
i   Loadbearing layer
j   Edge strip

Usually, green roofs have to include a 50 cm wide gravel strip at the edges, including those abutting any walls such as parapets; this is for fire safety reasons and to provide space for drainage outlets.

Flat roofs with a roof pitch of 1° to 5° are well suited to roof planting. In the case of roofs without any fall, it is important to consider the type of plant used, given that water may be ponding. Besides flat roofs, it is possible to apply roof planting on pitched roofs up to an incline of 45°; but with a roof pitch greater than about 20° it is necessary to install material with corrugation/ridges that prevent the sliding of vegetation support layers and help to control the water retention of the storage layers.

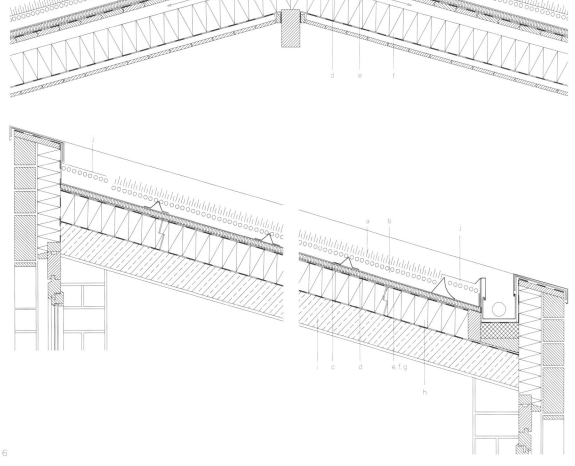

6

ENCLOSE | BUILD
EXAMPLES

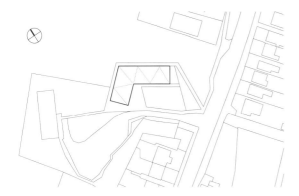

CHAPTER 5

ST. ANNE'S COMMUNITY CENTRE IN COLCHESTER,
GREAT BRITAIN
DSDHA, LONDON

The L-shaped community centre which, through its pro-portions and form, marks the transition between a small-scale residential development and heathland, provides a café as well as several rooms for public functions. In ad-dition, it has what is known as a 'Sure Start Centre', a government-funded facility for the provision of childcare, early education, health and family support.

The roof landscape is composed of eight triangles with opposing pitches and thereby cleverly mirrors the hilly topography of the area. It can be seen from afar from the roads and open areas, and makes the building into a lo-cal landmark. The outer skin features a uniform design for both the walls and the roof, without differentiation. It consists of timber slats and grey rendered areas.

The timber envelope has been designed as a back-ven-tilated construction in front of a diffusive facade mem-brane (wall) or above a sealing membrane (roof) which is the waterproof layer. The slatted facade consists of ther-mally modified timber, which has improved durability com-pared to untreated timber, owing to a combination of high-temperature drying and thermal treatment without the use of chemical wood preservatives. The primary con-struction consists of a timber stud wall, which in parts has been reinforced with steel sections and is lined with bitumen fibreboard made of wood fibres from waste material. The substrate for the render around the base of the building consists of WBP plywood sheets, which are coated and glued with phenolic resin and which are particularly suitable for damp environments. Special at-tention has been paid to the complicated joints of the outer cladding, which result from the complex building geometry. In order to create the acute mitre joints be-tween roof and wall which are integral to the design, the carpentry firm and the architects developed methods – using models up to a scale of 1:1 – that made a high-qual-ity and yet practical execution possible.

Location plan, 1:1000

South elevation
Layout of first floor
Layout of ground floor
Scale 1:500
a Café
b Community room
c Kitchen
d Storage
e WC
f Family room
g Day nursery
h Terrace
i Waiting area
j Medical area
k Office
l Staff room

Longitudinal section, 1:500

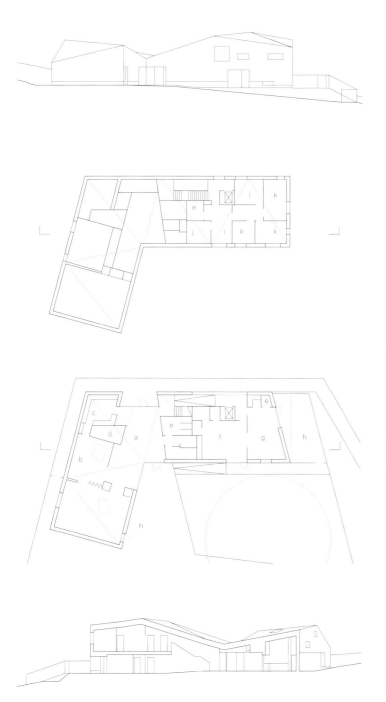

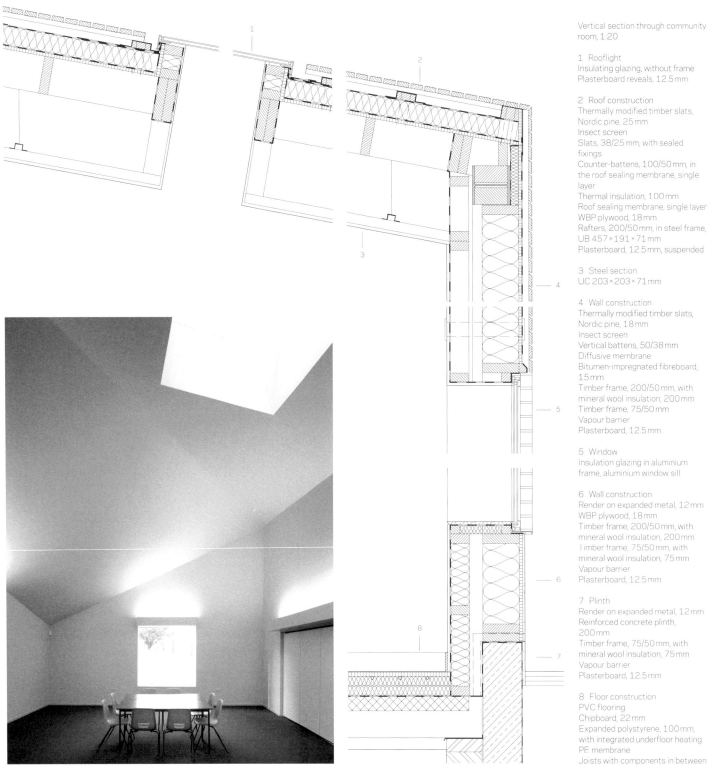

Vertical section through community room, 1:20

1 Rooflight
Insulating glazing, without frame
Plasterboard reveals, 12.5 mm

2 Roof construction
Thermally modified timber slats, Nordic pine, 25 mm
Insect screen
Slats, 38/25 mm, with sealed fixings
Counter-battens, 100/50 mm, in the roof sealing membrane, single layer
Thermal insulation, 100 mm
Roof sealing membrane, single layer
WBP plywood, 18 mm
Rafters, 200/50 mm, in steel frame, UB 457 × 191 × 71 mm
Plasterboard, 12.5 mm, suspended

3 Steel section
UC 203 × 203 × 71 mm

4 Wall construction
Thermally modified timber slats, Nordic pine, 18 mm
Insect screen
Vertical battens, 50/38 mm
Diffusive membrane
Bitumen-impregnated fibreboard, 15 mm
Timber frame, 200/50 mm, with mineral wool insulation, 200 mm
Timber frame, 75/50 mm
Vapour barrier
Plasterboard, 12.5 mm

5 Window
Insulation glazing in aluminium frame, aluminium window sill

6 Wall construction
Render on expanded metal, 12 mm
WBP plywood, 18 mm
Timber frame, 200/50 mm, with mineral wool insulation, 200 mm
Timber frame, 75/50 mm, with mineral wool insulation, 75 mm
Vapour barrier
Plasterboard, 12.5 mm

7 Plinth
Render on expanded metal, 12 mm
Reinforced concrete plinth, 200 mm
Timber frame, 75/50 mm, with mineral wool insulation, 75 mm
Vapour barrier
Plasterboard, 12.5 mm

8 Floor construction
PVC flooring
Chipboard, 22 mm
Expanded polystyrene, 100 mm, with integrated underfloor heating
PE membrane
Joists with components in between

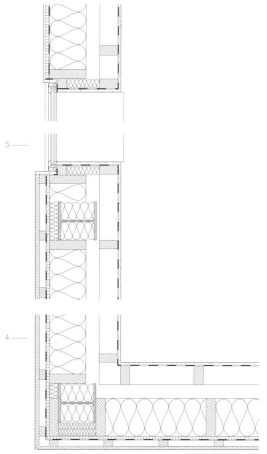

5 —

4 —

Horizontal section through
community room, 1:20

NORTH RHINE-WESTPHALIA STATE ARCHIVE
IN DUISBURG, GERMANY
ORTNER & ORTNER BAUKUNST, BERLIN

———————————

The clinker-brick grain store at the Duisburg river port dating from 1936, with its neatly built reinforced concrete frame, provided an ideal opportunity for a change-of-use conversion. The building, which was once used to store grain, now houses Europe's largest archive with approx. 148 km of shelving. A new archive tower rises 70 m in the centre of the former storage silo and is visible from beyond Duisburg's city boundaries. The openings and roof surfaces of the existing store were closed in order to protect the archive items from daylight and guarantee the necessary air-tightness, while ensuring a consistent room climate. The basic design element is a solid exterior brick skin, which lends a sculptural feeling to the archive tower. Functional components such as rainwater pipes and facade brackets have been kept unobtrusive. In this way, the structure and function of the historical building remains discernible.

The necessary thermal insulation has been applied to the inside in order to preserve the facade, which is under listed building protection. The existing brickwork consists of solid bricks with a historical format measuring 25×12×6.5 cm. The newly laid external brickwork was also manufactured in this format. The projections and recesses in the brickwork create a fine pattern with a textile effect. In their colouring and texture, the new bricks reflect the original surface of the existing ones, which have acquired a patina that bears witness to the industrial history of Duisburg. Nevertheless, the new brickwork remains distinct from that of the old grain store building in its colours and ornamentation.

Like a 'house within a house', the loadbearing structure of the new building is integrated into the existing substance which, following the conversion, transmits the horizontal loads and forms the building envelope in the lower part. The vertical structure of the largely enclosed reinforced concrete tower functions as a secondary support for the back-ventilated brick skin in the old format, while steel constructions on the inside are grouped like sleeves around the existing concrete columns in order to transmit the imposed loads from the archive into the ground, independent of the existing building.

Existing building prior to conversion

Section through archive tower, 1:1000

Elevation after conversion

Layout of ground floor,
Layout of 5th floor,
Layout of 18th floor,
1:1000

a   Repository
b   Library
c   Lecture hall
d   Reading room
e   Deliveries
f   Restoration workshop

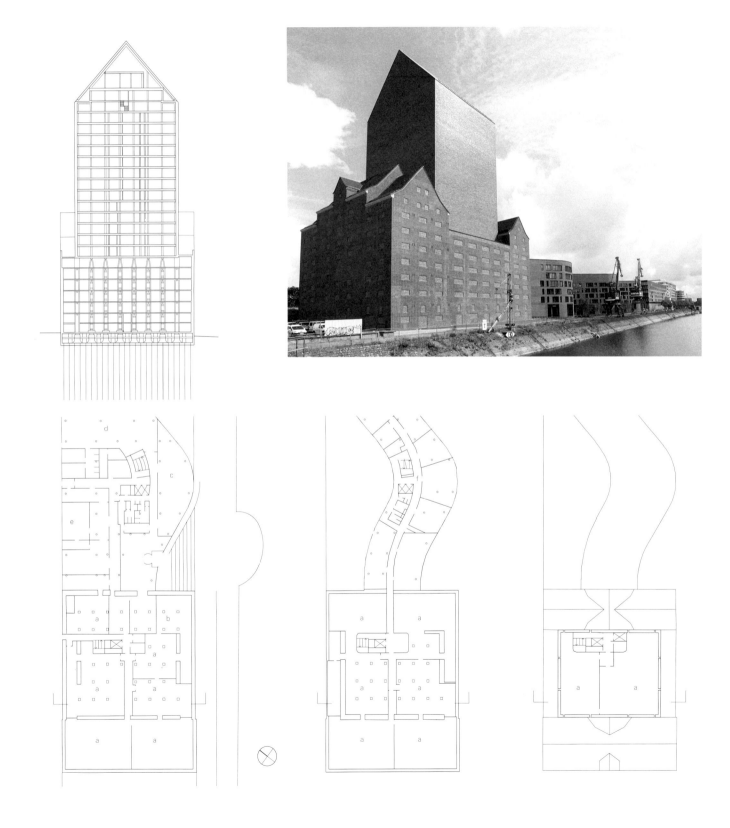

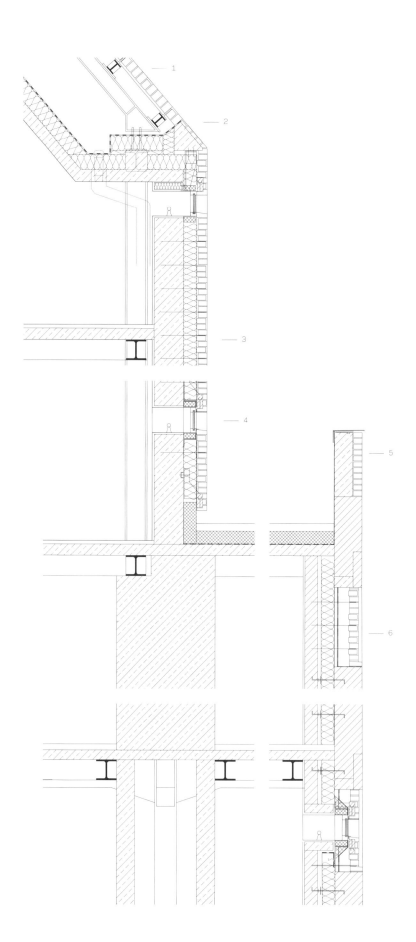

Vertical section through archive tower, 1:50

1   Roof construction – cold roof
Tower roof construction, slope 49°
Metal rail system
Brick piping threaded on aluminium core, retention
of the ornamental structure
Substructure, HEA 120
on main girder, IPE 600

2   Detail of tower roof eaves
Prefabricated concrete with clinker slips,
horizontal surfaces waterproofed in the factory
Fixing of prefabricated concrete component on
bracket
Three-layer sealing, diffusive, pressure-resistant
Insulation, 180 mm
Vapour check (emergency drainage - downstand
beam)

3   Detail of tower brick facade
Outer brick skin, 120 mm,
historical format, 250 × 120 × 65 mm
Air gap between brick skin and concrete wall,
200 mm,
part filled with insulation, 180 mm, with 20 mm
tolerance to the facing brick
Reinforced concrete, 400 mm
Internal plaster, 25 mm

4   Detail of tower window
Highly insulated aluminium window with highly
insulating triple-glazing with solar screening
Highly insulating sealed frame with airtight
and vapour-proof connection profiles
Lintel and parapet built as prefabricated concrete
component with clinker slips, parapet at least 2 %
fall, waterproofed horizontal surfaces with recesses
Fixed with brackets

5   Detail of wall upstand

Brick bond in the historical format of the building;
Concrete, 250 mm
Bitumen

6   Detail of existing external wall of archive
Existing brickwork approx. 380 mm,
historical format, 250 × 120 × 65 mm
Mineral insulation, 180 mm
Tolerance gap, 20 mm
Calcium silicate masonry, 175 mm
Tied using wall ties
Internal plaster, 25 mm

Horizontal section, 1:20

7   Verge of tower roof – horizontal section
Eaves of tower, slope 49°
Metal rail system
Pipe brick threaded to aluminium core in specific
form and thickness,
retaining the ornamental pattern
Substructure
Main beam (rafters), IPE 600

In the warm roof area:
Three-layer sealing, vapour-permeable,
insulation, 180 mm
Vapour check
Reinforced concrete slab

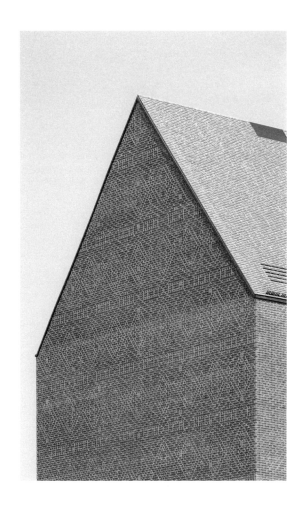

7 ——
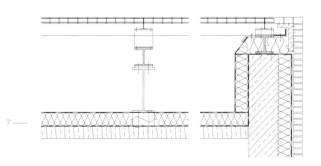

SVALBARD SCIENCE CENTRE IN LONGYEARBYEN, NORWAY
JARMUND/VIGSNÆS AS ARKITEKTER, OSLO

The Svalbard group of islands, which is located halfway between the Norwegian mainland and the North Pole, houses one of the world's most important laboratories for Arctic research. The Svalbard Science Centre increases the floor area of the existing university building from the 1990s four-fold and adds facilities such as a museum, a library, the Norwegian Polar Institute and rooms for the islands' local government. The shape of the building and the design of the facade are a response to the Arctic landscape and the prevailing climate conditions.

With the help of computer simulation and physical models, a shape has been developed for the building envelope that prevents the formation of snow drifts. Likewise, windows and entrances have been placed where they should remain accessible at all times. The building is raised on 390 drilled piles, which ensures that the wind can blow any fine snow away from underneath the building and thus prevent the melting of the loadbearing permafrost ground.

The expressive appearance of the building is enhanced by the design decision to use the same material for walls and roofs. Copper sheeting with standing seam joints covers the entire external surface and underscores the impression of a homogeneous envelope. In addition, copper has the advantage of being easy to process, even during periods of extreme cold such as are prevalent on Svalbard, which allows greater flexibility of scheduling during the construction phase. The loadbearing structure and fittings consist of timber, primarily in order to avoid thermal bridging, and secondly to allow easier processing of the elements, which were delivered to the site by ship. The interior rooms with their pine cladding and complex shapes have bright and warm finishes in order to counteract the monotony of the polar winter. In the generous foyer and circulation areas, the staircase handrails are of the same material as the external skin, hence contributing to the uniform design profile.

View of the Science Centre from the South against the backdrop of the snow-covered coastal mountain range

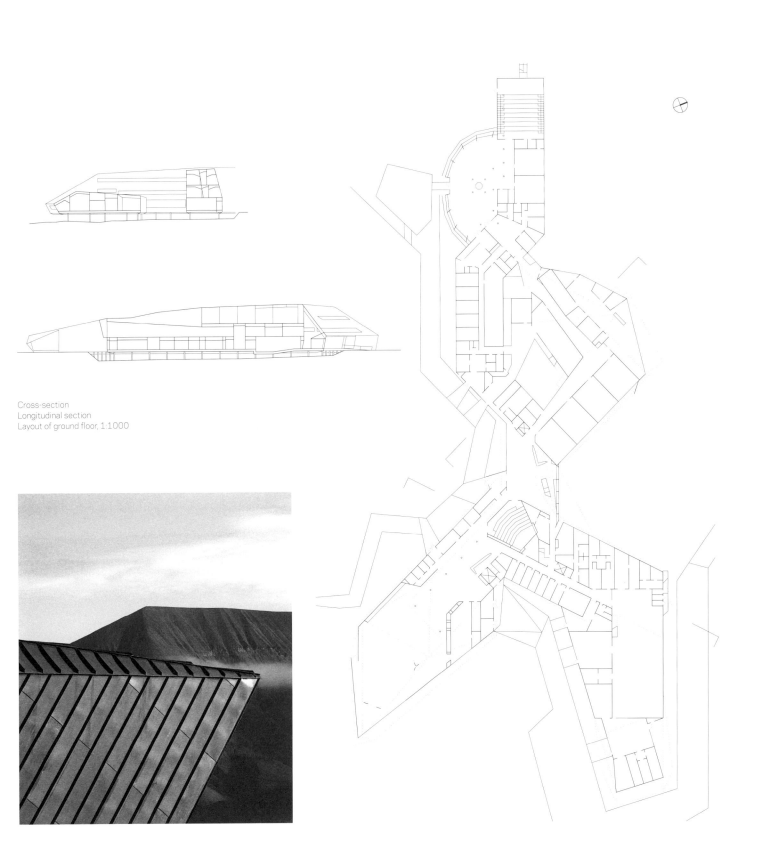

Cross-section
Longitudinal section
Layout of ground floor, 1:1000

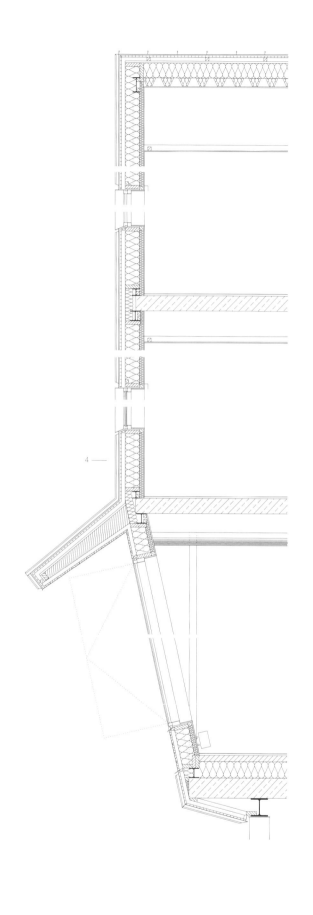

4 ——

Vertical section, 1:50
Teaching rooms and university
offices

Horizontal section, 1:20
Fenestration bands

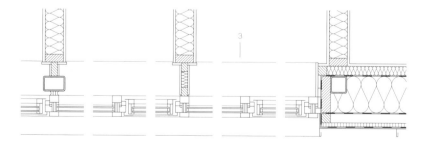

3

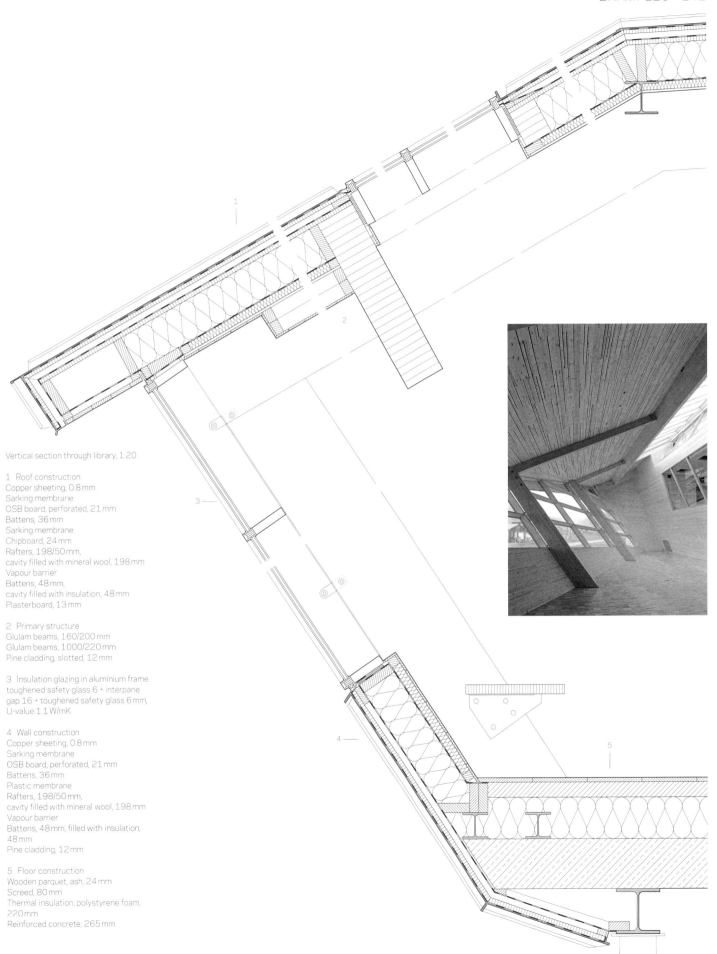

Vertical section through library, 1:20

1 Roof construction
Copper sheeting, 0.8 mm
Sarking membrane
OSB board, perforated, 21 mm
Battens, 36 mm
Sarking membrane
Chipboard, 24 mm
Rafters, 198/50 mm,
cavity filled with mineral wool, 198 mm
Vapour barrier
Battens, 48 mm,
cavity filled with insulation, 48 mm
Plasterboard, 13 mm

2 Primary structure
Glulam beams, 160/200 mm
Glulam beams, 1000/220 mm
Pine cladding, slotted, 12 mm

3 Insulation glazing in aluminium frame
toughened safety glass 6 + interpane
gap 16 + toughened safety glass 6 mm,
U-value 1.1 W/mK

4 Wall construction
Copper sheeting, 0.8 mm
Sarking membrane
OSB board, perforated, 21 mm
Battens, 36 mm
Plastic membrane
Rafters, 198/50 mm,
cavity filled with mineral wool, 198 mm
Vapour barrier
Battens, 48 mm, filled with insulation,
48 mm
Pine cladding, 12 mm

5 Floor construction
Wooden parquet, ash, 24 mm
Screed, 80 mm
Thermal insulation, polystyrene foam,
220 mm
Reinforced concrete, 265 mm

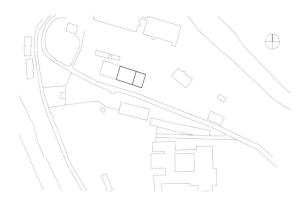

REFECTORY OF THE CANTONAL SCHOOL
IN WETTINGEN, SWITZERLAND
:MLZD, BIEL

The extension follows the outline of the historic barn known as 'Löwenscheune', dating from the early 19th century, but develops it in an unexpected way. On the inside there are four floors, which provide enough space in the sensitively refurbished barn for the infrastructure required to operate the cafeteria and the refectory hall.
The loadbearing structure, including that of the pitched roof, has been entirely constructed in reinforced concrete. Adequate thermal insulation is provided by 180 mm mineral wool installation. Four hundred perforated aluminium panels enclose the building as an external layer, without distinguishing between wall and roof. These have been anodised using a process in which the panels are placed in a metal salt solution and coloured electrolytically using alternating current. The choice of material makes refer-

ence to the importance of metal as a valuable raw material in the Middle Ages, and thus follows up the historical context of the neighbouring monastery buildings.
The rather severe formal simplification of the volume is alleviated by the floral ornament of the metal facade, which makes reference to the enclosed monastery garden. For this purpose, the artist Roland Herzog designed a punching tool consisting of six parts – a flower, a branch and four leaves of the clematis climbing plant. In some parts of the facade there are many holes punched closely together, while in others there are only a few.
Where there are the most holes, the external skin screens aluminium-framed windows and, on the ground floor, several large doors. In order to provide protection against the spread of fire within the facade cavity, all openings have been fitted with a surrounding frame consisting of steel sheeting and fire-protection panels. The play of light created by sunshine falling through the window openings playfully reflects the ornamental patterns in the otherwise clean and unembellished interiors, and thereby subtly connects the exterior with the inside space.

Location plan, 1:5000

With its dark abstract facade, the new building makes reference to the three-dimensional form of an archetypical house.

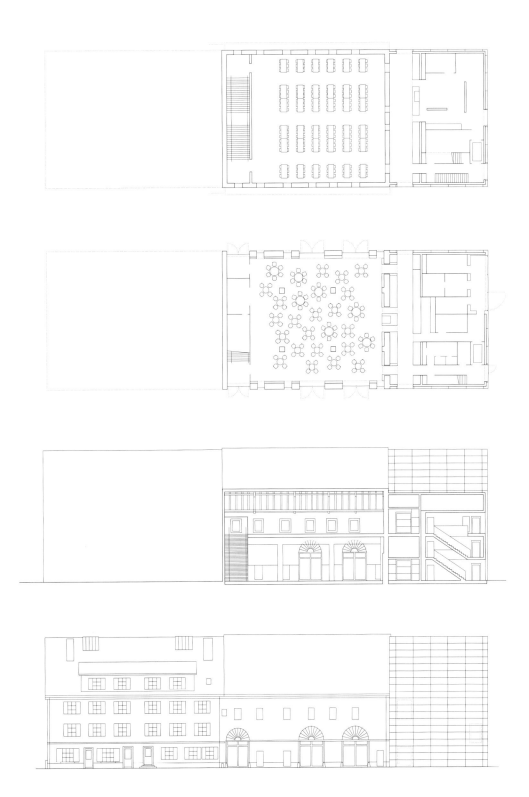

Layout of 2nd floor
Layout of ground floor
Longitudinal section
East elevation, 1:500

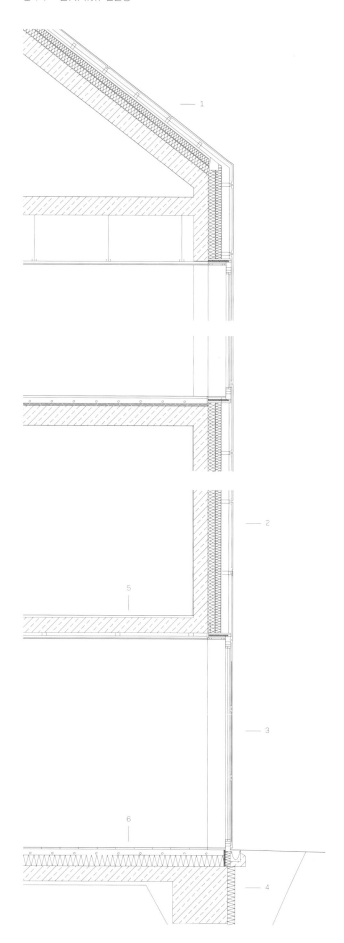

Vertical section, 1:50
Horizontal section through window, 1:20

1   Roof construction
Anodised aluminium sheeting,
coloured and punched, 2 mm
Back ventilation, 125 mm
Substructure, fixed at regular intervals,
sealed and thermally separated
Sarking membrane, diffusible
Mineral wool, 80 + 100 mm
Reinforced concrete, 250 mm,
Slope of roof, 38°
Integrated gutter,
Integrated metal gutter, 2 mm

2   Wall construction, metal facade
Anodised aluminium sheeting
coloured and punched, 2 mm
Back ventilation, 160 mm
Substructure, fixed at regular intervals,
sealed and thermally separated
Sarking membrane, vapour-permeable
Mineral wool, 80 + 100 mm
Reinforced concrete, 200 mm
Internal plaster, 15 mm

3   Window
Fireproof panel, 20 mm
Mineral wool, 20 mm
Fireproof panel, 20 mm
Sealing of frame and reinforced concrete
Fire protection frame, E160
Opening casement of insulated glazing
in aluminium frame, U-value 1.1 E/mK
Lintel and reveals: metal sheeting 1.5 mm,
concealed fixing
Threshold: metal sheeting 1.5 mm,
fixed concealed on wooden board
Metal facade continuous across the window,
daylight entering through punched holes

4   Wall construction of plinth
Damp-proof membrane
Foam glass, 160 mm
Reinforced concrete foundations
Drainage channel, 100 mm
Connection to window frame:
Vapour barrier
Impact sound membrane
Insulation strip

5   Floor construction, 1st floor
Granolithic screed, 30 mm
Reinforced concrete, 200 mm
Direct suspension, 13.5 mm

Substructure, CD section, 2 × 27 mm
Acoustic panel, 12.5 mm,
with straight perforation
Fleece, skimmed, 10 mm
Paint coating

6   Floor covering, GF
Natural asphalt tiles, 20 mm,
laid in mortar bed
Screed, 75 mm, with underfloor heating
PE membrane
Thermal insulation, EPS, 120 mm
Impact sound insulation, 20 mm
Damp-proof barrier
Reinforced concrete, 200 mm
Lean-mix concrete, 50 mm

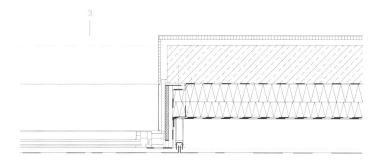

FRAC NORD-PAS DE CALAIS IN DUNKIRK, FRANCE
LACATON VASSAL, PARIS

The regional centres initiated by the Fonds Régionaux d'Art Contemporain (Frac) are present in all 22 regions of France and are the home of contemporary art collections; they all have rooms for exhibitions, events and libraries. For the FRAC Nord-Pas de Calais in Dunkirk in northern France, the architects deliberately ignored the specification in the competition that asked for the Frac to be accommodated in a former shipbuilding hangar. The AP2 hangar dating from 1949 is a unique architectural object and a historic relic of the now defunct industrial precinct, which is why they decided to leave it almost unchanged, except for installing a bridge crane, and to supplement it with a virtual mirror image. The new building adjoining it accommodates the art collection and exhibitions in a volume 75 m in length, 24.5 m in width and 35 m high at the ridge. The airy interior is an experience in its own right, which can nonetheless be used in the various ways associated with the spatial requirements of the FRAC brief. Loadbearing walls have been avoided by placing the fair-faced concrete floor slabs on a range of columns, thus allowing greater flexibility. Owing to its transparency and the choice of material, the new building does not compete with the former industrial structure. The lower floors have an internal envelope consisting of sliding panels with double-glazing, placed two metres inside the outer envelope. The latter is a transparent, bio-climatic building envelope of transparent polycarbonate panels and an inflatable double-skin ETFE plastic membrane.

Opening casements and solar screening blinds in the roof respectively ensure that there is adequate ventilation and prevent excessive heating of the space.

In addition to expressing the architectural idea and providing daylight to the exhibition rooms, the design also takes economic factors into account. The plastic material used here is more economical than conventional solutions with glass constructions; it can also be produced more cheaply owing to the greater use of prefabricated components – which does not prevent it from generating a distinct identity.

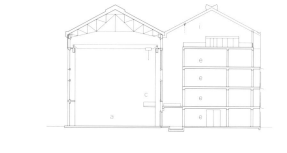

Location plan, 1:10,000

Elevation
Cross-sections
Layout of ground floor
Existing and new building
Scale 1:1000

a   Old shipbuilding hangar
b   Entrance with café
c   Internal balcony
d   Exhibition
e   Storage space
f   Loggia
g   Internal street
h   Forum
i   Belvedere

Forum exhibition area
Interior

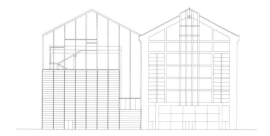

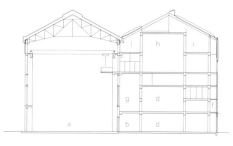

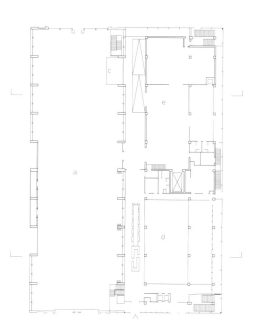

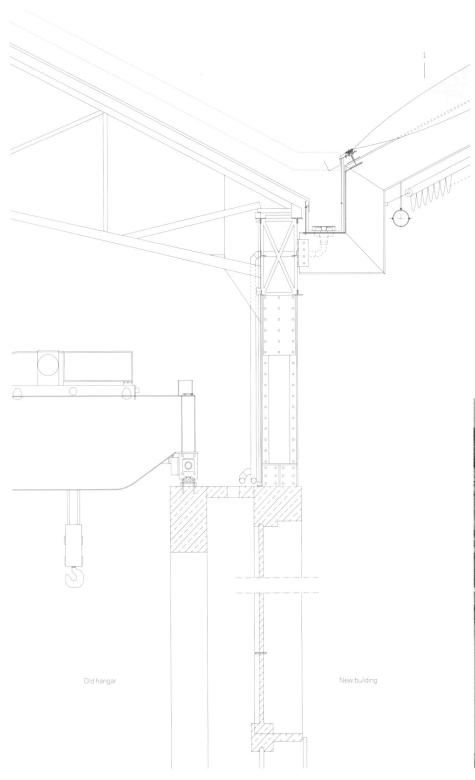

Old hangar

New building

Vertical section, 1:50

1 Construction of exterior skin
Transparent, inflatable double-skin ETFE cushion construction, membrane thickness 250 my
Panel size approx. 2.8 × 15.5 m
All-round restraining anchor for membrane
cushions
Substructure bearing on the primary steel
structure
Screw fixing to metal frame every 700 mm
Air supplied from a compressor with two fans
and one drainage valve at the lower membrane
cushion; nominal air pressure at 200/250 Pa,
the airlines are integrated into the primary
structure
plus openable elements for natural ventilation,
including bird screen
Solar screening blind
Lighting
Drainage via downpipes behind the thermal
envelope

2 Construction of interior facade
Interior facade consists of transparent
elements with double-glazing and sliding door
openings as well as closed elements consisting of thermal insulation board.
Reinforced concrete beam, prefabricated unit
Thermal insulation board, prefabricated
Floor slab:
Granolithic screed, ground and sealed on
prefabricated hollow prestressed concrete
slab

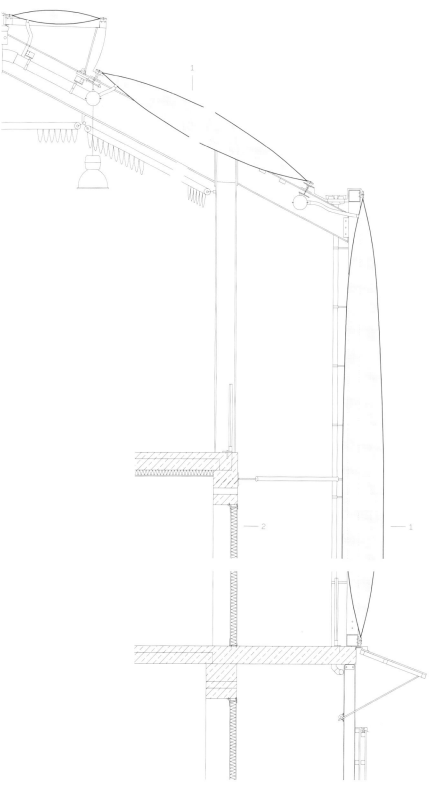

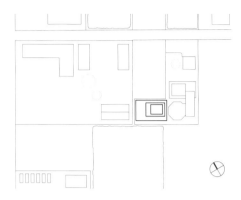

RESIDENCE IN MINAMITURU-GUNN, JAPAN
TAKESHI HOSAKA, YOKOHAMA

The desire to distance oneself from the surroundings on the one hand, and to open up the view of them on the other leads here to the varied use of closed and open facade elements. The three seemingly floating white bands that form an abstract pyramid protruding from the landscape, like stacked blocks, contrast sharply with the heterogeneous architectural character of the neighbourhood. The differently sized building volumes intersect and define spaces, each with a specific character. The degree of privacy increases as one progresses from the enclosed courtyard via the transparent living room to the discernible core of the building with staircase, kitchen, bathroom and master bedroom. This principle is continued in modified form on the upper floor, which is allocated to the three children.

A boundary wall at ground level and a high parapet on the first floor provide the required privacy. The all-round panoramic glazing opens the rooms to the attractive landscape with its mountains and paddy fields. The melding of interior and exterior spaces on the ground floor is not interrupted by horizontal or vertical frame elements. The 20 mm-thick acrylic glazing was prefabricated at the factory and delivered to the site as complete units; it offers absolute transparency without reflections and mirroring. Access to the courtyard and terrace is via four glazed sliding doors on each floor. The building envelope with its interior insulation is a type of curtain-wall steel structure tied to the building core via the floor slabs. The enclosed parts are lined with plywood board to which a glass-fibre reinforced plastic seal has been applied. Two existing large trees on the site become part of the architecture as they cast shadows on the purist white walls that are forever changing with the sunlight.

The abstract, seemingly floating, stacked white blocks contrast starkly with the rural landscape.

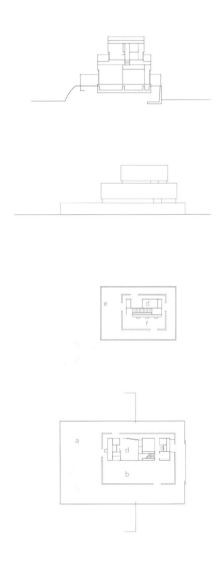

Cross-section
South elevation

Layout of first floor
Layout of ground floor
Scale 1:500
a Garden
b Living room
c Kitchen
d Bedroom
e Terrace
f Children's area

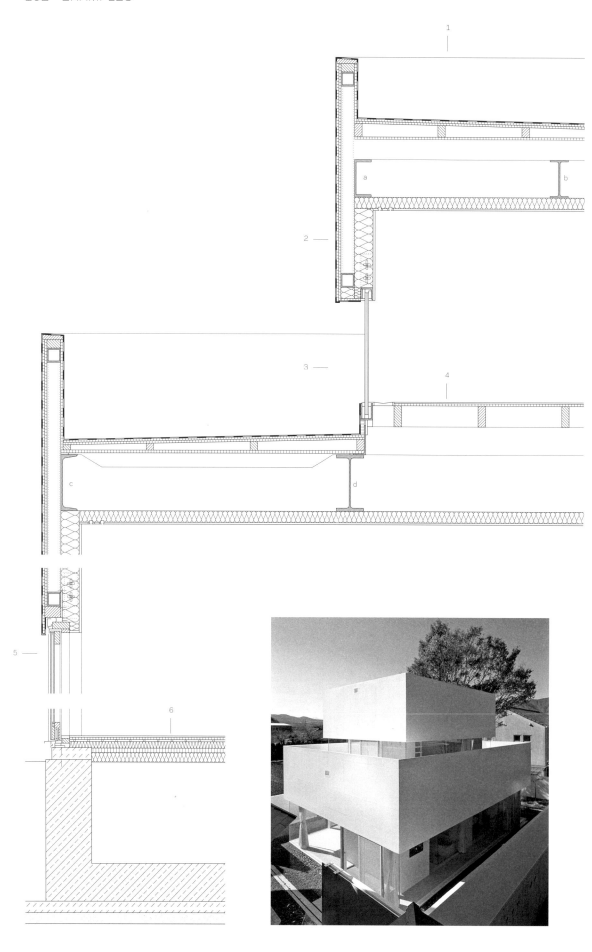

Vertical section, 1:20

1 Roof construction:
Plastic coating, white,
glass-fibre reinforced
Plywood board, 2 × 12 mm
Slats laid to fall
Plywood panel, 12 mm
Flat steel bar, 75/1.2 mm
Primary roof structure
a Steel channel, U 200/90 mm
b Steel beam, IPE 200/100 mm
Thermal insulation, 60 mm
Plasterboard, 9.5 mm
Curtain rail

2 Wall construction:
Plastic coating, white,
glass-fibre reinforced
Plywood board, 2 × 12 mm
Vertical steel tube, 75/40 mm
Horizontal steel pipe, 75/75 mm
Thermal insulation, 100 mm
Plasterboard, 9.5 mm
Paint coating

3 Fixed glazing
Steel anchor angle,
L-shaped, 90 × 90 × 7 × 180
Holder consisting of two steel
sections,
angle 65 × 65 × 8 and flat 50 × 9
Acrylic glass, 20 mm, fixed with
holding blocks and sealed all-round,
prefabricated at the factory
Drainage channel for condensate
at floor level

4 Floor construction, first floor
Carpet, 7 mm
Plywood panel, 12 mm
Timber section, 100/40 mm
Timber section, 150/60 mm
Primary floor structure
c Steel channel, U 300/90 mm
d Steel beam, IPE 300/150 mm
Thermal insulation, 60 mm
Plasterboard, 9.5 mm

5 Sliding doors
Timber section, 120/60 mm,
for fixing the sliding door frame
Toughened glass 5 mm + inter-pane
gap 12 mm + toughened glass
5 mm, in pine frame, painted white
Floor guide rail

6 Floor construction, ground floor
Carpet, 7 mm
Plywood panel, 12 mm
Battens 45/45 mm, impact sound
insulation and underfloor heating
Plywood panel, 24 mm
Battens, 50 mm, thermal insulation
Air space
Reinforced concrete, 200 mm
Lean-mix concrete, 60 mm
Blinding layer, 60 mm

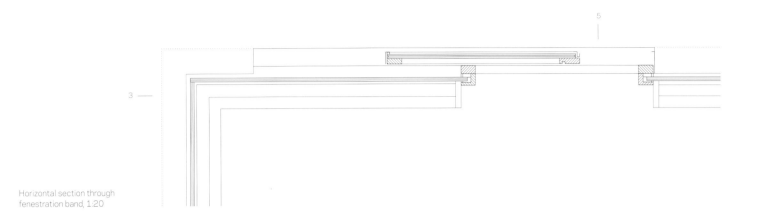

5

3

Horizontal section through
fenestration band, 1:20

ENCLOSE | BUILD
APPENDIX

TABLES AND INFORMATION

Building component / material	Years
Pad / strip foundations	≥ 50
Foundation slabs	≥ 50
Floor slab	≥ 50
Masonry wall	≥ 50
Concrete wall	≥ 50
Timber wall	≥ 50
Steel construction wall	≥ 50
Clay construction wall	≥ 50
Masonry blocks with concrete fill	≥ 50
Standard doors: metal	≥ 50
Standard doors: wood-based material	40
Standard doors: plastic	40
Fire doors	≥ 50
Special doors: sound reduction doors, glass doors	≥ 50
Windows (frame and casement): aluminium, compound aluminium and wood, compound aluminium and plastic, treated hardwood, steel	≥ 50
Windows (frame and casement): plastic, treated softwood	40
Glazing: safety insulation glass, triple / double thermal insulation glass, fire-resistant insulation glass, acoustic insulation glass, insulation glass resistant to manual attack, solar screening insulation glass	30
Sealing profiles	20
Sealants	12
Sealants against water (not under pressure)	35
Sealants to protect against groundwater (under pressure): sealing membranes	≥ 50
Waterproof concrete underground	≥ 50
Sealing material in contact with the ground (water not under pressure): bitumen sealing membranes, filler material	40
Sealing material in contact with the ground (water not under pressure): coatings and paint	30
Sealing material in contact with the ground: protective masonry walls (concrete, engineering brick, clinker brick)	≥ 50
Sealing material in contact with the ground: sealing panels made of polystyrene, dimpled membranes (polyethylene polypropylene), fibre-reinforced cement-based corrugated sheets	40
Sealing material in contact with the ground: sealing granulate mats, corrugated panels	30
Thermal insulation of components in contact with the ground: foam glass perimeter insulation	≥ 50
Thermal insulation of components in contact with the ground: extruded polystyrene perimeter insulation	40
External paint coating on mineral substrate: dispersion paint, dispersion silicate paint, white cement paint, plastic coating on concrete	20

Building component / material	Years
External paint coating on mineral substrate: silicone resin paint, silicate paint, polymer resin paint	15
External paint coating on mineral substrate: lime wash	8
External paint coating on mineral substrate: masonry impregnation	15
External timber protection coating: paints / stains for wood	8
External timber protection coating: wood oil / wax	5
External timber impregnation: pressure impregnation	18
Render on monolithic substrate: lime cement mortar, mortar with bonding agent, lime cement mortar, cement mortar with added air lime, cement mortar, air lime mortar, hydraulic lime mortar, semi-hydraulic lime mortar	45
Render on monolithic substrate: refurbishment render systems, mineral-based lightweight render systems on porous substrate	40
Render on monolithic substrate: silicate render, silicone resin render, synthetic resin render	30
Render on thermal insulation: mineral render systems, silicate render systems, synthetic resin render systems, silicone resin render systems	30
Cladding: clinker bricks, calcium silicate bricks, fair-faced concrete	≥ 50
Cladding: natural stone, artificial stone, concrete panels, fibre-cement panels, synthetic resin blocks, brick panels, ceramic tiles and panels, porcelain stoneware, stoneware / split tiles	≥ 50
Pointing/grouting compounds	30
Cladding: hard cladding materials on thermal insulation	30
Core insulation layer: mineral wool batts, polyurethane insulation boards, polystyrene, expanded slate granulate, foam glass granulate, expanded clay granulate	≥ 50
Insulation layer behind back-ventilated face layer: mineral foam boards, foam glass panels	≥ 50
Insulation layer behind face layer: vacuum insulation panels	30
Composite thermal insulation system: mineral wool batts, polystyrene insulation boards, polyurethane insulation boards, wood-fibre insulation boards, woodwool slabs, cork insulation boards	40
Composite thermal insulation system, transparent	20
Timber cladding: treated softwood, hardwood, wood-based systems	40
Timber cladding: untreated softwood	30
Timber cladding: wood shingles	≥ 50
Metal cladding: zinc, copper, anodised aluminium, paint-coated aluminium, non-rusting steel	≥ 50
Metal cladding: galvanised steel	40
Face layer with back ventilation: copper sheeting	≥ 50
Face layer with back ventilation: zinc, non-rusting steel	45

1   List of building components with their technical service life
The table contains the average service life of building components as input values for life-cycle calculations, grouped by construction element.

Source:
www.nachhaltigesbauen.de
BBSR table: Service life of building components for life-cycle analyses using the BNB assessment system for sustainable building
Research study on the service life of building components, research initiative ZukunftBau, study period: 2008 to 2010
Federal Ministry of the Environment, Nature Conservation, Building and Nuclear Safety, Department of Structural Engineering, Sustainable Building, Building Research, formerly the Federal Institute of Research on Building, Urban Affairs and Spatial Development (BBSR) within the Federal Office of Building and Regional Planning (BBR).

Building component/material	Years
Face layer with back ventilation: composite aluminium panels, low-corrosion steel, galvanised/coated steel	30
Face layer with back ventilation: glass	≥ 50
Transparent polycarbonate sheeting: acrylic glass panels	40
Transparent polycarbonate sheeting: polycarbonate panels	30
Face layer with back ventilation: fibre-reinforced composite resin panels	30
Wall cladding (systems): plastic, lightweight laminated construction board	40
Face layer: joint strip, pre-compressed sealing strip, pointing material, expansion joint profile	40
Face layer: sub-structure	≥ 50
Insulation panels: mineral foam insulation panels, calcium silicate panels	≥ 50
Loadbearing structure: slanted roof	≥ 50
Loadbearing structure: flat roof	≥ 50
Roof windows (frame): aluminium, plastic, aluminium/wood composite	≥ 50
Roof windows (frame): aluminium/plastic composite	35
Roof windows (frame): hardwood, treated	40
Roof windows (frame): softwood, treated	25
Skylights	25
Continuous roof lights	20
Roof escape hatches: hot-galvanised steel (dip-galvanised)	40
Roof escape hatches: plastic	30
Sealing membranes: elastomer membranes, plastic membranes beneath the insulation	40
Sealing membranes: bitumen membranes beneath the insulation	30
Sealing membranes: bitumen membranes, elastomer membranes, plastic membranes above the insulation, with heavy protective layer	30
Sealing membranes: bitumen membranes, elastomer membranes, plastic membranes above the insulation, with light protective layer	20
Sealing compounds: asphalt mastic, liquid sealant, melted asphalt beneath the insulation	40
Sealing compounds: asphalt mastic, liquid sealant, melted asphalt above the insulation, with heavy protective layer	30
Sealing compounds: asphalt mastic, liquid sealant, melted asphalt above the insulation, with light protective layer	20
Sealing compounds: liquid sealant above the insulation, without protective layer	20
Heavy protective layer: extensive roof greening	40
Heavy protective layer: gravel, slabs, intensive roof greening	30
Light protective layer: layer of chippings applied on site, factory-applied chippings	15

Building component/material	Years
Coatings: metallic paint coating	12
Roofing materials: slate	≥ 50
Roofing materials: tiles	≥ 50
Roofing materials: concrete, fibre-cement	≥ 50
Roofing materials: zinc, copper sheeting, non-rusting steel	≥ 50
Roofing materials: wood shingles	≥ 50
Roofing materials: galvanised and coated steel	45
Roofing materials: galvanised steel, aluminium	40
Roofing materials: bitumen shingles, bitumen corrugated panels	25
Strip metal roofing materials: non-rusting steel, copper	≥ 50
Strip metal roofing materials: galvanised and coated steel sheeting	45
Strip metal roofing materials: aluminium sheeting, galvanised steel sheeting	40
Roofing materials: thatch	30
Insulation layer on top and between rafters: foam glass panels, mineral wool batts, extruded polystyrene panels, expanded polystyrene panels, polyurethane panels, fibre-board made from wood, hemp or cellulose	≥ 50
Parapet coping: natural stone, artificial stone, precast concrete elements, concrete slabs, ceramic tiles and slabs, porcelain stoneware, stoneware, split tiles, copper, non-rusting steel, zinc	≥ 50
Parapet coping: aluminium, fibre-cement	40
Parapet coping: galvanised steel	30
Parapet coping: plastic	20
Drainage goods (gutters, rainwater downpipes, roof outlets): non-rusting steel, copper, zinc, aluminium	≥ 50
Drainage goods (gutters, rainwater downpipes, roof outlets): galvanised and coated steel	40
Drainage goods (gutters, rainwater downpipes, roof outlets): galvanised steel	30
Drainage goods (gutters, rainwater downpipes, roof outlets): plastic	20
Close boarding on the roof: bitumen wood-fibre board	≥ 50
Close boarding on the roof: impregnated fibre-board made of wood, hemp or cellulose	30
Close boarding on the roof: vapour-permeable plastic membranes	30
Insulation on, between and under rafters: mineral wool, polystyrene, polyurethane, expanded granulate, renewable insulation materials (e.g. wood-based insulation, cellulose, cork, light clay mixture, flax, meadow grass, hemp)	≥ 50
Fall guards, service treads and runs, snow and leaf guard rails, lightning protection systems: hot-galvanised steel (dip-galvanised), non-rusting steel	≥ 50
Roof ventilation: galvanised steel	25
Ventilation pipes: plastic	25

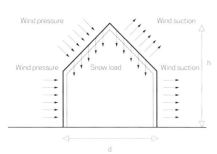

1 Map of wind zones

Wind load zone		Velocity pressure q in kN/m² for a building height h within limits of		
The data are valid for an altitude above sea level of < 800 m; above that, a factor is applied that increases the value. For buildings on the islands of the North Sea, the simplified method is only permitted up to a building height of 10 m.		$h \leq$ 10 m	10 m $< h \leq$ 18 m	18 m $< h \leq$ 25 m
☐ Wind load zone 1: 22 m/s	Inland	0.50	0.65	0.75
☐ Wind load zone 2: 25 m/s	Inland	0.65	0.80	0.90
	Coasts and islands of the Baltic Sea	0.85	1.00	1.10
☐ Wind load zone 3: 27.5 m/s	Inland	0.80	0.95	1.10
	Coasts and islands of the Baltic Sea	1.05	1.15	1.30
☐ Wind load zone 4: 30 m/s	Inland	0.95	1.15	1.30
	Coasts and islands of the Baltic Sea and North Sea	1.25	1.40	1.55

1 Wind load
Wind loads acting on buildings according to their locations, classified into zones under DIN EN 1991-1-4, Eurocode 1: Actions on structures – Part 1-4: General actions – Wind loads

The determination of the wind loads as fluctuating loads acting on the surfaces of the building envelope can be performed for buildings or parts of buildings that are sufficiently stiff and not susceptible to vibrations. The development of new, more lightweight construction materials, building shapes and construction methods has led to a revision of the existing standards.
The introduction of wind load zones ensures the generally required operative reliability for all types of building. The categories of terrain are classified either for each individual case, or using the standard classification.

Terrain category I
Open water; lakes with at least 5 km unobstructed surface in wind direction; smooth, flat land without obstructions

Terrain category II
Agriculturally used terrain enclosed with hedges, isolated farmsteads, houses or trees

Terrain category III
Suburbs of cities or industrial and commercial estates; forests

Terrain category IV
Urban areas in which at least 15% of the land is covered with buildings with an average eaves height of more than 15 m

2 Action of wind loads

2 Action on structures
The action of the wind load on a building depends on the building's shape. The total wind load is made up of pressure, suction and friction effects. Formula for the resulting wind load acting on the whole of a building:

$$W = [c_{pe} + c_{pi}] \cdot q \cdot A$$

c aerodynamic force coefficient; this depends on the shape of the building and the wind direction
c_{pe} = aerodynamic coefficient for external pressure
c_{pi} = aerodynamic coefficient for internal pressure

q velocity pressure of the wind in kN/m² (wind velocity v and air density ρ)
q_h distribution of velocity pressure
z_e reference height depending on shape and slenderness
A size of loaded area in m²
h height
b width of building at right angles to the wind flow
d building width
W Wind load

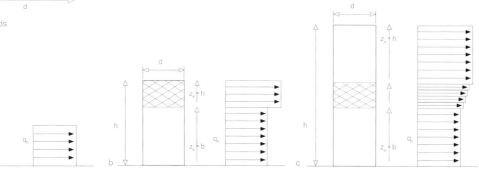

3 Calculation input variables for wind pressure

Reference height h, depending on slenderness; b is the building width perpendicular to the wind direction.
a Diagram of velocity pressure for buildings, h ≤ b and h ≤ 25 m
b Diagram of velocity pressure for buildings, b < h ≤ 2 × b
c Diagram of velocity pressure for buildings, h > 2 × b

4 Snow load

The characteristic value for snow loads (sk) at ground level is determined with different snow load intensities for the different regional zones (snow load zones). It depends on the geographic location and the altitude of the terrain above sea level.

Locations at an altitude of >1500m above sea level and certain locations within snow load zone 3 may have higher actual values than those resulting from the calculation. Information about the snow load in these locations should be obtained from the respective local authorities.

The characteristic value for snow load on the roof depends on the shape of the roof and the characteristic value for the snow load on the ground.

$s^i = s_k \cdot \mu$

s_i the snow load applicable to the building
s_k local characteristic snow load on the ground
μ shape coefficient

In each zone, a minimum snow load value (base amount) must be applied. Beyond that, the following formulas apply for the calculation.		Calculation formula A = altitude of terrain in metres above sea level	Snow load in kN/m²
☐ Zone 1	e.g. Rhine Valley, Rhine Lowlands	$s_k = 0.19 + 0.91 \cdot ((A+140)/760)^2$	> 0.65
Zone 1a	e.g. region around Munich and Augsburg	As zone 1, multiplied by 1.25	> 0.81
Zone 2	e.g. large parts of northern Germany	$s_k = 0.25 + 1.91 \cdot ((A+140)/760)^2$	> 0.85
Zone 2a	e.g. upper Black Forest, Sauerland, Rhön	As zone 2, multiplied by 1.25	> 1.06
Zone 3	e.g. Alp region, Thuringian Forest, Erzgebirge mountains	$s_k = 0.31 + 2.91 \cdot ((A+140)/760)^2$	> 1.10

Incline of roof α	0° ≤ α ≤ 30°	30° ≤ α ≤ 60°	α > 60°
μ_1	0.8	0.8 · (60−α)/30	0
μ_2	0.8 + 0.8 · α/30	1.6	1.6

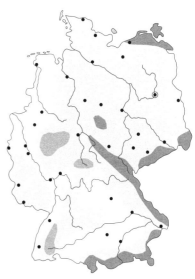

4 Map of snow zones

5 Driving rain

DIN 4108-3 – Thermal protection and energy economy in buildings Part 3: Protection against moisture subject to climate conditions, exposure groups
Driving rain:

Exposure group I:
Areas with an annual precipitation of below 600 mm, and locations that are particularly well protected against wind in areas with greater precipitation.

Exposure group II:
Areas with an annual precipitation of between 600 mm and 800 mm, and locations that are particularly well protected against wind in areas with greater precipitation. Tower blocks and buildings in exposed locations in areas with low exposure to driving rain owing to regional rain and wind conditions.

Exposure group III:
Areas with an annual precipitation of more than 800 mm and windy areas with less precipitation. Tower blocks and buildings at exposed locations in areas with medium exposure to driving rain owing to regional rain and wind conditions.

	Exposure group I Low exposure to driving rain:	Exposure group II Medium exposure to driving rain:	Exposure group III High exposure to driving rain:
Render	External render without special water-resistance requirements	Water-resistant external render	Water-resistant external render or synthetic resin render
	On external walls of masonry, wall construction panels, concrete etc., woodwool slabs and laminated lightweight construction panels		
Face brickwork	Single-skin face brickwork, 31 cm thick	Single-skin face brickwork, 37.5 cm thick	Double-skin wall with face brickwork, air gap and thermal insulation or core insulation
Wall tiles	External walls finished with tiles laid in standard mortar or tile adhesive		External walls finished with tiles laid in water-repellent mortar or tile adhesive
Concrete	External walls with an external high-density concrete layer		
Back-ventilated cladding	Walls with back-ventilated external wall cladding		
Composite thermal insulation systems (e.g. 'exterior insulation finishing system – EIFS)	Walls insulated externally using a rendered thermal insulation system or with an approved composite thermal insulation system		
Timber	External walls in timber construction with weather protection		

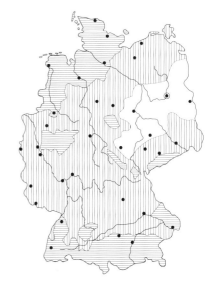

 Annual precipitation below 600 mm

 Annual precipitation between 600 and 800 mm

Annual precipitation over 800 mm, in windy areas over 700 mm

5 Driving rain protection map

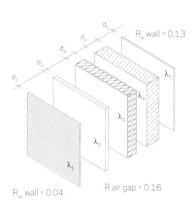

R_{si} wall = 0.13

R_{se} wall = 0.04   R air gap = 0.16

The U-value (thermal transmittance coefficient) is a measure of the transmittance of heat through one or several layers of material where the temperature on each side is different. It indicates the amount of energy that flows through an area of 1 m² in 1 second when the stationary air temperatures at the opposite surfaces differ by 1 K. Its SI unit of measure is therefore W/(m²K) (watt per square metre and degree Kelvin). The U-value is primarily determined by the thermal conductivity of the materials (λ-value) and the thickness of the component layers, as well as their arrangement in the construction. The lower the thermal conductivity of the components is, the lower the U-value is. A low U-value indicates good insulation properties. The inverse of the thermal transmittance coefficient is the thermal resistance RT (m²K)/W.

In the case of a homogeneous wall with infinite dimensions composed of layers with the thickness di and the thermal conductivity λ_i, the proportionality constant is calculated as follows:

$$U = \frac{1}{R_T} = \frac{1}{R_{se} + \frac{d_1}{\lambda_1} + \frac{d_i}{\lambda_i} + \ldots + R_{si}}$$

U: thermal transmittance coefficient in W/(m²K)
R_T: thermal resistance in (m²K)/W.
R_{se}: external heat transmission resistance in (m²K)/W
d: thickness of number of layers i in m
λ_i: specific thermal conductivity of layer in W/(m²K)
$1/\lambda_i = R\lambda$: specific thermal resistance of layer i in (m²K)/W
$d/\lambda_i = R_i$: thermal resistance of layer (m²K)/W
R_{si}: internal heat transmission resistance in (m²K)/W

1 Thermal transmittance coefficient
DIN EN ISO 6946:2008-04: Building components and building elements – Thermal resistance and thermal transmittance – Calculation method

2 Thermal conductivity λ; examples of characteristic values of selected materials

3 Examples of thermal transmittance coefficients of building components

Material	Material parameters		
	Dry bulk density in kg/m³	Thermal conductivity in W/mK	Water vapour diffusion resistance coefficient
Render	1200	0.35-0.87	10-35
Lime cement mortar	1800	0.87	15-35
Standard concrete	2400	2.10	70-150
Lightweight concrete	1600-2000	0.81-1.40	3-10
Autoclaved aerated concrete	500-800	0.19-0.29	5-10
Brick masonry	700-2000	0.30-0.96	5-10
Calcium silicate masonry	1000-2200	0.50-1.30	5-25
Insulating bricks	500-600	0.08-0.20	5-10
Vertically perforated bricks	1200-2000	0.50-0.96	5-10
Face brickwork	1800-2200	0.81-1.20	50-100
Natural stone	2600-2800	2.20-3.50	–
Solid timber	600-800	0.13-0.20	40
Cross-laminated timber	800	0.13-0.20	50-400
Gypsum fibreboard	1000	0.32	13-20
Plasterboard	900	0.21	8
Fibre insulation materials	8-500	0.035-0.05	1
Polystyrene, rigid foam	≥ 15	0.025-0.04	20-300
Polyurethane, rigid foam	≥ 30	0.03-0.045	30-100
Woodwool slab	360-570	0.093-0.15	2-5
Glass	2500	0.8-1.4	–
Steel	7800	60	–
Aluminium	2700	200	–

Building component	Thickness in m	U-value in W/(m²K)
External concrete wall without thermal insulation	0.25	3.3
External brick wall without thermal insulation	0.24 0.365	1.5 0.8
External brick wall with composite thermal insulation system	0.175 + 0.30	approx. 0.32
External wall with highly porous bricks with vertical perforations, not rendered	0.5	0.17-0.23
External timber frame wall, conventional construction	0.25	0.15-0.20
External solid timber wall (without thermal insulation)	0.205	0.5
External aerated concrete wall	0.365 0.40 0.50	0.183-0.230 0.163-0.210 0.125-0.146
External wall with brick cladding	0.35	0.75
Intermediate elastomer layers	0.002	0.2
Exterior door of wood or plastic	–	3.49
Windows with single glazing	–	2.8-3.0
Windows with thermal insulation glazing	–	1.3
Windows with triple-glazing	–	0.5-0.8
Lightweight polycarbonate construction element	0.005	approx. 0.83

2   3

4   Example of U-value calculation for wall constructions in accordance with DIN EN ISO 6946. The values are derived from the respective material thickness and the characteristic data, of which examples are given in the tables on page 160.

Example of U-value calculation for a multiple-skin solid wall consisting of a loadbearing layer, insulation, an air gap and brick cladding skin. Unless the brickwork ties are thermally separated or consist of carbon material, they are taken into account by a factor since they only penetrate the wall at certain points.

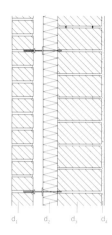

d_i		d_1		d_2	d_3	d_4	
	External transmission	Face brickwork skin	Air gap	Insulation layer	Load-bearing layer	Internal plaster	Internal transmission
R_T	$0.04 +$	$\dfrac{0.115\, +}{0.81}$	$0.16 +$	$\dfrac{0.10\, +}{0.035}$	$\dfrac{0.24\, +}{0.70}$	$\dfrac{0.015}{0.87}$	$+ 0.13$

$R_T = 0.04 + 0.14 + 0.16 + 2.86 + 0.34 + 0.02 + 0.13 = 3.69\ (m^2 \cdot K)/W$

$U = 1/R_T = 0.27\ W/(m^2 \cdot K)$

Example of U-value calculation for an external wall in timber construction, with back-ventilation and installation gap

d_i		d_1	d_2	d_3	d_4	d_5	d_6	d_7	d_8	d_9	
	External transmission	Timber cladding	Battens/membrane	Gypsum fibre-board	Construction timber	Wood-fibre insulation board	Cross-laminated timber	Battens	Mineral wool	Gypsum fibre-board	Internal transmission
R_T	$0.04 +$	$\dfrac{0.02\, +}{0.15}$	$\dfrac{0.03\, +}{0.13}$	$\dfrac{0.015\, +}{0.32}$	$\dfrac{0.20\, +}{0.13}$	$\dfrac{0.20\, +}{0.039}$	$\dfrac{0.094\, +}{0.13}$	$\dfrac{0.06\, +}{0.13}$	$\dfrac{0.05\, +}{0.04}$	$\dfrac{0.015}{0.32}$	$+ 0,13$

$R_T = 0.04 + 0.13 + 0.23 + 0.04 + 1.53 + 5.13 + 0.72 + 0.46 + 1.25 + 0.04 + 0.13 = 9.74\ (m^2 \cdot K)/W$

$U = 1/R_T = 0,10\ W/(m^2 \cdot K)$

5   Calculation of U-value for glazing (U_w)

The thermal transmittance coefficient (Uw) is calculated for the whole window. The value includes the U-values for the glazing unit (U_g) and the frame (U_f). In addition, the total U_w-value is affected by the linear thermal transmittance coefficient ψ_g (g = glazing) and the size of the window. In accordance with the Energy Conservation Directive (EnEv), the U_w-value for normal glazing must not exceed 1.3 W/m²K. Today, windows with a U_w-value of 0.8 W/m²K can be achieved with triple glazing. The calculation is carried out in accordance with DIN EN ISO 10077-1.

The following formula is used for determining the thermal transmittance coefficient:

$$U_w = \frac{A_g \cdot U_g + A_f \cdot U_f + l_g \cdot \psi_g}{A_g + A_f}$$

U_g = thermal transmittance coefficient of glazing unit
U_f = thermal transmittance coefficient of frame
ψ_g = linear thermal transmittance coefficient of edge bonding of insulating glazing unit, depending on the product
A_g = glass area
A_f = frame area
$A_w = A_g + A_f$
l_g = length of the inside edge of the frame profile (visible extent of the glass pane)

Timber window, 24 mm double glazing with argon filling, standard window size 1.23 m × 1.48 m, proportion of the frame area to the overall window area is 30%

$$U_w = \frac{1.27 \cdot 0,7 + 0.54 \cdot 1.6 + 4.19 \cdot 0.08}{1.27 + 0.54} = 1.15\ W/m^2 K$$

U_g 36 mm triple glazing with argon filling: 0.7 W/m²K
U_f timber frame: 1.6 W/m²K
ψ_g timber frame: 0.08 W/m²K

Window to Passive House standard, 36 mm triple glazing with krypton filling, standard window size 1.23 m × 1.48 m, proportion of the frame area to the overall window area is 30%

$$U_w = \frac{1.27 \cdot 0.5 + 0.54 \cdot 0.85 + 4.19 \cdot 0.08}{1.27 + 0.54} = 0.78\ W/m^2 K$$

U_g 36 mm triple glazing with krypton filling: 0.5 W/m²K
U_f timber-aluminium frame: 0.85 W/m²K
ψ_g timber-aluminium frame: 0.08 W/m²K

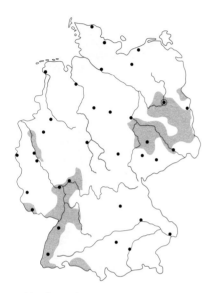

1 Map: Summer heat protection

The existing solar gain value S is calculated using this formula:

$$S = \sum_j \frac{A_{w,j} \cdot g_\perp \cdot F_c}{A_G}$$

S: solar gain value
$A_{w,j}$: the surface of the window (in m) facing in the direction j; the dimensions are for the clear dimensions of the opening in the shell construction
$g_\perp$: total energy transmission rate of the window
F_c: reduction factor for solar screening device
A_G: floor area of room in m²

Region A: cool in summer

Region B: moderate

Region C: hot in summer

Window glass type	Total energy transmission rate $g_\perp$
Single glazing	0.87
Double glazing	0.75
Double insulating glazing	0.50-0.70
Triple glazing, normal	0.60-0.70
Triple insulating glazing	0.35-0.50

Solar screening device	Reduction factor F_c
None	1.0
Internal, light colours	0.8
External, adjustable louvres	0.25
External, venetian blinds	0.4
External, roller shutters	0.3
External, awnings	0.5

1 Thermal insulation in summer
DIN 4108-2:2013-02, Thermal protection and energy economy in buildings – Part 2: Minimum requirements for thermal insulation
Thermal insulation in summer has the purpose of preventing overheating of rooms while using as little energy as possible for cooling. If the proportion of window area to the footprint area of the building exceeds 7 to 15% – depending on the orientation and inclination of the glass – proof of thermal protection in summer must be provided. Whereby $S \leq S_{zul}$ applies.
The permissible solar gain value S_{zul} is obtained by adding the contributory solar gain values S_x:
– for the climate region (A, B or C)
– for the type of construction (lightweight, medium or heavy)
– for optional night ventilation
– for any existing solar screening glazing, window tilt and orientation.

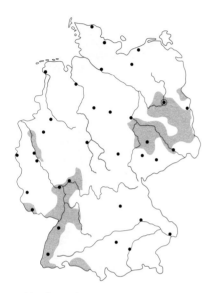

2 Requirements for facade scaffolds

w Width of the scaffold staging
c Clear distance between the uprights, c ≥ 600 mm
b Clear passage width,
   b ≥ max. {500 mm; c - 250 mm}
b_1 Distance to facade ≤ 300 mm
p Clear width at head height,
   p ≥ max. {300 mm; c - 450 mm}
h_1 Clear height between the scaffold stages h1 ≤ 2.0 m
h_2 Clear height between the scaffold stages and cross members/scaffold holders
h_3 Clear shoulder height
h_4 Height of side railing h4 ≥ 1.0 m, min. 0.95 m

Load class		Evenly distributed load max. kN/m²
1	Only inspection activities	0.75
2	Work that does not require the storage of material and building components	1.50
3	Width class W06 Painting and coating work, roofing and facade cladding work, pointing work	2.00
4	Min. width class W09 Bricklaying and rendering work,	3.00
5		4.50
6	reinforcement and installation work, work with tiles and natural stone, installation of composite thermal insulation systems	6.00

Width class	Width w of the scaffold stage in m
W 06	0.6 < w < 0.9
W 09	0.9 < w < 1.2
W 1.2	1.2 < w < 1.5
W 1.5	1.5 < w < 1.8
W 1.8	1.8 < w < 2.1
W 2.1	2.1 < w < 2.4
W 2.4	2.4 < w

2 Facade scaffolding
DIN EN 12811-1:2004-03, Temporary works equipment – Part 1: Scaffolds - Performance requirements and general design
Scaffolds are complex structures requiring careful design and coordination.
Scaffolds are temporary structures that provide a safe working platform for work to be carried out and for storing tools and materials; they provide protection against falling objects and the risk of persons falling. The construction of scaffolds is classified into six load classes and seven width classes, with three load categories:

Dead loads:
own load of the scaffold with all associated parts as well as necessary additional equipment, such as material lifts.

Live loads:
imposed loads, wind and snow loads

Exceptional loads:
loads from stored material or additional construction components

3 Sealing compounds
DIN 18540:2014-09, Sealing of exterior wall joints in building using joint sealants
This standard applies to external wall joints (movement joints) between building components made of in-situ concrete and/or prefabricated concrete elements forming a closed structure, and of un-rendered masonry and/or natural stone; the standard is also applicable to the interior.
The suitability of these compounds is determined by their extensibility and their resilience (the ability of the compound to return to the original dimensions once the effect of the forces causing the deformation ceases), both of which depend on the base material. In view of the fact that movement joints are subject to considerable and frequent changes in width, purely elastic base materials (tear easily) and purely plastic base materials (lasting deformation) are not suitable.

Place of application	Base material	Function	Extensibility in % of the joint width	Behaviour	Recovery capability in % of the joint width
Exterior	Polysulphide caoutchouc group of elastomers.	Permanently elastic sealing of construction joints, also where exposed to groundwater. Elastic, waterproof, resistant to chemicals.	≥ 25	Elastic	≥ 70
	Silicone caoutchouc group of elastomers.	Sealing profiles and sealing devices for window glazing. Repellent to water and to adhesives.	≥ 25	Elastic at temperatures from −70°C to +190°C, outside this range, plasto-elastic	≥ 70 ≥ 40 < 70
	Polyurethane seal group of elastomers.	Seals and covers for joints in concrete construction. Highly tear and abrasion resistant, highly impermeable to gases, resistant to acids, alkalis and solvents, resistant to ageing.	≥ 25	Elastic	≥ 70
Interior (not in wet rooms)	Butyl caoutchouc group of elastomers/co-polymers	Joint sealer, highly impermeable to gases, resistant to heat and chemicals, resistant to ageing.	≥ 5	Plastic to elasto-plastic	< 20 ≥ 20 < 40
	Acrylates, plastic emulsions or synthetic resin solutions based on acrylic resins or poly-acrylic resins.	In the form of a solution In the form of an emulsion Joints with little movement, joints between concrete, plaster and masonry. Fast drying, good response to tension.	≥ 5 ≥ 10	Plasto-elastic	≥ 40 < 70

4 Designation of roofing membranes
Material and method of application

Top layer	Abbreviation	Reinforcement and weight ≥ g/m2		Function	Thickness in mm	Method of application
Bitumen roofing membrane	G 200 DD J 300 DD PV 200 DD	Glass-fibre mesh Jute fabric Plastic fibre fleece	200 300 200	Sealing of roofs and buildings	– – –	Application with hot or cold adhesive
Bitumen roofing membrane for welding	V 60 S4 G 200 S4 PV 200 S5	Glass fleece Glass-fibre mesh Plastic fibre fleece	60 200 200	Sealing of roofs and buildings	4 4 5	Welding – heating the surfaces to be bonded with hot air and pressing them together.
Polymer bitumen roofing membrane Elastomer bitumen PYE, Plastomer bitumen PYP	PYE-G 200 DD PYE-J 300 DD PYE-PV 200 DD	Glass-fibre mesh Jute fabric Plastic fibre fleece	200 300 200	Roof sealing	– – –	Application with hot or cold adhesive
Polymer bitumen membrane for welding	PYE-G 200 S5 PYE-J 300 S4 PYE-PV 200 S5	Glass-fibre mesh Jute fabric Plastic fibre fleece	200 300 200	Sealing of roofs and buildings	5 5 5	Welding – heating the surfaces to be bonded with hot air and pressing them together.
Copolymer membrane	ECB-T1-2.5-K	Ethylene copolymer bitumen		Sealing of roofs and buildings	2-3	Application with hot or cold adhesive

Top layer	Material	Function	Thickness in mm	Method of application
Plastic membrane	Polyvinylchloride, with plasticiser (PVC-P-NB) Polyvinylchloride, fibre-reinforced (PVC-P-NB-PW) Polyvinylchloride, glass fleece-reinforced (PVC-P-NB-GV)	Roof sealing	1.2-2 1.2-2 1.2-2.4	Solvent welding – the surfaces to be bonded are dissolved with a solvent and then pressed together.
	Polyisobutylene, lined on one side (PIB-K)	Roof sealing	2.5	Solvent welding, bonding with adhesive
	Polyethylene, chlorinated, lined on one side (PE-C-K-PV) Polyethylene, chlorinated, fabric reinforcement (PE-C-K-PW)	Sealing of roofs and buildings	1.2-2 1.2-2	Solvent welding, bonding with adhesive
Elastomer membrane (synthetic caoutchouc)	Ethylene propylene dien monomers (EPDM) Chlorosulfonated polyethylene (CSM) Nitrile caoutchouc (NBR) Butyl caoutchouc (IIR)	Roof sealing	2.5-3.5 3-6 1.2-2.2 1.2-2.2	Bonding with a sealing tape, hot adhesive

STANDARDS AND GUIDELINES (SELECTION)

THERMAL INSULATION
- DIN 4108-3 Thermal protection and energy economy in buildings, replaced by DIN V 18599 Energy efficiency of buildings
- EnEV Energy Conservation Directive
- DIN EN ISO 10211 Thermal bridges in building construction
- DIN EN 13187 Thermal performance of buildings
- DIN EN ISO 14683 Thermal bridges in building construction
- DIN 55699 Application of composite thermal insulation systems
- DIN EN 13162 Thermal insulation products for buildings – Factory made mineral wool (MW) products
- DIN EN 13163 Thermal insulation products for buildings – Factory made expanded polystyrene (EPS) products
- DIN EN 13499/OENORM EN 13499/SN EN 12499 External thermal insulation composite systems (ETICS) based on expanded polystyrene
- DIN EN 13500/OENORM EN 13500/SN EN 13500 External thermal insulation composite systems (ETICS) based on mineral wool

PROTECTION AGAINST RAIN AND MOISTURE
- DIN 18195 Waterproofing of buildings
- DIN 18540 Sealing of exterior wall joints in building using joint sealants
- DIN 18531 Waterproofing of roofs
- DIN EN 13707/DIN V 20000-201 Waterproofing of roofs
- DIN EN 13969 Waterproofing of basements – tanking

SOUND INSULATION
- DIN 18005 Noise abatement in town planning
- DIN 4109 Noise abatement in buildings
- DIN EN ISO 717 Acoustics – Rating of sound insulation in buildings and of building elements
- DIN EN ISO 12354 Building acoustics – Calculation of the acoustic performance of buildings based on the performance of building components
- ISO 1996 Acoustics – Description, measurement and assessment of environmental noise – Part. 1: Basic parameters and assessment procedures
- VDI Guideline 4100 – Noise abatement in buildings

FIRE PROTECTION
- DIN 4102 Fire behaviour of building materials and components
- DIN EN 13 501 Fire classification of construction products and building elements
- DIN 18230 Structural fire protection in industrial buildings
- DIN 18234 Fire safety of large roofs of buildings

MASONRY – RENDER/PLASTER
- DIN 18 330 German construction contract procedures (VOB) – Part C: General technical specifications in construction contracts (ATV) – Masonry work
- DIN 1053 Masonry work
- EN 1996 Eurocode 6 – Structural design of masonry buildings
- DIN V 106 Calcium silicate bricks
- DIN V 4165 Autoclaved aerated concrete masonry units and high-precision units
- DIN 4166 Autoclaved aerated concrete slabs and panels
- DIN 18162 Lightweight concrete wallboards; unreinforced
- DIN 18550 Plastering/rendering and plastering/rendering systems
- DIN EN 13914 Design, preparation and application of external rendering and internal plastering
- DIN EN 846 Testing of masonry; determination of compressive strength and of modulus of elasticity
- DIN EN 998 Specification for mortar for masonry
- DIN 18555 Testing of mortars containing mineral binders; fresh mortar
- DIN EN 1062 Coating materials and coating systems for exterior masonry and concrete

CONCRETE
- DIN 18333 German construction contract procedures (VOB) – Part C: General technical specifications in construction contracts (ATV) – Concrete block work
- DIN 18203-1 Tolerances in building construction, prefabricated concrete elements
- DIN EN 206 Concrete

- DIN 1045 Concrete, reinforced and prestressed concrete structures
- DIN 4235 Compacting of concrete by vibrating
- DIN EN 1992 Eurocode 2: Design of reinforced and prestressed concrete structures, exposure classes DIN EN 1992-1-1
- DIN 18215 Timber form boards for concrete and reinforced concrete structures
- DIN 18216 Formwork ties
- DIN 18217 Concrete surfaces and formwork surface
- DIN SPEC 1021 Design of fastenings for use in concrete
- DIN V 18197 Sealing of joints in concrete with waterstops
- DIN EN 12350 Testing of fresh concrete
- DIN EN 12390 Testing of cured concrete
- DIN EN 12620 Aggregates for concrete
- DIN EN 13139 Aggregates for mortar
- DIN EN 932 Testing general characteristics of aggregates
- DIN EN 933 Testing geometric characteristics of aggregates
- DIN EN 1097 Testing mechanical and physical characteristics of aggregates
- DIN EN 1367 Testing thermal characteristics and weather resistance of aggregates
- DIN EN 1744 Testing chemical properties of aggregates
- DIN EN 13 055 Lightweight aggregates – Part 1: Lightweight aggregates for concrete, mortar and grout
- DIN EN 196 Methods of testing cement
- ISO 679 Cement – Methods of testing – Determination of strength
- DIN 1164 Cement with special properties
- DIN EN 14216 Composition, specifications and conformity criteria for special low-hydration heat cements
- DIN EN 12878 Pigments for the colouring of building materials based on cement and/or lime
- DIN EN 13263 Silica fume for concrete
- DIN EN 934 Admixtures for concrete, mortar and grout
- DIN EN 450 Fly ash for concrete
- DIN EN 480 Admixtures for concrete, mortar and grout
- DIN EN 13369 Common rules for precast concrete products
- DIN EN 14992 Precast concrete products – Wall elements
- DIN V 18500 Manufactured stone
- DIN 18516 Cladding for external walls; ventilated at rear – Part 5: Manufactured stone; requirements, design
- DIN EN 771-5 Specification for masonry units – Part 5: Manufactured stone
- DIN EN 13747-1 Precast concrete slabs with additional in-situ concrete – General requirements

TIMBER, WOOD-BASED MATERIALS
- DIN 18334 German construction contract procedures (VOB) – Part C: General technical specifications in construction contracts (ATV) – Carpentry and timber construction
- DIN 18203 Tolerances in building construction - Part 3: Building products made of timber and wood-based materials
- DIN 68100 Tolerance system for wood working and wood processing
- DIN 4074 Strength grading of wood
- DIN 68364 Properties of wood species – Density, modulus of elasticity and strength
- DIN EN 338 Structural timber – Strength classes
- DIN EN 335 Durability of wood and wood-based products
- DIN EN 350 Durability of wood and wood-based products
- DIN EN 1611 Softwood
- DIN EN 408 Timber structures – Structural timber and glued laminated timber
- DIN EN 594/596 Timber structures – Walls in timber panel construction
- DIN EN 595 Timber structures – Lattice girders
- DIN EN 1995 Eurocode 5: Design of timber structures
- DIN 1052 Design of timber structures
- DIN EN 12369 Wood-based materials – OSB, chipboard, fibreboard and solid wood panels
- DIN EN 14251 Structural round timber
- DIN 20000 Application of construction products in structures – Part 1: Wood based panels, Part 2: Prefabricated timber formwork beams
- DIN 68800 Wood preservation

ROOF AND ROOFING MATERIALS
- DIN 18338 German construction contract procedures (VOB) – Part C: General technical specifications in construction contracts (ATV) – Roofing and roof sealing work
- DIN 68119 Wood shingles
- DIN EN 490 Concrete roofing tiles and coping stones
- DIN EN 492 Fibre-cement slates and fittings
- DIN EN 494 Fibre-cement corrugated sheets and fittings
- DIN EN 501 Roofing products from metal sheet – Zinc sheeting
- DIN EN 502 Roofing products from metal sheet – Stainless steel sheeting
- DIN EN 504 Roofing products from metal sheet – Copper sheeting
- DIN EN 505 Roofing products from metal sheet – Steel sheeting
- DIN EN 506 Roofing products from metal sheet – Copper or zinc sheeting
- DIN EN 507 Roofing products from metal sheet – Aluminium sheeting
- DIN EN 508 Roofing products from metal sheet – Steel, aluminium or stainless steel sheeting
- DIN EN 534 Corrugated bitumen sheets
- DIN EN 544 Bitumen shingles with mineral and/or synthetic reinforcements
- DIN EN 12326-1 Slate and stone for overlapping roofing and external cladding
- DIN EN 14964 Rigid roofing underlays
- DIN EN 1304 Clay roofing tiles and fittings

FACADES IN GENERAL
- DIN 18202 Tolerances in building construction – Buildings
- DIN EN 1991 Eurocode 1, Actions on structures
- DIN EN 12152/DIN EN 12153 Curtain walling – Air permeability
- DIN EN 12154/DIN EN 12155/DIN EN 13050 Curtain walling – Watertightness
- DIN EN 12179 Curtain walling – Wind load resistance
- DIN EN 13119 Curtain walling – Terminology
- DIN EN 13830 Curtain walling – Product standard
- DIN EN 13947 Thermal performance of curtain wall facades
- DIN EN 14019 Curtain walling – Impact resistance
- DIN EN 1364 Fire resistance tests for non-loadbearing elements – Curtain walling
- DIN 18516 Cladding for external walls; ventilated at rear
- DIN 18351 German construction contract procedures (VOB) – Part C: General technical specifications in construction contracts (ATV) – Facade work/back-ventilated curtain wall facades
- DIN EN 15651 Sealants for facade elements
- DIN 18203 Tolerances in building construction – Prefabricated steel components
- DIN EN 12365 Gaskets and weatherstripping for doors, windows, shutters and curtain walling

FIBRE CEMENT
- ISO 8336/DIN EN 12467 Fibre-cement board
- DIN EN 15057 Corrugated fibre-cement panels

GLASS AND GLAZING MATERIALS
- DIN 18361 German construction contract procedures (VOB) – Part C: General technical specifications in construction contracts (ATV) – Glazing work
- DIN EN 572 Glass in building
- DIN 1249 Plate glass in building
- DIN 1259 Glass: Part 1: Terminology for glass types and groups, Part 2: Terminology for glass products
- DIN EN 1279 Glass in building: Insulating glass units
- DIN EN 1863 Glass in building: Heat-strengthened soda lime silicate glass
- DIN EN 14179 Glass in building – Heat-soaked thermally toughened soda lime silicate safety glass
- DIN EN 15683 Glass in building – Thermally toughened soda lime silicate channel-shaped safety glass
- DIN 18545 Sealing of glazing with sealants

- DIN EN 15434 Glass in building – Product standard for structural and/or ultra-violet resistant sealant (for use with structural sealant glazing and/or insulating glass units with exposed seals)
- DIN EN 13022 Glass in building – Structural sealant glazing
- ISO 28278 Glass in building – Structural sealant glazing
- DIN EN 1288 Glass in building – Determination of the bending strength of glass
- DIN EN 12600 Glass in building – Pendulum tests – Impact test method and classification of plate glass
- DIN 52338 Methods of testing flat glass for use in buildings; ball-drop test on laminated glass
- DIN EN 410 Glass in building – Determination of luminous and solar characteristics of glazing
- DIN 5034 Daylight in interiors
- DIN EN 13363 Solar protection devices combined with glazing
- DIN EN ISO 13791/DIN EN ISO 13792 Thermal performance of buildings without mechanical cooling

METAL
- DIN 18335 German construction contract procedures (VOB) – Part C: General technical specifications in construction contracts (ATV) – Steel construction work
- DIN 18360 German construction contract procedures (VOB) – Part C: General technical specifications in construction contracts (ATV) – Metal construction work
- DIN 18364 German construction contract procedures (VOB) – Part C: General technical specifications in construction contracts (ATV) – Corrosion protection work for steel and aluminium structures
- DIN 18203-2 Tolerances in building construction – Part 2: Prefabricated steel components
- DIN EN ISO 12944 Paints and varnishes: Corrosion protection of steel structures using protective paint systems
- DIN EN 988 Zinc and zinc alloys – Requirements for rolled flat construction products
- DIN EN 14782 Self-supporting metal sheet for roofing, external cladding and internal lining
- DIN EN 14783 Fully supported metal sheet and strip for roofing, external cladding and internal lining
- DIN 24041 Perforated plates – Dimensions
- VDI 3137 Forming – Terms, designations, characteristic quantities
- DIN EN 14509 Self-supporting, double-skin metal-faced insulating panels

PLASTICS AND TEXTILES
- DIN EN 1013 Light-transmitting single-skin profiled plastic sheets for internal and external installation to roofs, walls and ceilings
- DIN 18204 Components for enclosures made of textile fabrics and plastic films (tent fabric) for structures and tents
- DIN EN ISO 11963 Plastics – Polycarbonate sheets
- DIN EN 16153 Light-transmitting flat multiwall polycarbonate (PC) sheets for internal and external installation to roofs, walls and ceilings
- DIN EN 16240 Light-transmitting flat solid polycarbonate (PC) sheets for internal and external installation to roofs, walls and ceilings
- DIN EN 1013 Light-transmitting single-skin profiled plastic sheets for internal and external installation to roofs, walls and ceilings

NATURAL STONE
- DIN 18332 German construction contract procedures (VOB) – Part C: General technical specifications in construction contracts (ATV) – Natural stone work
- DIN 18516-3 Cladding for external walls – Part 3: Natural stone
- DIN EN 1341 Slabs of natural stone for external paving
- DIN EN 1469 Natural stone products – Slabs for cladding
- DIN EN 12326 Slate and stone for overlapping roofing and external cladding
- DIN EN 13364 Natural stone test methods – Determination of the breaking load at dowel hole

ASSOCIATIONS (SELECTION)

MASONRY - RENDER / PLASTER

Bundesverband der Deutschen
Ziegelindustrie e.V.
Schaumburg-Lippe-Straße 4
53133 Bonn
Tel.: +49 228 914930
www.ziegel.de

Bundesverband
Kalksandsteinindustrie
Entenfangweg 15
30419 Hannover
Tel.: +49 511 279540
www.kalksandstein.de

Bundesverband Leichtbeton e.V.
Sandkauler Weg 1
56564 Neuwied
Tel.: +49 2631 22227
www.leichtbeton.de

Bundesverband Porenbeton
Kochstraße 6-7
10969 Berlin
Tel.: +49 30 25928214
www.bv-porenbeton.de

Deutsche Gesellschaft für
Mauerwerksbau
Kochstr. 6-7
10969 Berlin
Tel.: +49 30 25359640
www.dgfm.de

Fachverband der Stuckateure
für Ausbau und Fassade
Wollgrasweg 23
70599 Stuttgart
Tel.: +49 711 451230
www.stuck-verband.de

Verband Österreichischer
Ziegelwerke
Wienerbergstraße 11
A-1100 Wien
Tel.: +43 1 58733460
www.ziegel.at

Verband Schweizerische
Ziegelindustrie
Elfenstraße 19
CH-3006 Bern
Tel.: +41 31 3565757
www.domoterra.ch

INSULATION

Fachverband WDVS
Fremersbergstraße 33
76530 Baden-Baden
Tel.: +49 7221 3009890
www.fachverband-wdvs.de

Gesamtverband
Dämmstoffindustrie GDI
Friedrichstraße 95 (PB 138)
10117 Berlin
Tel.: +49 30 206189790
www.gdi-daemmstoffe.de

Institut Bauen und Umwelt e.V.
Panoramastraße 1
10178 Berlin
Tel.: +49 30 30877480
www.bau-umwelt.com

CONCRETE

BetonMarketing Deutschland
GmbH
Steinhof 39
40699 Erkrath
Tel.: +49 211 280481
www.beton.org

BETONSUISSE Marketing AG
Marktgasse 53
CH-3011 Bern
Tel.: +41 31 3279787
www.cemsuisse.ch

Bundesverband der Deutschen
Transportbetonindustrie e.V.
Kochstraße 6-7
10969 Berlin
Tel.: +49 30 25922920
www.transportbeton.org

Bundesverband der Deutschen
Zementindustrie e.V.
Postfach 51005066
50941 Köln
Tel.: +49 221 376560
www.BDZement.de

Bundesverband Deutsche
Beton- und Fertigteilindustrie e.V.
Schlossallee 10
53119 Bonn
Tel.: +49 228 9545656
www.fdb-fertigteilbau.de

Verein Deutscher Zementwerke
e.V.
Tannenstraße 2
40476 Düsseldorf
Tel.: +49 211 4369260
www.vdz-online.de

Vereinigung der Österreichischen
Zementindustrie
Reisnerstraße 53
A-1030 Wien
Tel.: +43 1 71466810
www.zement.at

CEMBUREAU – Vereinigung der
Europäischen Zementindustrie
www.cembureau.be

ERMCO – Europäischer
Transportbetonverband
www.ermco.eu

TIMBER, WOOD-BASED
MATERIALS

Fachverband der Holzindustrie
Österreichs
Schwarzenbergplatz 4
A-1037 Wien
Tel.: +43 1 7122601
www.holzindustrie.at

Hauptverband der Deutschen
Holzindustrie und Kunststoffe
verarbeitenden Industrie und
verwandter Industrie- und
Wirtschaftszweige e.V.
Flutgraben 2
53604 Bad Honnef
Tel.: +49 2224 93770
www.holzindustrie.de

Holzbau Deutschland – Bund
Deutscher Zimmermeister im
Zentralverband des Deutschen
Baugewerbes e.V. (ZDB)
Kronenstraße 55-58
10117 Berlin
Tel.: +49 30 203140
www.holzbau-deutschland.de

Informationsdienst Holz
Esmarchstraße 3
10407 Berlin
www.informationsdienst-holz.de

proHolz Austria
Arbeitsgemeinschaft der
österreichischen Holzwirtschaft
Uraniastraße 4
A-1011 Wien
Tel.: +43 1 7120474
www.proholz.at

Lignum, Holzwirtschaft Schweiz
Mühlebachstrasse 8
CH-8008 Zürich
Tel.: +41 44 2674777
www.lignum.ch

Studiengemeinschaft Holzleimbau
e.V.
Heinz-Fangman-Str. 2
42287 Wuppertal
Tel.: +49 202 76972732
www.studiengemeinschaft-
holzleimbau.de

ROOF AND ROOFING MATERIALS

Zentralverband des deutschen
Dachdeckerhandwerks e.V.
Fachverband Dach-, Wand- und
Abdichtungstechnik
Fritz-Reuter-Straße 1
50968 Köln
Tel.: +49 221 3980380
www.dachdecker.de

Fassaden allgemein
Fachverband Baustoffe und
Bauteile für vorgehängte
hinterlüftete Fassaden e.V.
Kurfürstenstraße 129
10785 Berlin
Tel.: +49 30 21286281
www.fvhf.de

Österreichischer Fachverband für
hinterlüftete Fassaden (ÖFHF)
Campus 21, Europaring F15 /303
A-2345 Brunn am Gebirge
Tel.: +43 1 8903896
www.oefhf.at

Schweizerischer Fachverband für
hinterlüftete Fassaden (SFHF)
Industriestraße 25
CH-3178 Bösingen
Tel.: +41 31 7475868
www.sfhf.ch

VFT – Verband für Fassadentechnik
Ziegelhüttenstr. 67
64832 Babenhausen
Tel.: +49 6073 712650
www.v-f-t.de

Society of Facade Engineering
(SFE)
www.facadeengineeringsociety.org

vdd Industrieverband Bitumen-
Dach- und Dichtungsbahnen e.V.
Mainzer Landstr. 55
60329 Frankfurt am Main
Tel.: +49 69 25561315
www.derdichtebau.de

GLAS UND GLASBAUSTOFFE

Bundesverband Flachglas
Mülheimer Straße 1
53840 Troisdorf
Tel.: +49 2241 87270
www.bundesverband-flachglas.de

Fachverband Konstruktiver Glasbau
Aachener Straße 1019a
50858 Köln
Tel.: +49 221 9488714
www.glas-fkg.org

Schweizerisches Institut für Glas
am Bau
Rütistrasse 16
CH-8952 Schlieren
www.sigab.ch

Verband Fenster + Fassade (VFF)
Walter-Kolb-Str. 1-7
60594 Frankfurt am Main
Tel.: +49 69 9550540
www.window.de

NATURAL STONE

Deutscher Naturwerkstein-
Verband e.V.
Sanderstraße 4
97070 Würzburg
Tel.: +49 931 12061
www.naturwerksteinverband.de

Fachverband Fliesen und
Naturstein
Kronenstrasse 55-58
10117 Berlin
Tel.: +49 30 203 140
www.fachverband-fliesen.de

Naturstein-Verband Schweiz
Seilerstrasse 22
Postfach 5853
CH-3001 Bern
Tel.: +41 31 3102010
www.nvs.ch

MANUFACTURERS (SELECTION)

FASTENINGS/FORMWORK

Adolf Würth GmbH & Co. KG
Reinhold-Würth-Str. 12–17
74653 Künzelsau
Tel.: +49 7940 150
www.wuerth.de

BWM Dübel + Montagetechnik
GmbH
Ernst-Mey-Str. 1
70771 Leinfelden-Echterdingen
Tel.: +49 711 903130
www.bwm.de

compriband-Dichtungen GmbH
Hanfpointstraße 101
A-4050 Traun
Tel.: +43 7229 724960
www.compriband.at

DYWIDAG-Systems International
GmbH
Südstraße 3
32457 Porta Westfalica
Tel.: +49 5731 76780
www.contec-bau.de

Gerlinger GmbH & Co. KG
Klebeband- und Dichtstoffwerke
Dietrich-Gerlinger-Str. 1
86720 Nördlingen
Tel.: +49 9081 2130
www.gerband.de

H-BAU Technik GmbH
Am Güterbahnhof 20
79771 Klettgau
Tel.: +49 7742 921520
www.h-bau.de

HALFEN
Vertriebsgesellschaft mbH
Katzbergstr. 3
40764 Langenfeld
Tel.: +49 2173 9700
www.halfen.de

ISO-Chemie GmbH
Röntgenstraße 12
73431 Aalen
Tel.: +49 7361 94900
www.iso-chemie.de

JORDAHL GmbH
Nobelstr. 51
12057 Berlin
Tel.: +49 30 682 83433
www.jordahl.de

KEIL – Befestigungstechnik GmbH
Im Auel 42
51766 Engelskirchen
Tel.: +49 2263 8070
www.keil.eu

Max Frank GmbH & Co. KG
Mitterweg 1
94339 Leiblfing
Tel.: +49 9427 1890
www.maxfrank.de

Migua Fugensysteme GmbH
Dieselstraße 20
42489 Wülfrath
Tel.: +49 2058 7740
www.migua.com

PERI GmbH
Rudolf-Diesel-Straße
89264 Weißenhorn
Tel.: +49 7309 9500
www.peri.de

PFEIFER Seil- und Hebetechnik
GmbH
Dr.-Karl-Lenz-Str. 66
87700 Memmingen
Tel.: +49 8331 9370
www.pfeifer.de

Ramsauer GmbH & Co. KG
Sarstein 17
A-4822 Bad Goisern
Tel.: +43 6135 82050
www.ramsauer.at

Wilhelm Flender GmbH & Co. KG
Herborner Straße 7–9
57250 Netphen
Tel.: +49 2737 59350
www.flender-flux.de

CONSTRUCTION CHEMICALS,
MORTAR

B.T. innovation GmbH
Sudenburger Wuhne 60
39116 Magdeburg
Tel.: +49 391 73520
www.bt-innovation.de

BASF SE
67063 Ludwigshafen
Tel.: +49 621 600
www.construction.basf.com

Uzin Utz AG
Dieselstraße 3
89079 Ulm
Tel.: +49 731 40970
www.codex-x.de

Dyckerhoff GmbH
Biebricher Straße 69
65203 Wiesbaden
Tel.: +49 611 6760
www.dyckerhoff.com

HASIT Trockenmörtel GmbH
Landshuter Straße 30
85356 Freising
Tel.: +49 8161 6020
www.hasit.de

HENKEL AG & Co. KGaA
Henkelstr. 67
40131 Düsseldorf
Tel.: +49 211 7970
www.ceresit-bautechnik.de

KauPo Plankenhorn e.K.
Max-Planck-Str. 9/3
78549 Spaichingen
Tel.: +49 7424 958423
www.kaupo.de

MAPEI GmbH
Bahnhofsplatz 10
63906 Erlenbach/Main
Tel.: +49 9372 98950
www.mapei.de

maxit Gruppe – Franken Maxit
Mauermörtel GmbH & Co.
Azendorf 63
95359 Kasendorf
Tel.: +49 9220 18 0
www.franken-maxit.de

MEM Bauchemie GmbH
Am Emsdeich 52
26789 Leer
Tel.: +49 491 925800
www.mem.de

Moll Bauökologische Produkte
GmbH
Rheintalstraße 35–43
68723 Schwetzingen
Tel.: +49 6202 27820
www.proclima.com

Murexin AG
Franz-von-Furtenbach-Straße 1
A-2700 Wiener Neustadt
Tel.: +43 2622 274010
www.murexin.com

OTTO-CHEMIE Hermann Otto
GmbH
Krankenhausstraße 14
83413 Fridolfing
Tel.: +49 8684 9080
www.otto-chemie.de

quick-mix Gruppe GmbH & Co. KG
Mühleneschweg 6
49090 Osnabrück
Tel.: +49 541 60101
www.quick-mix.de

Remmers Baustofftechnik GmbH
Bernhard-Remmers-Str. 13
49624 Löningen
Tel.: +49 54 32 830
www.remmers.de

Saint-Gobain Weber GmbH
Schanzenstr. 84
40549 Düsseldorf
Tel.: +49 211 913690
www.sg-weber.de

Schöck Bauteile GmbH
Vimbucher Straße 2
76534 Baden-Baden
Tel.: +49 7223 9670
www.schoeck.de

SCHOMBURG,
Unternehmensgruppe
Aquafinstraße 2-8
32760 Detmold
Tel.: +49 5231 95300
www.schomburg.de

Sika Deutschland GmbH
Kornwestheimer Straße 103–107
70439 Stuttgart
Tel.: +49 711 80090
www.sika.de

Sopro Bauchemie GmbH
Biebricher Straße 74
65203 Wiesbaden
Tel.: +49 611 17070
www.sopro.com

StoCretec GmbH
Gutenbergstr. 6
65830 Kriftel
Tel.: +49 6192 401104
www.stocretec.de

tremco illbruck GmbH & Co. KG
Werner-Haepp-Str. 1
92439 Bodenwöhr
Tel.: +49 9434 2080
www.tremco-illbruck.de

WEBAC-Chemie GmbH
Fahrenberg 22
22885 Barsbüttel bei Hamburg
Tel.: +49 40 670570
www.webac.de

BRICKS/CLINKER BRICKS

ABC-Klinkergruppe
Grüner Weg 8
49509 Recke
Tel.: +49 54 5393330
www.abc-klinker.de

Adolf Zeller GmbH & Co.
POROTON Ziegelwerke KG
Märkerstr. 44
63755 Alzenau
Tel.: +49 6023 97760
www.zellerporoton.de

Agrob Buchtal GmbH
Servaisstraße
53347 Alfter-Witterschlick
Tel.: +49 228 3910
www.agrob-buchtal.de

August Lücking GmbH & Co. KG
Eggestr. 2
34414 Warburg
Tel.: +49 5251 13400
www.luecking.de

Bisotherm GmbH
Eisenbahnstraße 12
D-56218 Mülheim-Kärlich
Tel.: +49 2630 98760
www.bisotherm.de

Bockhorner Klinkerziegelei
Uhlhorn GmbH & Co. KG
Hauptstraße 34
26345 Bockhorn-Grabstede
Tel.: +49 44 5291280
www.bockhorner.de

CRH Clay Solutions GmbH
Wellie 65
31595 Steyerberg-Wellie
Tel.: +49 50 2398 0110
www.crh-ccs.de

Deppe Backstein-Keramik GmbH
Neuenhauser Straße 52
49843 Uelsen-Lemke
Tel.: +49 59 4292100
www.deppe-backstein.de

Egernsunder Ziegel GmbH
Osterlükken 2
24955 Harrislee
Tel.: +49 461 773080
www.egernsunder-ziegel.de

Feldhaus Klinker Vertriebs GmbH
Nordring 1
49196 Bad Laer
Tel.: +49 5424 29200
www.feldhaus-klinker.de

Gillrath Ziegel- und Klinkerwerke
GmbH & Co. KG
Wockerather Weg 38
41812 Erkelenz
Tel.: +49 2431 2200
www.gillrath.de

Girnghuber GmbH
Ludwig-Girnghuber-Straße 1
84163 Marklkofen
Tel.: +49 87 32240
www.gima-ziegel.de

Hagemeister GmbH & Co. KG
Klinkerwerk Appelhülsener Straße
48301 Nottuln
Tel.: +49 25 028040
www.hagemeister.de

Heidelberger Kalksandstein GmbH
Malscher Str. 17
76448 Durmersheim
Tel.: +49 7245 8060
www.heidelberger-kalksandstein.de

HKS Hunziker Kalksandstein AG
Aarauerstr. 75
CH-5200 Brugg
Tel.: +41 56 4605466
www.hksag.ch

Janinhoff GmbH & Co. KG
Thierstraße 130
48165 Münster-Hiltrup
Tel.: +49 25 0196340
www.janinhoff.de

Keller Systeme AG
Ziegeleistrasse 7
CH-8422 Pfungen
Tel.: +41 52 3040300
www.Keller-Systeme.ch

Klimaleichtblock GmbH
Lohmannstr. 31
56626 Andernach
Tel.: +49 2632 25770
www.klb.de

Klinkerwerk Rusch KG Ritscher
Außendeich 2
21706 Drochtersen
Tel.: +49 41 48610130
www.rusch-klinker.de

KS-ORIGINAL GMBH
Entenfangweg 15
30419 Hannover
Tel.: +49 511 279530
www.ks-original.de

Moeding Keramikfassaden GmbH
Ludwig-Girnghuber-Str. 1
84163 Marklkofen
Tel.: +49 8732 24600
www.moeding.de

NBK Keramik GmbH & Co. KG
Reeser Straße 235
46446 Emmerich
Tel.: +49 2822 81110
www.nbk.de

Neue Ziegelmanufaktur
Glindow GmbH
Alpenstraße 47
14542 Werder (Havel), OT Glindow
Tel.: +49 33 2766490
www.ziegelmanufaktur.com

OLFRY Ziegelwerke GmbH & Co.
KG
Friesenstraße 9-11
49377 Vechta
Tel.: +49 44 419590
www.olfry.de

Petersen Tegl A/S
Nybølnorvej 14
DK-6310 Broager
Tel.: +45 74 441236
www.petersen-tegl.dk

Randers Tegl Deutschland GmbH
Tegelbarg 9
24576 Bad Bramstedt
Tel.: +49 41 9287930
www.randerstegl.de

Röben Tonbaustoffe GmbH
Klein Schweinebrück 168
26340 Zetel
Tel.: +49 44 52880
www.roeben.com

THERMOPOR Ziegel-Kontor
Ulm GmbH
Postfach 43 45
89033 Ulm
Tel.: +49 731 966940
www.thermopor.de

UNIKA GmbH
Am Opel-Prüffeld 3
63110 Rodgau-Dudenhofen
Tel.: +49 6106 280910
www.unika-kalksandstein.de

Unipor – Xella Gruppe
Düsseldorfer Landstraße 395
47259 Duisburg
Tel.: +49 203 608800
www.unipor.de

Wehrmann-Ziegel GmbH
Rieder Str. 2
28844 Weyhe-Sudweyhe
Tel.: +49 4203 81290
www.wehrmann.de

Wienerberger GmbH
ArGeTon
Oldenburger Allee 26
30659 Hannover
Tel.: +49 610 700
www.wienerberger.de

Wienerberger AG
Wienerberg City,
Wienerbergstraße 11
A-1100 Wien
Tel.: +43 1 60 1920
www.wienerberger.com

Wittmunder Klinker
Mühlenstraße 69
26409 Wittmund
Tel.: +49 44 6294740
www.wittmunder-klinker.de

Ziegelei Hebrok Natrup-Hagen
Ziegeleiweg 5
49170 Hagen
Tel.: +49 5405 98020
www.ziegelei-hebrok.de

Ziegelwerk Blomesche Wildnis
Heinrich Pollmann jun. KG
An der Chaussee 47-51
25348 Glückstadt
Tel.: +49 41 24604830
www.zbw-klinker.de

Ziegelwerk Freital EDER GmbH
Wilsdruffer Straße 25
01705 Freital
Tel.: +49 351 648810
www.ziegel-eder.de

CONCRETE

Bürkle Betonfertigteile GmbH & Co.
Fellbacher Str. 68
70736 Fellbach
Tel.: +49 711 951600
www.buerkle-baugruppe.de

CEMEX Deutschland AG
Theodorstr. 178
40472 Düsseldorf
Tel.: +49 211 44700
www.cemex.de

CREABETON MATERIAUX AG
Oberes Kandergrien
CH-3646 Einigen
Tel.: +41 33 334 2525
www.creabeton-materiaux.ch

Dennert Baustoffwelt GmbH & Co.
KG
Veit-Dennert-Str. 7
96132 Schlüsselfeld
Tel.: +49 9552 710
www.dennert.de

Ducon Europe GmbH & Co. KG
Farmstr. 118
64546 Mörfelden-Walldorf
Tel.: +49 6105 275831
www.ducon.eu

Dyckerhoff AG
Biebricher Straße 69
65203 Wiesbaden
Tel.: +49 611 6760
www.dyckerhoff.com

F.C. NÜDLING BETONELEMENTE
GmbH + Co. KG
Ruprechtstraße 24
36037 Fulda
Tel.: +49 661 83870
www.nuedling.de

Hebel – Xella Gruppe
Düsseldorfer Landstraße 395
47259 Duisburg
Tel.: +49 203 608800
www.hebel.de

Heidelberger Beton GmbH
Berliner Str. 10
69120 Heidelberg
Tel.: +49 6221 48139503
www.heidelberger-beton.de

Hermann Rudolph Baustoffwerk
GmbH
Steinbißstr. 15
88171 Weiler-Simmerberg
Tel.: +49 8384 82100
www.rudolph-baustoffwerk.de

Holcim (Deutschland) AG
Hannoversche Str. 28
31319 Sehnde
Tel.: +49 5132 927432
www.holcim.de

Liapor GmbH + Co. KG
Industriestr. 2
91352 Hallerndorf – Pautzfeld
Tel.: +49 95454 480
www.liapor.com

LUCEM GmbH
PratTel.sackstraße 25
52222 Stolberg
Tel.: +49 2402 1246694
www.lucem.de

Rieder Smart Elements GmbH
Mühlenweg 22
A-5751 Maishofen
Tel.: +43 6542 690844
www.rieder.cc

Schlagmann Poroton GmbH & Co.
KG
Ziegeleistr. 1
84367 Zeilarn
Tel.: +49 8572 170
www.schlagmann.de

Silka / Ytong – Xella Gruppe
Düsseldorfer Landstraße 395
47259 Duisburg
Tel.: +49 203 608800
www.ytong-silka.de

Syspro-Gruppe Betonbauteile e.V.
Hanauer Str. 31
63526 Erlensee
Tel.: +49 700 70002005
www.syspro.de

Thermodur Wandelemente
GmbH & Co KG
In Metzlerskaul 20
56567 Neuwied
Tel.: +49 2631 97420
www.thermodur.de

NOE-Schaltechnik Georg
Meyer-Keller GmbH + Co. KG
Kuntzestraße 72
73079 Süssen
Tel.: +49 7162 131
www.noeplast.com

RECKLI GmbH
Gewerkenstr. 9a
44628 Herne
Tel.: +49 2323 17060
www.reckli.de

Faserzement
AURiA Deutschland GmbH
Feringastr. 6
85774 München/Unterföhring
Tel.: +49 89 99216156
www.auria.de

Eternit AG
Im Breitspiel 20
69126 Heidelberg
Tel.: +49 6224 7010
www.eternit.de

Eternit (Schweiz) AG
CH-8867 Niederurnen
www.swisspearl.ch

FibreCem Deutschland GmbH
Lohmener Str. 15
01833 Dürrröhrsdorf-Dittersbach
Tel.: +49 35026 940
www.fibrecem.de

COMPOSITE THERMAL
ELEMENTS

Aluform System GmbH & Co. KG
Dresdener Straße 15
02994 Bernsdorf
Tel.: +49 35723 990
www.aluform.com

ArcelorMittal Construction
Deutschland GmbH
Münchener Straße 2
06796 Sandersdorf-Brehna
Tel.: +49 34954 4550
www.arcelormittal.com/arval

Metawell GmbH
Schleifmühlweg 31
86633 Neuburg/Donau
Tel.: +49 8431 67150
www.metawell.com

Metecno Bausysteme GmbH
Am Amselberg 1
99444 Blankenhain
Tel.: +49 36454560
www.metecno.de

Hoesch Bausysteme GmbH
Hammerstraße 11
57223 Kreuztal
Tel.: +49 2732 5991599
www.hoesch-bau.com

Ruukki Deutschland GmbH
Schifferstraße 92
47059 Duisburg
Tel.: +49 203 317390
www.ruukki.com

INSULATION / SEALANTS

alsecco GmbH
Kupferstraße 50
36208 Wildeck
Tel.: +49 369 22880
www.alsecco.com

Baumit GmbH
Reckenberg 12
87541 Bad Hindelang
Tel.: +49 8324 9210
www.baumit.com

Dörken GmbH & Co. KG
Wetterstraße 58
58313 Herdecke
Tel.: +49 2330 630
www.doerken.de

Doser Holzfaser-Dämmsysteme
GmbH
Vilstalstr. 80
87459 Pfronten
Tel.: +49 8363 96000
www.doser-dhd.de

FDT FlachdachTechnologie GmbH
& Co. KG
Eisenbahnstraße 6–8
68199 Mannheim
Tel.: +49 621 85040
www.fdt.de

Fermacell GmbH
Düsseldorfer Landstr. 395
47259 Duisburg
Tel.: +49 800 5235665
www.fermacell.de

GUTEX Holzfaserplattenwerk
Gutenburg 5
79761 Waldshut-Tiengen
Tel.: +49 7741 60990
www.gutex.de

IsoBouw Dämmtechnik GmbH
Etrastr. 1
74232 Abstatt
Tel.: +49 7062 6780
www.isobouw.de

KEMPER SYSTEM GmbH & Co. KG
Holländische Straße 32–36
34246 Vellmar
Tel.: +49 561 82950
www.kemper-system.com

POLYFIN AG
Ziegelhäuser Straße 25
69250 Schönau
Tel.: +49 6228 92490
www.polyfin.de

RYGOL DÄMMSTOFFE
Werner Rygol GmbH & Co. KG
Kelheimer Str. 37
93351 Painten
Tel.: +49 9499 94000
www.rygol.de

Saint-Gobain Isover
Bürgermeister-Grünzweig-Straße 1
67059 Ludwigshafen
Tel.: +49 621 501200
www.isover.de

Sto SE & Co. KGaA
Ehrenbachstr. 1
79780 Stühlingen
Tel.: +49 7744 571010
www.sto.com

Wilhelm Flender GmbH & Co. KG
Herborner Straße 7–9
57250 Netphen
Tel.: +49 2737 59350
www.flender-flux.de

METAL

Alcoa Architectural Products
1 rue du Ballon
F-68500 Merxheim
Tel.: +33 3 89 744763
www.alcoaarchitecturalproducts.eu

ALUCOBOND®/3A Composites
Schweiter Technologies AG
Neugasse 10
CH-8810 Horgen
Tel.: +41 44 7183303
www.schweiter.com

Belu TecVertriebsgesellschaft mbH
Technische Systeme
Am Seitenkanal 3
49811 Lingen (EMS)
Tel.: +49 591 912040
www.belu-tec.de

Dillinger Fabrik gelochter Bleche
GmbH
Franz-Méguin-Straße 20
66763 Dillingen
Tel.: +49 6831 70030
www.dfgb.de

Gebr. Kufferath AG
Metallweberstraße 46
52348 Düren
Tel.: +49 2421 8030
www.gkd.de

Hans Laukien GmbH
Borsigstraße 23
24145 Kiel
Tel.: +49 43171870
www.laukien.de

Haver & Boecker Drahtweberei und
Maschinenfabrik
Ennigerloher Straße 64
59302 Oelde
Tel.: +49 2522 30684
www.diedrahtweber-architektur.
com

Hueck GmbH & Co. KG
Loher Straße 9
58511 Lüdenscheid
Tel.: +49 2351 1510
www.hueck.de

Kalzip GmbH
August-Horch-Str. 20-22
56070 Koblenz
Tel.: +49 261 98340
www.kalzip.com

Colt International GmbH
Briener Straße 186
47533 Kleve
Tel.: +49 2821 9900
www.colt-info.de

KME Germany GmbH & Co. KG
Klosterstr 29
49074 Osnabrück
Tel.: +49 541 3212000
www.kme.com/tecu

MN Metall GmbH
Industrieweg 34
23730 Neustadt
Tel.: +49 4561 51 790
www.mn-metall.de

Novelis Europa
Sternenfeldstr. 19
CH-8700 Küsnacht
Tel.: +41 44 386 2150
www.novelis.com

PREFA GmbH
Aluminiumstr. 2
98634 Wasungen
Tel.: +49 36941 78510
www.prefa.de

proMesh GmbH
In den Waldäckern 10
75417 Mühlacker
Tel.: +49 7041 954460
www.alphamesh.de

RAICO Bautechnik GmbH
Gewerbegebiet Nord 2
87772 Pfaffenhausen
Tel.: +49 8265 9110
www.raico.de

RHEINZINK GmbH & Co. KG
Bahnhofstraße 90
45711 Datteln
Tel.: +49 2363 6050
www.rheinzink.de

RMIG GmbH
Hallesche Strasse 39
06779 Raguhn – Jeßnitz
Tel.: +49 34 906500
www.rmig.com

ThyssenKrupp Steel Europe AG
Kaiser-Wilhelm-Str. 100
47166 Duisburg
Tel.: +49 203 520
www.thyssenkrupp-steel-europe.
com

Umicore Bausysteme GmbH
Gladbecker Straße 413
45326 Essen
Tel.: +49 201 836060
www.vmzinc.de

Reynaers GmbH Aluminium
Systeme
Franzstrasse 25
45968 Gladbeck
Tel.: +49 2043 96400
www.reynaers.com

GLASS - FACADE SYSTEMS

AGC Glass Europe
Chaussée de La Hulpe
B-1661170 Brussels
Tel.: +32 2 6743111
www.yourglass.com

BGT Bischoff Glastechnik AG
Alexanderstrasse 2
75015 Bretten
Tel.: +49 7252 5030
www.bgt-bretten.de

BRUAG
Bahnhofstrasse 8
CH-8594 Güttingen
Tel.: +41 71 4140090
www.bruag.ch

Dobler Metallbau GmbH
Hansastr. 15
80686 München
Tel.: +49 89 5709240
www.dobler-metallbau.com

FRENER & REIFER GmbH
Alfred Ammon Straße 31
I-39042 Brixen (BZ)
Tel.: +39 0472 270111
www.frener-reifer.com

GIP GmbH
An der Katharinenkirche 2
38100 Braunschweig
Tel.: +49 531 70211244
www.gip-fassade.com

Glas Marte GmbH
Brachsenweg 39
A-6900 Bregenz
Tel.: +43 5574 67220
www.glasmarte.at

Glasfabrik Lamberts GmbH & Co.
KG
Egerstraße 197
95624 Wunsiedel
Tel.: +49 9232 6050
www.lamberts.info

Interpane Glas Industrie AG
Sohnreystraße 21
37697 Lauenförde
Tel.: +49 5273 8090
www.interpane.com

Jansen AG
Industriestrasse 34
CH-9463 Oberriet SG
Tel.: +41 71 7639111
www.jansen.com

Josef Gartner GmbH
Gartnerstrasse 20
89423 Gundelfingen
Tel.: +49 9073 840
www.josef-gartner.de

Lindner Group
Bahnhofstraße 29
94424 Arnstorf
Tel.: +49 8723 203700
www.lindner-group.com

Okalux GmbH
Am Jöspershecklein 1
97828 Marktheidenfeld-Altfeld
Tel.: +49 9391 9000
www.okalux.de

Pilkington Deutschland AG
Haydnstraße 19
45884 Gelsenkirchen
Tel.: +49 209 1680
www.pilkington.com

RAICO Bautechnik GmbH
Gewerbegebiet Nord 2
87772 Pfaffenhausen
Tel.: +49 8265 9110
www.raico.de

Reynaers GmbH Aluminium
Systeme
Franzstraße 25
45968 Gladbeck
Tel.: +49 2043 96 400
www.reynaers.com

RODECA GmbH
Freiherr-vom-Stein-Straße 165
45473 Mülheim an der Ruhr
Tel.: +49 208 765020
www.rodeca.de

Schollglas Holding
Schollstraße 4
30890 Barsinghausen
Tel.: +49 5105 7770
www.schollglas.com

SCHOTT Architektur
Hattenbergstraße 10
55122 Mainz
Tel.: +49 6131 661812
www.schott.com/architecture

Schüco International KG
Karolinenstraße 1-15
33609 Bielefeld
Tel.: +49 521 7830
www.schueco.com

Sky-Frame, R&G Metallbau AG
Bergwisstrasse 2
CH-8548 Ellikon an der Thur
Tel.: +41 52 3690230
www.sky-frame.ch

SOLARLUX Aluminium Systeme
GmbH
Gewerbepark 9-11
49143 Bissendorf
Tel.: +49 5402 4000
www.solarlux.de

Joh. Sprinz GmbH & Co. KG
Lagerstr. 13
88287 Grünkraut-Gullen
Tel.: +49 751 3790
www.sprinz.eu

WICONA Sapa Building Systems
GmbH
Einsteinstr. 61
89077 Ulm
Tel.: +49 731 39840
www.wicona.de

INPEK GmbH
Pfitschtalstraße 57/E
I-39049 Wiesen Sterzing (BZ)
Tel.: +39 0472 760575
www.inpek.it

WAREMA Renkhoff SE
Hans-Wilhelm-Renkhoff-Str. 2
97828 Marktheidenfeld
Tel.: +49 9391 200
www.warema.de

PROFILED STRUCTURAL
GLASS - POLYCARBONATE
PANELS

Bayer MaterialScience GmbH
Otto-Hesse-Str. 19/T9
64293 Darmstadt
Tel.: +49 6151 13030
www.bayersheeteurope.com

Deutsche Everlite GmbH
Am Keßler 4
97877 Wertheim
Tel.: +49 9342 96040
www.everlite.de

E.M.B. Products AG
Rudolf-Diesel-Straße 6
46446 Emmerich
Tel.: +49 2822 69710
www.roda.de

FDT FlachdachTechnologie GmbH
Eisenbahnstr. 6–8
68199 Mannheim
Tel.: +49 621 85040
www.fdt.de

Flachglas (Schweiz) AG
Zentrumstrasse 2
CH-4806 Wikon
Tel.: +41 62 7450030
www.flachglas.ch

Pilkington Bauglasindustrie GmbH
Hüttenstr. 33
66839 Schmelz
Tel.: +49 6887 3030
www.pilkington.com

prokuwa Kunststoff GmbH
Meinhardstr. 5
44379 Dortmund
Tel.: +49 231 90720
www.prokulit.de

RODECA GmbH
Freiherr-vom-Stein-Str. 165
45473 Mülheim
Tel.: +49 208 765020
www.rodeca.de

Wacotech GmbH & Co. KG
Querstraße 7
33729 Bielefeld
Tel.: +49 521 9620080
www.wacotech.de

Wilkes GmbH
Heidestraße 23-29
58332 Schwelm
Tel.: +49 2336 93700
www.wilkes.de

NATURAL STONE

Alfredo Polti SA Gneiss Calanca
Via alla Sega
CH-6543 Arvigo
Tel.: +41 91 8272442
www.alfredopolti.ch

Bamberger Natursteinwerk
Hermann Graser GmbH
Dr.-Robert-Pfleger-Str. 25
96052 Bamberg
Tel.: +49 951 96480
www.bamberger-natursteinwerk.de

Die STEINWERKSTATT Weiler
GmbH
Kristinusstraße 30
88171 Weiler im Allgäu
Tel.: +49 8387 923380
www.diesteinwerkstattweiler.com

Grünig Natursteine GmbH
Jaufenstrasse 102
I-39049 Sterzing
Tel.: +39 0472 765465
www.gruenig-natursteine.com

Heinrich Quirrenbach Naturstein
Produktions- und Vertriebs GmbH
Eremitage 6
51789 Lindlar
Tel.: +49 2266 47460
www.quirrenbach.de

HOFMANN NATURSTEIN GmbH &
Co. KG
Anton-Hofmann-Allee 2
97956 Werbach-Gamburg
Tel.: +49 9348 810
www.hofmann-naturstein.com

JUMA GmbH & Co. KG
Kipfenberger Str. 22
85137 Walting
Tel.: +49 8465 9500
www.juma.com

Lauster Steinbau GmbH
Natursteinwerke
Enzstraße 46
70376 Stuttgart
Tel.: +49 711 59670
www.laustersteinbau.de

Rauriser Naturstein Zentrum GmbH
Wörtherstraße 42
A-5661 Rauris
Tel.: +43 6544 62790
www.rauriser.at

Schön + Hippelein GmbH & Co. KG
Industriestraße 1
74589 Satteldorf
Tel.: +49 07951 4980
www.schoen-hippelein.de

Stone Group AG
Zürcherstrasse 77
CH-8730 Uznach
Tel.: +41 55 280 3979
www.stonegroup.ch

Stonepark GmbH
Stauffenbergstraße 23
49356 Diepholz
Tel.: +49 5441 98680
www.stone-park.de

TRACO GmbH
Poststraße 17
99947 Bad Langensalza
Tel.: +49 3603 852121
www.traco.de

TIMBER/WOOD

ABA Holz van Kempen GmbH
Streitheimer Str. 22
86477 Adelsried
Tel.: +49 8294 8033130
www.aba-holz.de

Abderhalden Holzbau AG
Industriestraße 19
CH-9630 Wattwil
Tel.: +41 71 9881657
www.abderhalden-holzbau.ch

Anton Ambros GmbH
Hauptstraße 5
87659 Hopferau
Tel.: +49 8364 983430
www.ambros-haus.de

Binderholz GmbH
Zillertalstraße 39
A-6263 Fügen
Tel.: +43 5288 6010
www.binderholz.com

Dobler Holzbau GmbH
Interpark Focus 2
A-6832 Röthis
Tel.: +43 5523 65311
www.dobler-gruppe.at

ERNE AG Holzbau
Werkstraße 3
CH-5080 Laufenburg
Tel.: +41 62 8698181
www.erne.net

Gebr. Schneider GmbH, Holzwerk
Kappel 28
88436 Eberhardzell
Tel.: +49 7355 93200
www.schneider-holz.com

Hecht Holzbau AG
Rigistrasse 11a
CH-6210 Sursee
Tel.: +41 41 9251840
www.hecht-holzbau.ch

HESS TIMBER GmbH & Co. KG
Am Hundsrück 2
63924 Kleinheubach
Tel.: +49 9371 40030
www.hess-timber.com

Holzbau Erni AG
Guggibadstr. 8
CH-6288 Schongau
Tel.: +41 917 38 88
www.holzbau-erni.ch

Kaspar Greber Holz- und Wohnbau
GmbH
Ellenbogen 632
A-6870 Bezau
Tel.: +43 5514 2360
www.kaspargreber.at

Kaufmann Bausysteme GmbH
Vorderreuthe 57
A-6870 Reuthe
Tel.: +43 5514 314400
www.kaufmannbausysteme.at

Kebony AS
Hoffsveien 48
N-0377 Oslo
Tel.: +47 7702 104182
www.kebony.com

KLH Massivholz GmbH
Mur 202
A-8842 Katsch
Tel.: +43 3588 88350
www.klh.at

Lignatur AG
Herisauerstr. 30
CH-9104 Waldstatt
Tel.: +41 71 3530410
www.lignatur.ch

Lignotrend Schweiz
Kreuzmatt 2
CH-6242 Wauwil
Tel.: +41 41 9841309
www.lignotrend.ch

Marti AG Holzbau
Dorfstrasse 9
CH-8766 Matt
Tel.: +41 55 6421148
www.martimatt.ch

Meiberger Holzbau GmbH & Co. KG
Lofer Nr. 304
A-5090 Lofer
Tel.: +43 6588 83060
www.holzbau-meiberger.at

Merk Holzbau GmbH
Menhardsweiler 1
88410 Bad Wurzach-
Unterschwarzach
Tel.: +49 7564 93200
www.merk-holzbau.de

MERKLE Holzbau GmbH
Fabrikstraße 31
73266 Bissingen an der Teck
Tel.: +49 7023 900590
www.merkle-holzbau.de

müllerblaustein HOLZBAUWERKE
Pappelauer Str. 51
89134 Blaustein
Tel.: +49 7304 96160
www.muellerblaustein.de

Neuhauser Holzbau GmbH
Gewerbestrasse 9
A-6710 Nenzing
Tel.: +43 5525 636660
www.neuhauser-holzbau.at

oa.sys baut GmbH
Zoll 887
A-6861 Alberschwende
Tel.: +43 5579 202570
www.oa-sys.com

Parklex - Composites Guera
Composites Guera, S. A.
Zelain Auzoa 13
E-31780 Vera de Bidasoa, Navarra
Tel.: +34 948 625045
www.parklex.com

Pfeifer Timber GmbH
Fabrikstraße 54
A-6460 Imst
Tel.: +43 5412 69600
www.pfeifergroup.com

Prodema
B San Miguel, s/n
E-20250 Legoretta Gipuzkoa
Tel.: +34 943 807000
www.prodema.com

Renggli AG
Gleng
CH-6247 Schötz
Tel.: +41 62 7482222
www.renggli-haus.ch

Rubner Holding AG
Handwerkerzone 2
I-39030 Kiens
Tel.: +39 0474563777
www.rubner.com

Sohm HolzBautechnik
Bühel 818
A-6861 Alberschwende
Tel.: +43 5579 71150
www.sohm-holzbau.at

Thoma Forschungszentrum
für Holzverarbeitung
Hasling 35
A-5622 Goldegg
Tel.: +43 6415 8910
www.thoma.at

Trespa International B. V.
Niederkasseler Lohweg 18
40547 Düsseldorf
Tel.: +49 800 1860422
www.trespa.com

Tschopp Holzbau AG
An der Ron 17
CH-6280 Hochdorf
Tel.: +41 41 9142020
www.tschopp-holzbau.ch

Wyler Holzbau AG
Stockmatte
CH-3855 Brienz
Tel.: +41 33 9521325
www.wylerholzbau.ch

Zimmerei Gerhard Bilgeri e.U.
Baser 93b
A-6943 Riefensberg
Tel.: +43 5513 8855
www.zimmerei-bilgeri.at

COMPOSITE THERMAL
INSULATION SYSTEMS

Brillux GmbH & Co. KG
Weseler Str. 401
48163 Münster
Tel.: +49 251 7188759
www.brillux.de

CAPAROL Farben Lacke
Bautenschutz GmbH
Roßdörfer Str. 50
64372 Ober-Ramstadt
Tel.: +49 6154 710
www.caparol.de

HAGA AG Naturbaustoffe
Hübelweg 1
CH-5102 Rupperswil
Tel.: +41 62 8891818
www.haganatur.ch

HOMATHERM GmbH
Ahornweg 1
06536 Berga
Tel.: +49 346 5141661
www.homatherm.com

Knauf Gips KG
Am Bahnhof 7
97346 Iphofen
Tel.: +49 9323 310
www.knauf.de

Linzmeier Bauelemente GmbH
Industriestraße 21
88499 Riedlingen
Tel.: +49 7371 18060
www.linzmeier.de

PAVATEX
Wangener Str. 58
88 299 Leutkirch
Tel.: +49 7561 98550
www.pavatex.de

puren GmbH
Rengoldshauser Str. 4
88662 Überlingen
Tel.: +49 7551 80990
www.puren.com

SCHWENK Putztechnik GmbH &
Co. KG
Hindenburgring 15
89077 Ulm
Tel.: +49 731 93410
www.schwenk-putztechnik.de

VARIOTEC GmbH & Co. KG
Weißmarterstraße 3–5
92318 Neumarkt/OPf.
Tel.: +49 9181 69460
www.variotec.de

HECK Wall Systems GmbH
Thölauer Strasse 25
95615 Marktredwitz
Tel.: +49 9231 8020
www.wall-systems.com

Multipor – Xella Gruppe
Düsseldorfer Landstraße 395
47259 Duisburg
Tel.: +49 203 608800
www.multipor.de

MEMBRANES/PLASTIC

CENO Membrane Technology
GmbH
Am Eggenkamp 14
48268 Greven
Tel.: +49 2571 9690
www.sattler-global.com

Hightex GmbH
Nordstraße 10
83253 Rimsting
Tel.: +49 8051 68880
www.hightexworld.com

Koch Membranen GmbH
Kunststofftechnologie
Nordstraße 1
83253 Rimsting
Tel.: +49 8051 690980
www.kochmembranen.de

LAMILUX Heinrich Strunz Holding
GmbH & Co. KG
Postfach 1540
95105 Rehau
Tel.: +49 9283 5950
www.lamilux.de

Membranteam GmbH
Möllenbronn 7
88273 Fronreute
Tel.: +49 7505 957891
www.membranteam.de

Seele GmbH
Gutenbergstr. 19
86368 Gersthofen
Tel.: +49 821 24940
www.seele.com

Sefar AG
Hinterbissaustrasse 12
CH-9410 Heiden
Tel.: +41 71 898 5700
www.sefar.com

Serge Ferrari, Ferrari S.A
BP 54 F
F-94857 La Tour du Pin – Cedex
Tel.: +33 4 74974133
www.ferrari-textiles.com

Taiyo Europe GmbH
Mühlweg 2
82054 Sauerlach
Tel.: +49 8104 628980
www.taiyo-europe.com

Texlon HSP GmbH
Hirsernriedstrasse 6
CH-6074 Giswil
Tel.: +41 41 6766644
www.texlon.ch

Vector Foiltec GmbH
Steinacker 3
28717 Bremen
Tel.: +49 421 693510
www.vector-foiltec.com

ROOFS

alwitra GmbH & Co.
Am Forst 1
54296 Trier
Tel.: +49 651 91020
www.alwitra.de

Braas GmbH
Frankfurter Landstraße 2–4
61440 Oberursel
Tel.: +49 6171 61014
www.braas.de

climacell GmbH
Etzwiesenstr. 12
74918 Angelbachtal
Tel.: +49 7265 91310
www.climacell.com

Creaton AG
Dillinger Straße 60
86637 Wertingen
Tel.: +49 8272 860
www.creaton.de

DEUTSCHE ROCKWOOL
Mineralwoll GmbH & Co. OHG
Rockwool Str. 37–41
45966 Gladbeck
Tel.: +49 2043 4080
www.rockwool.de

Erlus AG
Hauptstraße 106
84088 Neufahrn/NB
Tel.: +49 8773 180
www.erlus.com

Jacobi Tonwerke GmbH
Osteroder Straße 2
37434 Bilshausen
Tel.: +49 5528 9100
www.dachziegel.de

Nelskamp GmbH, Dachziegelwerke
Waldweg 6
46514 Schermbeck
Tel.: +49 2853 91300
www.nelskamp.de

Porextherm Dämmstoffe GmbH
Heisinger Straße 8/10
87437 Kempten
Tel.: +49 831 575360
www.porextherm.com

Rathscheck Schiefer und
Dach-Systeme
St.-Barbara-Str. 3
56727 Mayen
Tel.: +49 2651 9550
www.rathscheck.de

Schiefergruben Magog GmbH &
Co. KG
Alter Bahnhof 9
57392 Fredeburg
Tel.: +49 2974 96200
www.magog.de

Walther Dachziegel GmbH
Lohmühle 3–5
90579 Langenzenn
Tel.: +49 9101 7080
www.dachziegel.de

The addresses of the associations
and manufacturers have been
grouped by building component and
material, and are in alphabetical
order.

REFERENCES / PICTURE CREDITS

Andritschke, Dünisch, Herres: Holz im Außenbereich, Munich 2012
Baus, Siegele: Holzfassaden, Stuttgart Munich 2000
Baus: Sichtbeton, Munich 2007
Block, Gengnagel, Peters: Faustformel Tragwerksentwurf, Munich 2013
Boake: Understanding Steel Design, An Architectural Design Manual, Basel 2011
Bollinger, Grohmann, Feldmann, Giebeler, Pfanner, Zeumer: Atlas Moderner Stahlbau, Munich 2011
Colling: Holzbau - Grundlagen und Bemessung nach EC 5, Vienna 2014
Deplazes: Constructing Architecture, Basel 2013
Dierks, Schneider, Wormuth: Baukonstruktion, Düsseldorf 1993
Döring, Meschke, Kind-Barkauskas, Schwerm: Fassaden, Düsseldorf 2000
Eisele: Grundlagen der Baukonstruktion, Berlin 2014
Frick, Knöll, Neumann, Weinbrenner: Baukonstruktionslehre, Wiesbaden 2015
Giebeler, Fisch, Krause, Musso, Petzinka, Rudolphi: Refurbishment Manual, Basel 2009
Guttmann, Eder, Schober: Fassaden aus Holz, Vienna 2010
Hauschild: Konstruieren im Raum / Spatial Construction, Munich 2003
Hegger, Auch-Schwelk, Fuchs, Rosenkranz: Construction Materials Manual, Basel 2006
Hegger, Fuchs, Stark, Zeumer: Energy Manual, Basel 2008
Herzog, Krippner, Lang, Werner: Facade Construction Manual, Basel 2004
Hildner, Hübener: Wand. Materialität, Konstruktion, Detail, Munich 2011
Hirsch, Lohr: Energiegerechtes Bauen und Modernisieren, Wuppertal 1996
Holschemacher: Entwurfs- und Konstruktionstafeln, Berlin 2013
Huckfeldt: Praxis-Handbuch Holzschutz, Cologne 2014
Hugues, Greilich, Peter: Großformatige Ziegel, Munich 2003
Hugues, Steiger, Webe: Timber Construction, Basel 2004
Hugues, Steiger, Weber: Building with Large Clay Blocks, Munich 2013
Jeska, Pascha, Hascher: Emergent Timber Technologies, Basel 2014
Johannes: Entwerfen. Architektenausbildung in Europa von Vitruv bis Mitte des 20. Jahrhunderts. Geschichte - Theorie - Praxis, Hamburg 2010
Kaltenbach: Translucent Materials, Munich 2012
Kind-Barkauskas, Kauhsen, Polonyi: Beton Atlas, Basel 2002
Knaack, Chung-Klatte, Hasselbach: Prefabricated Systems, Basel 2012
Knaack, Klein, Bilow, Auer: Façades, Principles of Construction, Basel 2014
Knippers, Cremers, Gabler, Lienhard: Atlas Kunststoffe + Membranen, Munich 2010

Koch: Membrane Structures, Munich Berlin London New York 2004
Krampe, Reich, Weller: Glasbau-Praxis, Berlin 2012
Lohmeyer, Ebeling, Baar: Stahlbetonbau, Wiesbaden 2012
Moro: Baukonstruktion - vom Prinzip zum Detail, Vienna 2008
Neuenhagen: Grundwissen moderner Holzbau, Cologne 2014
Pech, Pommer, Zeininger: Fassaden, Basel 2014
Peck: Atlas Moderner Betonbau, Munich 2013
Peck: Baustoff Beton, Munich 2008
Pfeifer, Ramcke, Achtziger, Zilch: Masonry Construction Manual, Munich 2001
Pfundstein, Rudolphi, Spitzner, Gellert: Dämstoffe, Munich 2008
Pottgiesser: Fassadenschichtungen – Glas, Mehrschalige Glaskonstruktionen, Berlin 2004
Pottgiesser: Prinzipien der Baukonstruktion, Stuttgart 2008
Rice, Dutton: Transparente Architektur, Glasfassaden mit Structural Glazing, Basel 1995
Schittich, Staib, Balkow, Schuler, Sobek: Glass Construction Manual, Basel 2007
Schittich: best of DETAIL Holz / Wood, Munich 2014
Schittich: In Detail: Building Skins, Basel 2001
Schmitt: Hochbaukonstruktion, Wiesbaden 1993
Schöwer, Leukefeld: Das Baustellenhandbuch der Maßtoleranzen, Merching 2007
Schunck, Oster, Barthel, Kießl: Roof Construction Manual, Basel 2003
Sedlbauer, Schunck, Barthel, Künzel: Flat Roof Construction Manual, Munich 2010
Seidel: Textile Hüllen – Bauen mit biegeweichen Tragelementen, Berlin 2008
Staib, Dörrhöfer, Rosenthal: Components and Systems: Modular Construction; Design, Structure, New Technologies, Basel 2008
Steiger: Basics Holzbau, Basel 2013
von der Heyde-Platenius: Gestalten mit Beton, Cologne 2014
Watts: Modern Construction Facades, Vienna 2005
Weller: Glass in Building, Munich 2008
www.baunetzwissen.de
www.proholz.at / www.dataholz.com

Achtermann, Jens: p.15 5
Alwitra, S. Tornow: p.124 2,3; 125 2,3
Amunt Architekten: p.51 5
ANO, DAICI: p.29 6
ArGeTon, D. Malagamba: p.85 3
Bercy Chen Studio: p.127 5
Bitter, Jan: p.75 3
Bryant, Richard: p.23 9
Callejas, Javier: p.70 1
Carter, Earl: p.8
Croce, Michael: p.48 1
Dale, Nils Petter: p.128; 138–141
derdichtebau.de: p.125 1
Dietzsch & Weber Architekten: p.84 2
Dold und Hasenauer OG / Superlab: p.59 7
Doradzillo, Marc: p.45 2
Druot, Frédéric: p.42 1
Dujardin, Filip: p.52 3
E.M.B. Products AG: p.97 4,5
eckertharms Architekten / Innenarchitekten: p.93 3
Eternit (Schweiz) AG: p.93 4
Eternit, Stefan Marquard: p.64 2
Eternit/IBA: p.93 5
Feiner, Ralph: p.27 9; 58 3
Ferrero, Alberto: p.75 2
Flickr / Laura Manning: p.23 8
Flyout: p.15 4
Forward Stroke inc.: p.21 7
Frances, Scott: p.30 3

Frost, Mikkel: p.102
Gallardo, José Javier: p.112 1
Griffith, Tim: p.126 4
Halbe, Roland: p.84 3
Hart, Rob 't: p.27 10
HECK Wall Systems: p.101 5b
Heinrich Quirrenbach, Andrea Dingeldein: p.50 1
Heinrich, Michael: p.100 2
Hennings, Dirk: p.110 2
Herrmann, Eva: p.13 2,4; 14 2; 21 5; 22 5; 27 4,5,7; 30 1,2; 43 2b; 45 3; 46; 51 5; 52 2; 54 2,3; 56 3,4; 57 5,6; 60; 64 2; 70 2; 80 1; 83 6; 90 2,3; 98 2; 120
Highsmith, Carol M.: p.22 3
Hirai, Hiroyuki: p.11 3
Hisgett, Tony: p.22 7
Holzherr, Florian: p.14 3; 77 6
Hufton + Crow: p.64 2
Hursley, Timothy: 96 1
Huthmacher, Werner: p.105 5
Jantscher, Thomas: p.27 2
JORDAHL GmbH, Andreas Achmann: p.83 6
JORDAHL GmbH: p.83 4,5
Kemper System, Wolfgang Hauck Fotodesign: p.124; 125 4
Kida, Katsuhisa: p.105 4
Kirchner, Jens: p.66 2
Knerer Lang Architekten: p.43 2a
Lignum.ch: p.58 1,2
Lill, Edmund: p.13 7

Lindman, Åke E:son: p.111 5
Lins, Marc: p.27 8
Louage, Kevin: p.111 6
magma architecture: p.99 4
Marinescu, Ioana: p.111 4
Max Dudler Architekten: p.66 3
Mayer, Thomas: p.91 4
Membranteam: p.99 6
Metawell GmbH: p.81 3
Miguletz, Norbert: p.15 6
Müller-Naumann, Stefan: p.96 2; 115 3
Müller, Stefan: p.14 1; 29 4; 110 3
Multipor: p.101 5a
Nagel, Norbert: p.29 1
Neue Ziegelmanufaktur Glindow: p.50 1
O&O Baukunst: p.134–137
Oliv Architekten: p.43 3a,b
Passoth, Jens: p.11 4
Pegenaute, Pedro: p.21 8
PERI GmbH: p.55 7,8
Radon, Norman: p.95 6
Rathscheck Schiefer: p.120
Reckli: p.77 9
Reichel, Alexander: p.116; 125
RENGGLI AG: p.95 4
Rheinzink: p.91 5; 120; 121
Richers, Christian: p.29 3; 90 1
Ricola AG: p.45 5; 154
Rieder: p.76 4
Rosier, JM: p.10 2
Ruault, Philippe: p.146–149
Salewa, Oskar DaRiz: 69 5

Schels, Sebastian: p.97 7
Schüco International KG: p.72 1
Schultz, Kerstin: p.27 6
Sobajima, Toshihiro: p.150–153
Spehr, Daniel: p.45 1
Stanserhornbahn: p.99 5
Steiff: p.62 2
Steinbach: p.21 4
Sumner, Edmund: p.130–133
Tchoban Foundation, Roland Halbe: p.77 8
Van der Hoek, Allard: p.43 4
Vervoorts & Schindler, Bochum, Schüco International KG: p.73 4
Vitra, Julien Lanoo: p.124 1
Völkel, Thomas: p.43 5
Wacotech: p.96 3
WAREMA: p.73 5
Weber, Jens: p.86 1; 95 5
Wehrli, Dominique: p.142–145
Wiel Arets Architects: p.77 7
Wienerberger/ Norbert Prommer: p.17 3; 45 4
wikiarquitectura: p.62 1
wikimedia commons: p.13 1,3,6,8; 17 1,2; 20 1,2; 21 3,6; 22 2,4,6; 29 5; 58 1; 62 3,4; 86 3; 104 2; 120; 121
Wolff Architekten: p.120
Wollenweber, Jörg: p.111 7
Zerdoun, Yohan: p.100 3
Zillerplus, GBW: p.48 2; 78 4
Zimmerei & Holzbau Ehrlich: p.114
Zucchi, Cino: p.27 3

INDEX

Editors: Alexander Reichel, Kerstin Schultz
Concept: Alexander Reichel, Kerstin Schultz, Andrea Wiegelmann
Authors: Eva Maria Herrmann, Martin Krammer, Jörg Sturm, Susanne Wartzeck
Authors' Assistants: Michael Grobbauer, Dan Kröning

Translation from German into English: Hartwin Busch
Copy editing and proofreading: Richard Toovey
Project management: Odine Oßwald, Petra Schmid

Layout: Eva Maria Herrmann
Drawings: Eva Maria Herrmann, Dan Kröning, Virginia Marini, Anna Tomm, Anna Tschochner
Design concept SCALE: Nadine Rinderer
Typesetting: Amelie Solbrig

The technical and construction recommendations contained in this book are based on the present state of technical knowledge. They should be checked in each case against the relevant instructions, standards, laws etc. as well as local regulations before applying them. No liability is accepted.

Library of Congress Cataloging-in-Publication data
A CIP catalog record for this book has been applied for at the Library of Congress.

Bibliographic information published by the German National Library
The German National Library lists this publication in the Deutsche Nationalbibliografie; detailed bibliographic data are available on the Internet at http://dnb.dnb.de.

This publication is also available as an e-book (ISBN PDF 978-3-0356-0336-1;
ISBN EPUB 978-3-0356-0351-4)
and in a German language edition (ISBN 978-3-0346-0206-8).

© 2015 Birkhäuser Verlag GmbH, Basel
P.O. Box 44, 4009 Basel, Switzerland
Part of Walter de Gruyter GmbH, Berlin/Boston

Printed on acid-free paper produced from chlorine-free pulp. TCF ∞

Printed in Germany

ISBN 978-3-0346-0207-5

9 8 7 6 5 4 3 2 1

www.birkhauser.com